Weeding the Flowerbeds

Weeding the Flowerbeds

Sarah Mkhonza

Copyright © 2009 by Sarah Mkhonza.

Library of Congress Control Number: 2008902307
ISBN: Hardcover 978-1-4257-9999-1
Softcover 978-1-4257-9976-2

All rights reserved. No part of this book may be reproduced or transmitted in any form or by any means, electronic or mechanical, including photocopying, recording, or by any information storage and retrieval system, without permission in writing from the copyright owner.

This book was printed in the United States of America.

To order additional copies of this book, contact:
Xlibris Corporation
1-888-795-4274
www.Xlibris.com
Orders@Xlibris.com
45057

In memory of Gordon James "Chaucer" Thomas who passed away on August 20, 2006, of malignant melanoma cancer at the age of fifty-six. Gordon Thomas worked at Manzini Nazarene High School, Swaziland, from 1973 to 1976 and later at Endzingeni Nazarene High School, Swaziland, from 1983 to 1985. He was teaching at Nazarene Bible College in Manchester, England, when he died.

Chapter One

Freedom is not procured by a full enjoyment of what is desired, but by controlling the desire.

—Epictetus

* * *

Half past five and the bell rang. I woke up. I heard the bell nicely and clearly since I was in dormitory 34. We were in the dorm that was closest to the kitchen. When the bell ringer took the bell off the table, we could hear the first *tlink*, *tlink* and get ready to jump out of bed. It is just that jumping out of bed is never easy at the age of thirteen. It is easier to pull back the blankets and shove your head further under them. I knew that it was time to attend morning prayers, and I dreaded it.

    I peeped through the door to see who the bell ringer was. I knew even the sermon we would hear! It would be about Much Afraid, a girl who was always afraid. I don't know why this student teacher always preached about Much Afraid. Not that the name sounded phony, but just that at the age of thirteen, I was being told about the girl who feared everything when my whole life had been born in tremendous fear. It did not make much sense to me. I wanted to be told about Much Courageous. Maybe that would make sense because where I was, in this hostel, at Manzini Nazarene High School, I needed to be more than courageous. If I wasn't, I was going to be the laughingstock of all the girls. I discovered this when I told the girls on the first day that I was from Phonjwane Primary School. This was a lowveld school that was out in the countryside. After that everybody called me "Pho" as if the whole word had made me grow the *Phondo* (horn) in Phonjwane on my head. I didn't know how to deal with the laughter of young girls at that time. I was giggly myself. I just thought I should leave them alone or pretend that the name does not mean anything to me. I was wrong. I was Pho way into adulthood. Even now, maybe I am still Pho.

    I jumped out of bed, pulled off my nightdress and put on my skirt and shirt, and rushed to the bathroom to brush my teeth. I hated singing hymns with my morning breath all over me. By the time I got back to the dormitory to take my Bible and file with the others to the chapel, the matron was closing the door and disappearing behind the wall on her way to the morning service. I decided to cheat and not attend the morning prayers. I gently pulled the clothes that were on the coat hangers and squatted into the space below them and sat down. I did this after making sure that I had taken the "spookie" out of the door. The spookie was the small square metal piece that makes the door to lock. If I took it out, nobody could open the door and come in. I did morning prayers in hiding, very happy that I escaped one ordeal of our endless prayers that I doubted if God heard when we were so sleepy that we were cursing under our breaths for being awakened so early to serve a God we neither knew nor loved. It is not that I did not revere God. I knew him in my own secret heart. He was up there and listening to me very intently when I was sad. When I was broke, he gave me a rand. When I was lonely, he sent angels to play with me in my mind. I named them Sindi and Kuhle. They were black like me, and so was my God. He looked like me. I knew that I was the light of God trapped into myself. I could see this in my fingers. God lived in them. I wrote with him, and even as I hid under the clothes that day, he was in the space that surrounded me. It is just that he was not asking me why I had cheated morning prayers. He was laughing at my naughtiness and saying, "I love you even though you will get into trouble for what you are doing." I felt it in the pounding of my heart. I took my book *Hatter's Castle* and pretended to read. That was when I heard the knock on the door.

I was scared. My heart started to pound even harder. I called on God and said a little prayer, "Get me through this, O Father." With those words, I went to the door. "Bulelo, open the door," the voice said. I quickly recognized the voice. It was the voice of the junior matron Ms. Cele. She was trying the handle of the door from outside. I knew that she could not open the door. When I turned to the window where I had put the spookie, I was shivering. I stuck it into the hole and looked for the handle so that I could turn the door. I could not find it. I started shivering. Where was the handle? I had put it down here. I looked on the top of the bookshelf. It was not there. I looked for it on all the five beds. It was not there. I was in serious trouble because the voice outside was still calling. I threw my glance under the bookshelf on the second drawer, and there it was, the glimmer of silvery metal that looked like an oversized comma. It was the handle of the door, the part that you turned to open it. I put it over the spookie and opened the door. We had broken the handle of the door so that we could lock people out of the dormitory. The part called the spookie actually turns inside the door when you turn the handle. We would take it out and lock people out and put it in to open. This could only be done from inside. As if it was not enough trouble to lock the matron out! Now I was adding insult to injury by taking forever to open the door. When I finally pulled the door toward me, the matron was looking at me. She did not have a ferocious look on her face. She was smiling as if she could sense the slight amusement that was hidden in my stomach. I was stifling a laugh that was in half shame and in half disdain. I did not have to answer why I had not gone to the prayers. I was told to go out and join the others in weeding the flower beds. At that time, my friend Sisile was laughing slyly and looking at me through the corner of the eye. How come she had always stayed and not gone to morning prayers and never got caught? To say that she was lucky was an understatement. I had just done it now, and here I was in the biggest mess I had even been in. Not to say I had not been in bigger "scandals." I already had my fair share of sins recorded in the matron's black book. I was already the "bad fig" in the bag.

I walked out of the dormitory to go and find group 10. We were grouped according to the tables in the dining hall. There were twelve of us. We had one table leader whom we called "mother," with a deep American accent. She was very kind to us. She did all the dishing of food and going back to check if we had enough. We liked her. She also made sure that we did our fair share of the work. Now that I had disgraced her by being found missing when she had not reported, I had to see to how I would get myself out of that fix. I knew that I owed her an apology. Like any good leader, she deserved to hear me express my own humiliation about what I had done. I made it easy for myself and took her to the side and spoke into her ear. "Mother, I was sick. I had a stomachache, truly." I could not bring myself to apologize without making an excuse. She brushed it aside and showed me the section of the flower beds I had to weed. I went there and knelt besides my friend Makhosi who was already laughing at me.

"Rebel, you see, you got into trouble," Makhosi said, stifling a laugh. She was bending down and speaking softly so that the others would not hear.

"You lucky, naughty Rebel 1. You are the one who started this. Yet now I am the one who is in trouble," I said, feigning anger. She laughed until tears came out of her eyes. Whenever I was in a spot, Makhosi would laugh in order to make me laugh at myself. At first I resented her laughter, but now I was used to it. It was what made our friendship. After reading a book about a rebel, we decided that we would be the Sisters Three and also be Rebel 1, 2, and 3.

"Did the junior matron ask you about the spookie?" she asked, trying to find out if we had been discovered.

"What do you think? Of course." I knew I was lying even when I said it. "She knows that you broke the door. She said she will deal with you when the time comes." Makhosi knew that "the time" was in the afternoon when we came back from school. This was when all the other girls were relaxing. It was a time to discipline those who did not do what they were supposed to do. I wanted

Makhosi to be afraid and tell Sisile that we were in trouble. I saw Sisile coming toward us and moved toward the farthest side of the flower bed so that she could come and weed the bed next to mine.

"Hey, Rebel 2, you thought you would get away with it." She was giggling as she dug her hands into the sand and crouched next to me. She was whispering something to Makhosi. I knew that both of them were worried about the spookie since I had told them that we had to see the matron about breaking down the door. I could see fear in Sisile's face, and I felt very good. I felt glad that even though I was the one who had been in trouble, I now had control because I knew something they did not know. It felt very good to have this ace against these two.

I knelt down and pretended not to be concerned about what they were doing. I decided to give my work my full attention. I pulled hard at the grass that was growing in between the daisies. It was a rough, strong type of grass that had dried up. It was nestling in between the Namaqualand daisies as if it belonged there. There was something funny about these daisies. I liked their red flowers, but I hated the fact that here at our school, they were so many. It was as if they were the only flower. I liked their rareness and hated their abundance. Nowhere in Swaziland had I seen so many Namaqualand daisies. I saw the Harmattan lilies, the dahlias, and the wild daisies. They were in most households in the highveld where I came from. Just this one flower, with its rough green roundly serrated leaves, was all over. I decided to take care of them. I went and made a circle around each flower and gave it my best tending. I was trying to make sure that it is well grounded in the soil. I weeded everything that could possibly harm it and made a wish. My wish was that these daisies would always bloom and multiply and never ever disappear. I wanted generations to come and find them still blooming. I did not want the weeds to kill them. I did not want the harsh weather to spoil the flowers. I spoke to the petals. I spoke to each strip of the daisy petal and told it why it was important that it should be there when life moves over it. It was not supposed to give in to defeat. It was supposed to be hardy like a real desert flower. Life was no different from a desert; but a flower, a real flower, bloomed against the odds. After having weeded the whole flower bed, I moved back and looked at my work.

I was pleased with what I had done. Sisile would be surprised when I showed her this flower bed. I made sure that wherever we weeded, I left a mark of perfection that only I could leave. I wanted my work to be seen years after I had gone because I was me, a very special specimen of the human race. Something in me told me that I had to do this so that everybody would know. I did not want to embrace mediocrity. I wanted to chase excellence. This I did everywhere I went. This is why I was ashamed of myself when I went to the bathroom to wash and get ready for school that day. It was as if everybody knew that I had missed morning prayers. I could not handle being the center of attention for doing something bad like cheating and not going for prayers. I reacted sheepishly and hoped that this moment, like all moments, of shame would pass.

I had already reserved my washing space by placing my towel in the bathroom. We had to do this because there were only sixteen sinks and five showers in the bathroom. Some students had to wash out of buckets. The bathroom was full when we went in to wash with Makhosi. I took off my clothes and started to bathe. I had already come to terms with my body at that time. The days of feeling like everybody was looking at me were gone. I washed my hair first and did my whole bath in twenty minutes. After that I went to the dormitory and prepared to go to the dining hall. I had to wash the dishes for my punishment. I did that very quickly and prepared to go to school. I did not want to be late for morning prayers. The school chapel was only two hundred yards from the hostel.

We wore red tunics, white shirts, black jerseys, and black shoes and socks at our school. It was twenty past seven, and the day scholars were already flocking toward the school. The boys wore grey trousers and shirts. They were coming toward the school from their hostel, which was near the hospital. The high school is set right in the middle of the Church of the Nazarene grounds. To go from the boys' hostel to the school takes about fifteen minutes. In between the school and the boys' hostel is the teacher training college. It is a school for training primary school and secondary school teachers. There is also a nurses' college near the hospital. The Church of the Nazarene started in 1911 when Harmon Schmelzenbach, a missionary of the Church of the Nazarene, started work at Endzingeni. The institutions like hospitals and schools then spread all over the country. The Church of the Nazarene has some of the finest schools and clinics and has a Bible school in Siteki today. Manzini, the hub of Swaziland, is a hub for the Church of the Nazarene activities as well since it is in a central place. The high school in Manzini makes a significant contribution in that is has a fine education that is exemplary to most of the institutions. The grantee of the Nazarene schools also has an office on the premises of the church in Manzini.

At seven thirty the bell would ring, and all the students would file into the school auditorium. This was a hall that had a floor that was staggered into steps. There were solid, dark wooden benches for the students to sit on. The teachers sat in the front. Standing behind the podium, the teacher who was in charge of assembly would read the Bible and preach to us once more. Right now the girls were leading the chorus: "He taught me how to watch and pray and live rejoicing every day."

Today it was Mr. Nkonzo, the Bible knowledge teacher, who would lead the prayers. We knew what the sermon would be about even before it began. It would be about the ant. "Look to the ant, oh, sluggard," he would repeat. If the message about the ant did not get into our heads, it was because nothing would. Mr.

Nkonzo liked to give us life lessons. He would talk to us about destiny. "Decision decides destiny," he would say. Even though we did not know what destiny was at the time, the alliteration in the phrase made it stay in our minds. We had to be decided all the time, and all things would fall into place. Life is funny because it is the things you hear about the most that catch up with you when you are older. Even though I was bored with the lessons from the teachers, I remembered them and took them with me into my future. That is why it is easy to repeat them to you today. Whether I practiced them is another story.

"Turn to hymn number two forty-five," Mr. Nkonzo said and moved a bit back from where he stood behind the podium. Standing where he was, Mr. Nkonzo looked like a clown. He was a short man with a bald head and a round face. His hair reminded me of the soapstone images that are sculptured by craftsmen in the highveld because of the way it formed a quarter moon around the shiny part of his head. He always wore a jersey even when it was not cold. He had fine-looking teeth when he flashed his usual smile. His short whiskers of a moustache would recede to the side, and his clever eyes would twinkle as they settled on you with a wisdom that was unusual and out of this world. He liked to teach about Bible stories in a way that made you feel he was a figure that had come out of biblical times in his sincerity. He would talk about the children of Israel, and we could see ourselves in these stories. I saw a Moses in myself, and I vowed that I would fight for the oppression of others even if it meant that I would die doing so. Such was the passion with which Mr. Nkonzo taught Bible lessons.

After the song was mentioned, a brave soprano from the back would start it, and the hall would reverberate with the sound of the song. That day the song could be heard from afar. We were singing from small red hymnals called Alexander's hymns. I did not know who Alexander was, but even though we all did not know who he was, we had to agree that the hymns in the hymnal were a good selection of the standard Christian music that was used in schools those days. We got the hymnbooks with the rest of the books that we bought in the first year in high school. We got two Bibles and two hymnbooks: one hymnbook in English and one in Zulu, just like the Bible. There was a Zulu Bible and an English Bible. The rest were books that we needed for class.

We bellowed the music into the morning air inside the fully packed auditorium. "Who is on the Lord's side? Who will serve the king?" we asked in song. "Who will be his helpers other lives to bring?" we continued. "Who will leave the world's side? Who will face the foe? Who is on the Lord's side other lives to bring? Who for him will go?" Question after question we sang on and wondered which side we were on. Were we on the side of the foe as we sang in that hall, or were we on the side of the Lord? There were times when we knew that the students were on the side of the foe. They would sing obscenities and laugh under their breath when some choruses were sung because they had invented their own words for the songs. On those days, I felt sorry for us students and felt that we needed other things to do than being asked questions such as "Will you not try to win someone back to the narrow way?" I knew that no matter how many times the way was described as narrow, some of us could not imagine it beyond a winding Swazi path out in the countryside. The whole saga of the cross was a story that had to be taught and retaught to the children of Swazis who still believed in *muti* and *sangomas*. Whether there was a heaven or not was not the issue; the issue was how we would deal with the knowledge of witches, demons, and ancestors. Would the stories of the Bible transplant our beliefs and transform them into the story of the cross and the death of Jesus, or would we go to the *sangomas* when we were old? These were questions that were not discussed at the personal level. Stories about repentant *sangomas* (shamans) and *inyangas* (traditional healers) were featured once or twice in the sermons of the evangelists who came to our school to preach, but as for whether we were going to hell or heaven, most of us did not know. We just knew that hell was a fierce place, and to set out to go there was not a clever thing to do indeed. It seemed to be very difficult to become prim and proper so that we could feel fit enough to go to heaven. One thing was clear though: it was that God loved even the sinner, which was always a comfort. We did not understand how a young person of thirteen could stop sinning. If I was dealing with my friends Makhosi and Sisile who were always telling lies to catch me and laugh at me, how could I even begin to think that we were heaven bound? One place worked itself into our reality even though we did not want it, and that was hell. Fearful though it was to go there, we did not work hard at trying not to go there. We did not work hard at getting there either. Somewhere in between hell and heaven, we seemed to be stuck and unable to proceed. The gate was narrow, but it was so invisible in the reality of our lives that we decided to live on and not ask these questions too deeply. They were enough to make us unhappy forever. While we were together in that hostel, we needed to have fun, and fun we would have.

After prayers we went to class. The first lesson was the history lesson. Our Form I teacher for history was Mr. Thiki, a fat man who wore thick glasses. "Thiki" was the nickname that we gave him because Sisile thought that he walked as if he was shaking himself in a manner that showed that there was no hurry in his world. She would imitate his behind, and we would laugh in the dorm as we watched Sisile's thin behind imitating Mr. Thiki. "Thiki-thiki-thiki," she would say as she shook her backside to imitate the history teacher after taking each step. We would roar with laughter, and she would continue imitating him. Sisile was light in complexion, and imagining her as Mr. Thiki added to the laughter. I would throw my leg in the air as I laughed at how Mr. Thiki walked. When I saw him climbing the stairs and coming toward our class, I would watch his behind, and the "thiki" thing that Sisile was describing could be seen in the slight shaking that his lazy walk exhibited, and I would quickly walk past him and go to class. I would remember the part where Sisile asked us in the dorm how Mr. Thiki would run if a mamba was chasing him. She would shake all over, and the relaxed intervals would create another circus as the imaginary mamba snake chased Mr. Thiki and made his backside joggle. She would vibrate till there was no breath in me and tears were rolling down my eyes. Watching Mr. Thiki and imagining the mamba snake as he walked to class made me focus on his brown shoes and laugh even more. The front of the shoes were slightly upturned with use. They were what Sisile called "gimme some," which was a phrase used for shoes that are old. The girls thought that they were like hands faced up and saying, "Please give me some of what you are eating."

Mr. Thiki would teach us about the history of the church. He taught us about Martin Luther and Zoroastrianism. He taught us about Timbuktu and the silent trade. He also taught us about Shaka Zulu, Stalin, Hitler, and Mussolini. We learned the history of southern Africa that begins with the arrival of Jan van Riebeeck and never learned that there were two women in the *Dromedaris* when it was shipwrecked and landed at the Cape of Good Hope in 1652. We did not learn about the gardener's wife and the priest's wife. It was a history where women were silent. Apart from the history of the queens of England, there was very little that we learned about women. We did however learn about Queen Labotsibeni. It was not her revolutionary work, but about her sending the young Sobhuza to school. The seventies was not a time when you learned about women in southern Africa. It was a time when life was seen through the system of apartheid that was the order of the day in the whole of southern Africa. In Mozambique, which was the neighboring country, the Portuguese were oppressing the black people; and there was a belief that they beat them with *spakatane*, an object that had holes that would pull off the flesh on the back of a black Mozambican. In Zimbabwe, the Unilateral Declaration of Independence by the government of Ian Smith was sitting like a yoke on the back of the black people. In Namibia, the blacks were reeling under apartheid. The newly independent states of Botswana, Lesotho, and Swaziland had formed a coalition called Boleswa to try to deal with the issues of the development of their landlocked and poor states. All around them were white people who played boss with black people who succumbed to the harshness of the rule of the day.

Even in the Nazarene mission, most senior administrative jobs were occupied by white people. The grantees of the schools were white, and so was the head of the Nazarene mission. Such messages did not create a psyche that would strongly oppose apartheid and create a mind-set that would bring about change in Swaziland, yet we needed to become very strong if we were to succeed in taking over the lives ahead of us and become citizens of a newly independent country. Break time was at ten, and we would go out and play in the school yard. Sisile,

Makhosi, and I would walk out of the classroom and make for the tap to drink some water. It was nice to run down the steps of the school and go and search for guavas in the grounds just below the school. We would shout at each other as we went guava hunting in the summer. Just the smell of the guavas gave us the feeling of what it was like to be out and running instead of being confined. I liked the white guavas and felt very good when I ate them. My friends liked the red ones. We would trade if we got one that we did not like. After that we would go and stand near the assembly hall and bask in the sun with all the other students. Walking up the steps in our school made us feel that we were at home. We loved the school that was made of a double-storied building that had an office and a woodwork shop. It felt like our home while we were students.

I was not good at spelling when I was in Form I. I was always misspelling words. I did not know how to spell *porridge* and *pocket*. In English class, my teacher would read my spelling mistakes to the class, and I would feel embarrassed. I would try to improve by reading and taking more care when I wrote my compositions.

At break time the bell rang, and we made our way downstairs in order to bask in the sun. It was early in the year, and the classrooms were cold on rainy days. We walked out of the class and went downstairs in a group. It was as if all the girls who stayed at the hostel wanted to be together. We made our way to play table tennis in the space that was between the office and the outside entrance to the school. There were already some boys on the table. We decided to join them with Sisile. She was very good at table tennis. We won the first game even though I could tell that my concentration was poor. We vowed that we would maintain our position even in the second game. It is when you concentrate on something like table tennis that you make the most mistakes. I missed the ball on our last game, and that was how we lost the game. I felt very bad when the bell rang because I was determined to win and maintain the position of being the best table tennis player among the girls.

We went back to class for more lessons. We were going for the Zulu lesson. Our Zulu teacher was Mr. Khoza, a man who was better known as "UBaba" (Father) to all the students. He was a funny man who spoke with a continuous uncontrollable wink on his face. He called every student "idiot." One time a girl fell in class, and he said, "The idiot was so confused that all she could do was fall." When Mr. Khoza entered the classroom, he had the Zulu grammar book *Uhlelo* in his hand. We took our books and turned to the page where there were pronouns in Zulu. He used to make us recite the pronouns word for word. Because we read this grammar book every year, we were tired of the lists that were in it. We wished that there were other books for grammar besides this one. The Zulu class passed without any consequence. Once in a while he would tell us stories. One of his stories was about a man who married an ugly woman just because she had a beautiful voice. He said one day the man found the woman asleep, and he looked at the woman's ugly face and said, "Woman, wake up. Wake up and sing." The woman woke up slowly, and then the man looked at her and said, "Woman, sing." It was not the way the woman sang that was funny. It was the way Mr. Khoza told the story. He repeated, "Woman, wake up and sing, and the woman bellowed." When he said that, we laughed because we could imagine the ugliest woman in the world doing the thing she could do best, bellowing the notes into the air. After telling a funny story, Mr. Khoza would leave and go back to the staff room. Our class would still be noisy from the laughter. We had to settle down for the next teacher.

When our English teacher came in, she was wearing a short-sleeved navy blue crimplene two-piece that had grey on it, flat wedge shoes, and a mohair beret on her head. Her elbows were white as if she had been kneeling on them on the part where the lower part of the arm and the upper part meet. The fatness of her buttocks made a nice tablelike bulge at the back, and as she swung her legs and entered the class, the fatness of her arms jingled a little as if in protest about the manner in which the owner handled herself. She came into class about five minutes late and pulled the chair after greeting us and looked through the window. Her not-so-good-looking smile that revealed slightly chipped teeth showed itself as she spoke to us the usual greeting that was about papers on the floor and telling the boys to sit up straight. "Dlamini, sit up, man, you are not an old man. Your back is not that of an old person." She had her knitting in her hands; and after pulling out her chair, she took out the book, opened it, pulled the yarn, pulled over the knitting needle with her left hand, and talked about how we should behave if we wanted to be decent women. She would knit on and on as she spoke to us, and we would listen to her advice. She always talked about playing house and "getting married in the grass." She would say, "Mantombazane, ningakyateli o'tshanini" in Xhosa. This meant that we should not have boyfriends who were after getting pleasure from our bodies. We were supposed to get engaged in church and then marry in the Christian way. She told us how children in Zakhele liked to play house *ubuyokuyoku*. Sometimes she would break into her limited Latin phrases and state in Latin how we should speak to her and say, "Dici mihi in verbis puella stulta." She said this meant "Speak to me in words, silly girl," and we would speak to her in words.

We enjoyed her stories and read the book *Practical English* by Tregidgo and Ogundipe. It was a red book that had pictures of two students on its cover. The girl was wearing red and white like us, and the boy was wearing grey shorts and a white shirt. We used to do conversations and then read a passage and then do some grammar from it. Things were smooth sailing in English because we were reading a lot. I was reading *Hatter's Castle*, and other girls were reading books like *Wuthering Heights*. These simplified versions of the English classics were from Longman. They were abridged and at a level of English that we would understand. Sometimes when we were bored, we would read picture dramas like *Chunkie* and other cartoons. Our teacher would be furious with us. "Never read these picture things. Even an illiterate can read these. Bring this here. I don't want to see it here," she would say as she confiscated our picture dramas. Since these were cheap and bought in the stores and passed on from one person to another, we felt very bad when they were taken from us.

    She would tell us to write a composition, and that would be time for me to think of all the things I knew that I could write about. My eyes would wander, and I would look at the blue sky through the window. I could see the clouds and the top part of the trees from the upstairs classroom where we had our Form I class. I thought about the time when I had arrived at the school. It had been in January 1970. I had come from Phonjwane Primary School where I had been among the only three second-class passers in Standard V. Coming to Manzini Nazarene was a complete change from walking eight miles a day. It was sheer luxury compared to the long walks I had taken to go to school each day. I would sit and look at the other students. Most of them were from the Practicing Primary School and the Manzini Nazarene Primary School, both of which were on the premises of the Nazarene mission. Those of us who had come from other schools were from the other Nazarene primary schools like Mbuluzi, Sidvokodvo, Mliba, and Balekane. I would think about the first day when I had arrived and made to sit outside on the bench that was outside the office. It was after I was admitted that I went to join the other students in the line that was going to the assembly hall. My thoughts would wander from outside to the open door through which I could see the girls' hostel far out toward the west and then come back to the teacher. Eventually I would jot down a sentence or two after coming up with a topic and then start thinking again. The other students were also struggling with their writing. They also did not know what to write. They sat with their pens in the air, thinking what word to put down next. Before we knew it, it would be time to submit our composition, and we would ask to take it home because we were not done. Our teacher would tell us to make sure that we had it ready the next time we met and tell us to read the books, not picture books because that was why we could not think in English. She told us that we had to know English and even dream in it. That is when we would begin to find it easy to write a composition.

    I used to think about the way my English was different from that of the students who had gone to the schools that were in town. I did not understand the present simple tense. I thought these town students were wrong, and they did not know English the way I did when they added an *s* to the third person for everyday happenings. I thought I knew better until I started reading more books and then settled into my own way of understanding English. I laughed at myself whenever those thoughts came back. English class would end with our teacher picking up her book and rolling the knitting and leaving our class. As soon as she stepped out, the students would start talking and playing. They would pass notes about messages, and we would read them. My friend Sisile would pass her novel and show me funny things in the book. Some of them were very naughty things that we did not want teachers to know about. We were surprised that books had such funny things in them. We would chatter among ourselves until the next teacher came. If it was study time, we would read our books while the other students marched up and down. We would keep busy with different things, happy that we had a few minutes to ourselves, and all the fun would come to an end when it was time for lunch.

Lunch would be announced by the long whine of a siren that announced break throughout the mission. We were looking forward to this sound because we were hungry. We would once again get ready to go to the hostel. The day scholars went to a window behind the assembly hall. This is where they were served a meal of samp mealies and peanut butter. Sometimes they had meat, and at times they had peas or beans. We would go to the hostel for our lunch that often consisted of mealie rice and meat. Only on Wednesdays and Sundays did we have something different. Wednesday was the day for dry peas. We called this pea soup *smanga*, which means "surprise" because it was a pea soup by all standards, but its yellow color was a surprise. I think this is how it got its name. Sundays we had chicken. All the girls liked the back of the chicken. These pieces of meat were passed around on the tables. We were very happy when it was our turn to be dished the back of the chicken. On Mondays we had liver. We thought liver was a special treat just like the chicken.

After lunch we would go back to the dorms. Some girls would wash and powder their faces. Some like me, who never thought that it was necessary to wash and powder the face, would just rely on the morning application of Snow White. Anybody in the school who did not have money used this pomade or a slightly inferior version called Snowene. The girls who had money bought creams that were expensive. Some of the creams were dangerous for the skin because they peeled off the pigmentation and made the girls lighter. The girls would talk about having *ikhompi*, meaning that their complexion was lighter from these. These were days when being lighter was considered a better thing in southern Africa. When I went back to the dorm, I would take my novel and read it to pass time. We were not allowed to go to school before the bell rang. As soon as the bell rang, we would make our way to school. At two o'clock, we had to be in class.

The last two hours of class passed quickly no matter what we were doing. We had library classes, music, or sports once a week. Apart from those, the afternoons were just class days like any other day.

In the athletics season, we had sports practices every day. We would wait for the after-school bell to ring and make our way to the playground. My friends

WEEDING THE FLOWERBEDS

Sisile and Makhosi were in the athletics team. Makhosi was the sprinter of the school. She had brought many trophies to the school because she was the fastest runner in the nation. Sisile was the high jumper of the school. I envied her how she could lift herself up like a bird. She would head for the storeroom that was under the stairs to fetch the steel rod that was used for the high jump. You would see her holding the rod as if she owned it. Even when we were in Form I, she was already jumping over six feet, which was even taller than her. I had come to terms with my own abilities. I did not wait for the athletes. I made my way to the fitness exercise stop that was under the gum trees. I was doing ordinary physical exercises for all the students. We were supposed to pass three of these exercises. Our teacher Ms. Savage would record our scores. I decided to pass near the guava trees on my way to the fitness exercises. I had seen a juicy guava at break time, and I knew that it was way inside the tree and hidden from the other students. I was reaching for it when my foot stepped on something soft. I looked down, and lo and behold! It was a snake. I quickly made my way shouting, and the snake started to chase me. "It is the snake which is attracted by something red! Run!" the girls who were behind me shouted. I ran back toward the cement steps that were outside the school. "It is coming up this way," I heard the girls saying as they ran toward the steps. Right then I saw a boy picking up a big rock from the ones that lined the flower bed. He beat the snake on the head, and I saw it squirm under the rock. The tail moved this way and that way. The head could not be seen as it was under the rock. Another boy took a rock and beat the tail.

"Is it still alive and moving?" the boy who had beaten the snake on the head asked.

"No," I answered. I had moved back to see what was happening. The boys kicked the stones off the snake and picked it up with a stick. They were going to throw it on the other side of the school where there were some sisal-like plants. Right then I saw the biology teacher Ms. Mngadi. She was coming to talk to the boys. Some students had told her about the snake, and she came and told the boys to take the snake to the biology lab. The lab had all sorts of amphibians. All of them were inside bottles that had watery solutions.

"Bulelo, I am back. I am going to run down there." It was Makhosi. She was pointing at the sports ground.

"What is wrong with the primary school grounds?" I asked.

"The student teachers and the primary school children are using the ground. We are too crowded. We are going to run down there," she said as she hugged me. She was pointing at the big football field that was way beyond the gum trees.

"Twigza, be careful. I just saw a snake," I said, pointing at the guava trees.

"Is that why you look so frightened? I don't fear snakes. I fear frogs. If it was a frog, I would be shaking," Makhosi said as she continued toward the sports ground of the high school.

"Frogs don't bite; that snake could have bitten me, Twigza. It was this close. I was way in that clump of trees reaching for a guava and what! It just turned and started chasing me. It was *phempetfwane*, the tiny snake that is attracted by red things. You could have seen how all the girls ran because they knew it would chase them. I hate snakes. My brother was once bitten by a small snake called inhlangwane. His whole foot was swollen for a week. My mother had to take him to the hospital at night," I said as we walked down to the gum tree.

"When I was young, a snake called *imfeti* spat into my eyes. We were playing behind bags of maize. My father shot it with a gun," Makhosi said as we walked.

"Let's not talk about snakes anymore. I am still scared," I said as we neared the place for the fitness exercises. I could still feel the creepiness of the aftereffects of seeing the snake. I felt funny all over my body.

"I am going down now. Last time I was late and the physical education teacher did not like it. I must move fast," Makhosi said as she ran toward the sports field. We could already see the physical fitness teacher. He was a young man from Oregon in the United States. He was agile, and he seemed to enjoy getting the students to prepare to run. At the age of around twenty, he had the energy of an athlete and could have been one of the students himself. His name was Mike Allen.

I put my exercise books down near a small tree and made my way to the ropes. I was supposed to climb up the gum tree using a rope. I took off my shoes and lifted my arms to pull the rope. I heaved my weight and held on tight to the rope. It was very difficult for me to pull up all my weight and climb up at the same time. I kept going, and luckily I seemed to be making progress. The last time I had tried this exercise I had stopped because of the pain from the rope that was cutting into my hand. I held on this time and moved about. I had made six feet when I decided to look down. Suddenly it did not make sense to proceed when the ground was so low. I looked up and then decided to keep going. I made one final jump, and now it became very difficult to go farther. My mind was no longer focusing on continuing. I wanted to be done. I felt myself going down and then looked up. The rope was coming off the pole. I wondered how this had happened. Since the rope seemed to have become detached and was coming down, I decided to jump. I fell and landed with a thud. I hit the ground with my behind and hurt my elbow on the tree near the poles that supported the rope. It was a small jacaranda tree that seemed to be stunted because of trying to grow under the big gum trees. I sat there for some time before going on to the next exercise. It was push-ups. I went and lay down and started on my push-ups. The last time I had done them, I had only fallen short by six. The total we were supposed to do was thirty sit-ups. That earned us three points. I wanted more than three points, so I continued. I surprised myself by doing 60 push-ups. Ms. Savage, the sports teacher, was happy that I had done so many. She told me that I had broken the record of the school! I was very pleased with myself.

When I took the road that went back to the hostel, I was the happiest person that day. I went past the tall poplar trees that lined the right-hand side of the road and felt as if they were also celebrating my success. I made it to the dorm and then took some money and went to the tuckshop. I needed some washing soap and a toothbrush and black polish for my shoes. I decided to celebrate by buying myself the things I needed for my morning bath. After that I went back to the room, and realizing that I still had fifty cents, I went to buy myself fat cakes from the matron's niece who used to sit outside the kitchen with a dish full of fat cakes.

"Bule, where are you going? I heard that you were almost bitten by a snake. I heard this from Makhosi." It was Sisile. She was back from the field where she had been doing high jump.

"I don't want to talk about that story, Twigza. How high did you jump today?" I asked, looking at her.

"I barely made six feet. I did not perform very well. I have to set myself new goals. Ever since I stopped competing with others, I have been improving. I just set myself a goal and then see what I can do to take my jump over that. I continue increasing the distance little by little. I think this way, I will improve a great deal. I did not know that if you challenge yourself little by little, things improve. You also work harder because you are working against yourself. How about you? How was your fitness practice?"

"Let me tell you, Twigza," I said, whispering into her ear, "I made sixty sit-ups. Tomorrow I will do push-ups. I am not expecting a miracle, but if I can do ten, I will be happy. It is important for me to create realistic goals too. I am not an athlete like you, but I can also improve at my own pace. I will do that. I will also take part in the cross-country race." Everybody knew that I stood a chance in winning the cross-country race. That race was not about being fast as much as it was about being clever and strategic in finding the pieces of the puzzle that were hidden on the route. We ran toward the farm and looked for pieces of cloth or other instructions and ran back on the road that passed below the head of the mission station's house and into the gum trees. Then after touching all the spots, we came back to win prizes at the school. I did win the cross-country once. "I think I will win this time again, Twigza. I am willing to try. It will be an improvement on my part," I said, looking at her as if seeking her approval.

"I also think it will. I am just glad that you are also improving," Makhosi said as we walked toward the wire lines, which were used for hanging clothes to dry in the sun. We took the ball and decided to go and play a ball game we called "die." We would try to hit someone with the ball, and if they were touched by the ball, they had to sit down and someone else would go in. Everybody took a turn to try to be the one who would stay in the longest. It was fun to be out there playing. When we got tired, we would go and sneak into the dormitories of the student teachers and visit them. They liked chatting with us even though the matron did not want us to go to them. They were nice to us and ironed our uniforms on Saturday and also bought fat cakes for us. It was nice to be pampered by them.

Our after-school time would be terminated by the bell for supper. We had time to run around as much as we wanted to until that bell rang. We were allowed to go anywhere around the hostel except beyond the chapel because we knew that those areas were out of bounds. There was a cement ring outside one of the entrances. Inside this cement ring, there was a tree we called *umsilinga*. In spring, it had small purple flowers; and after the flowers, there would be round seedy fruits that were used as seeds. The fruits would ripen into a brownish color, and they would leave a fleshy pulp when we crushed them. These were often used to make beads. We would go sit under the tree on the ring or go out to pick pawpaws on the trees that were all around the hostel. We would take the pawpaws to the cooks sometimes. Sometimes they would disappear between the dormitories and the kitchen when our honesty levels were low. Once in a while a girl who sold dry peanuts would come to the gum tree that was near the chapel. We would go and buy a small tin of peanuts for five cents. We would share these among ourselves. It was good to have a little bit of money to spend on these extras. They made life interesting to children who were far away from home.

The hostel doors were locked at five thirty. The bell for locking the doors would ring, and we would know that it was time to go to the chapel. They would be opened when we were done with bathing, and we would go to the chapel, and then afterward they were closed for good. Chapel time was time for another sermon. If we could count how many sermons we heard in high school, we can go beyond thousands. If one's salvation depended on the number of times they read the Bible, we would have been saved at that time. Unfortunately it is the things people have the most that they end up lacking. Deep down our souls, we're crying for a different education than the one we were getting. We were being given a very Christian education when our country just got its independence. What we needed was an education for a newly independent nation, one that would allow us to create our own worlds.

There should have been a drastic change in our way of life that should have characterized the changes that our nation was faced with. We should have been transforming the inside to lead itself in whatever situation it was because we were living in a southern Africa that was characterized by the forceful rule of racist South Africa. The important thing was to be a thinker no matter what the situation one was in. The world we were going out to, though characterized by apartheid, was no longer going to remain a world of the Christian who obeys the rules. It was a world of the Christian who says no. These would be people who would say no to poverty, no to inferiority of blacks, and no to being ruled by others. Instead they would rule the world themselves. They would quickly establish the needs of communities and work on plans and goals of achieving these. They had to know how to address the needs of others the way they knew their own needs. It was interesting that we were in the hostel far away from every noise and being molded into young people who would be followers of rules. If we followed rules in the world, we would be correct; but if the rules were oppressive, without an understanding of the rules of the Christian that says no, success would be a wild dream. This is when the campaign to reread and the rules of the hostel began. It began one day when were in the big dormitory called "Enqabeni."

I was standing on the table and repeating what our teacher Mr. Khoza used to say. He used to begin his own sermons the moment we got to class. He would say, "The Bible says, 'Seek ye first the kingdom of God,'" but I say, "Seek ye first the kingdom of money and all things shall be added unto you." The first rule said, "Every girl shall eat the food that is provided by the hostel." In real life, the girls were not forced to eat all the food that was provided. They ate what they felt like eating. It was interesting that the rule read like that.

We did not argue with this rule. We appreciated the food, and we ate most of it, but when we were protesting, I heard one girl read, "Every girl shall eat the chaff that is provided by the hostel." On the whole, the food was not chaff. We knew this very well, but there was a need to query things in that dormitory. Everybody wanted to be heard. The girls wanted to have been there when the rules were made rather than for the rules to be handed to them as if they were a must. That is why we were going through them. We, the people who were affected by the rules, had not been consulted when the rules were made. We decided that we would make this clear the next time we were asked about the rules.

There were rules that we did not understand the need for. An example would be the rule on waiting for the bell before we went to school after lunch. It did not make sense why we had to wait. It did not bother us, but some of those rules seemed to be there just because somebody was enjoying writing rules. It was clear that we did not want rules for rules' sake. We wanted rules that stated the reason why they were there. Rules about noise at night were understandable because making noise when others wanted to sleep was not good. We all wanted such rules to be enforced. After our meeting, we decided to hold a separate meeting with the prefects. It was important to tell them that they were in the school administration system to help us understand how we were led, not to bring the system down to us for their own benefit. We did not want people who betrayed the course. We wanted people who supported the school system so that there would be progress for all. It was important for us to educate our prefects ourselves. We could not afford to have people who wanted to rule when they did not know who we were and what we wanted. We were not in the school to duplicate generations. Ours was a generation that had been born in very difficult times. We were going to go out into a world where jobs were scarce. We needed to have living skills and not just to learn the three *r*'s and then go out to be incompetent.

It was Makhosi who expressed our resolutions very well that day. She said that if the teachers loved us, they were going to make sure that we are taught how to talk about ourselves and our needs. We did not want rules that said we should not wear sleeveless dresses when we did not know why. We did not want rules about food in the lockers when we did not know why there should be no food there. We wanted lessons on sex education because we were teenagers. We wanted to understand the biology of our lives because of its importance in our own development. When we left school, we wanted to be prepared to live in the world that was ahead of us and bring about the improvement that was needed.

We did not know that there was a whistle-blower among the girls who were at that meeting. The consequences of speaking when there is a whistle-blower caught up with us in the evening. We were going to study in the dining hall when the matron came to our dormitory. Makhosi, Sisile, and I and some of the girls who had called the meeting were summoned to go to the matron's office. We did not hesitate to tell her what we were discussing. It was the way we spoke that convinced the matron that we were not talking about making trouble. Time and again, she would hint that we could lead a strike, and we assured her that we wanted to have the best stay ever at the hostel. There was no way we would want to make trouble. We wanted every student to be happy. We told her how we had discussed stealing among the students. We told her how some of those habits were difficult for her to check and how we were going to work together to make sure that nobody stole from other girls. We talked about the sister's-keeper system and how it would work such that people would not hide things from others if they were bad. We were going to be our own sister's keeper and look out for each other. We told her how we would teach each other how to talk with respect and power. When we left her office, she was convinced that we were up to improving things for the best for our lot.

Life improved after we had had discussions with the matron. We felt more like people who could decide their destiny the way Mr. Nkonzo had said at morning prayers. We tried to live lives that were more focused on the future. We talked about how we would practice interpreting so that we can be useful in the communities when we go back to our homes. We were determined to become students who understood the life ahead of them. We studied more and read more books.

I remember how we started to read more books. It was Sisile who liked to read at first. I just liked to laugh. I was envious when we were walking in the street, and she started laughing at people she thought looked like Humpty Dumpty. I did not know who Humpty was. I wanted to know, and she would tell me that she would show me when we go to the library. She would pick a book in the library, and just because I wanted to laugh with her, I would read it and laugh at the man and his stomach and his thin legs. After that we were reading everything we could lay our hands on. We read Jerzy Kosinski's *The Painted Bird* and Charlotte Bronte's *Wuthering Heights*. These books made us laugh. The phrases of people "shaking as if they had been treated with some inner wind" became our everyday talk. We would read and make sure that we were watching every comma and every period. Our compositions had to show that we were reading daily so that our spelling and expression would improve. Even in Zulu, we were reading and using idioms whenever we could because we wanted to improve. We wanted our time in school to be memorable.

There was a lot of improvement in our first year. It became clear that if things went the way we're working, we would do well in all areas in our lives. We had set out on the right path. Take away the spiritual world of the Bible and anything that was done in this world, in this consciousness, and you had three successful human beings in the Sisters Three. This was the life that my friend Makhosi, Sisile, and I had come to begin to conquer at Manzini Nazarene High School.

Chapter Two

Freedom is not merely the opportunity to do as one pleases; neither is it merely the opportunity to choose between set alternatives. Freedom is, first of all, the chance to formulate the available choices, to argue over them—and then, the opportunity to choose.

—C. Wright Mills

* * *

Sunday morning was a bit lax. We did not wake up very early. We would go and wash after a breakfast of three fish sandwiches and cocoa in a mug and thin porridge. We would go out and polish our shoes out in the sun on a cement wall under a gum tree on the way to the chapel. After applying the polish, we would wait for it to set and then shine our shoes with a brush. We would finish off by wiping them with a pantyhose in order to give the shoes a real shine. Our wake-up time was seven o'clock. We went for breakfast at eight o'clock and then filed into the chapel at nine o'clock. On this day, we wore checkered skirts and white blouses. Our short cropped hair shone with Vaseline petroleum jelly, which was the standard pomade for both body and hair. Equipped with the smells of the cheapest perfume called Country Club for those who could afford it, we would be on our way to church.

We parted with the older girls and the student teachers and made our way to the old church for Sunday school. This church was surrounded by the nurses' home, the nurses' college, and the Raleigh Fitkin Memorial Hospital. Sometimes we would see the boys on their way to church as we walked up the road that was marked by the tall poplar trees. Other girls went to different classes. Makhosi, Sisile, and I would be joined by the girls from the orphanage and the other girls who lived on the mission station who were around the ages of twelve and thirteen. Our Sunday school class was taught by one of the student nurses. She would take any Bible story and keep us occupied for the hour. We would sing songs and discuss stories from the Bible. It was nice to meet with the children of the Nazarenes who went to other schools. Some of the girls whose parents were Nazarenes went to Saint Theresa's High School. We would enjoy having them in our class.

We would walk out of the old church and go past the nurses' college. There was a clump of bamboo trees near a tap just outside the nurses' college. We would pass and drink water from this tap. We would look inside the nurses' college and see that some of the nurses were asleep. Sometimes the girls from the orphanage would go in and talk to some student nurses that they knew; and Makhosi, Sisile, and I would join them. It was interesting to see where the nurses lived. We would take in the whole premises and look at it with wonder. There seemed to be some knowledge lurking in this building, which seemed to have been built years ago judging from the flaking bluish white paint and the black watercolor paint boundary that marked the foundation. There were mango trees inside the fence, and the lines on which the nurses dried their clothes could be seen near these trees. We would pass near the fence and go through a small gate and then cross the dirt road that cars use to go to the parking lot of the Sharpe Memorial Church and then go down some steps to get to the church. After that we would go and join the other members of the congregation who were waiting for the Sunday school services of the adults to finish. These were still going on in the main church. We would watch the buses on the road or send some of the day scholars to Lewis Store to buy us chewing gum and Toff-O-Luxe, a chewy caramel sweet that we loved because of the milky taste that it left in our mouths.

Some of the nurses would join us as we stand out and watch the buses passing on the road. They were wearing their white aprons, caps, and blue shirts. Some of them had badges on their shoulders, and some did not. The Sister Tutors wore all white and caps that had black stripes on them. To me, nursing seemed to be a rigidly graded career like being in the army. It was just one reason why I did not find it attractive even though our high school literature book required us to read the biographies of Florence Nightingale and Albert Schweitzer. I knew that a life of philanthropy such as the one that these two had lived would not make me the person I wanted to be. We would watch the cars of the missionaries as they drove into the parking lot under the conifers. It was an interesting time for us because those of us who had parents who were Nazarenes got a chance to greet them. Makhosi's grandmother would arrive, and we would go and talk to her. She would be wearing her usual *doek* with a cloth over her shoulders and carrying a walking stick and walking barefooted if not wearing a black pair of slippers. She would greet us in her hoarse voice, and we would chat with her. We loved Grandmother Ndlaleni Vilakati with our whole hearts. When looking at her wrinkled face and fine sunken eyes, we would feel as if we were with someone from another world. Just the thought of being with an octogenarian was a blessing like no other. She would sometimes bring avocado pears from her orchard, and we would tell her to give them to us after the main service because we did not have anywhere to hide them.

At half past eleven, we would go into the main service. It was led by the main pastor of the mission station who lived near the house that was near the nurses' college. It lasted from half past eleven to one o'clock. It was difficult to sit and listen for so long. Sometimes the sermons were interesting. At other times, they were not. We would all sing from the only hymnal *Ezokudumisa*. We almost knew the songs by heart. The church was shaped like a cross from inside. All the four sides focused on the pulpit that was on the joint of the cross, if you know what I mean. There is the long part of the cross and the short part. All the parts meet at the center. If you get the picture, then you have a clear picture of what Sharpe Memorial Church looks like. It is a tall building that is made of red bricks with small windows that line all the sides from about halfway to the roof. The roof is made out of red corrugated iron. There is a podium and a curtained section that demarcates the part where the pastors sit. In front of the curtained section are two benches that mark the altar. This is where we rolled off the burden of sins when the altar call was made. I remember walking up there after my heart was "pierced" by the word. I would pray that the Lord Jesus would have mercy on me and save me. The kind of salvation we were after was not the one where you become one with all and love all. We were after a salvation that would elevate you from the ordinary man you are, a black African sinner and child of the devil.

Many sermons advocated the idea of a heart of sin. There was one pastor who used to use a chart that had the snake, the pig, and the devil and his horns among other horrifying animals. The fact that all these were inside one's heart was unbearable. It made sense to want to repent and leave the devil with his animals. We did not want to go to hell and be with these animals. The thought that if we did not repent they would be inside us was even more unbearable. I remember wishing that the Lord Jesus would have mercy on me and take away the pride of the peacock. I am not sure if he heard me because my conceit still showed in some of my deeds.

I think salvation is very difficult to comprehend at the age of thirteen. It is coveted but difficult to lay hands on, let alone to get into one's heart. The biology and the language confuse and confound a child. The idea of the mind, body, and spirit is too complex and a bit too vague at this age. That is why we ended up thinking about other things instead of the sermon. Food at lunch, what our parents were doing at home, and the sound of a car passing on the road to Mbabane were occasional distractions that made the mind wander. If what was happening behind the podium was not funny, we would sit like really bored African children who could not hide that our playtime would yield better results than listening to the sermons in such a big church. Once in a while an incident that would cause us to listen attentively would help us focus. These incidents were rare. An example would be like the jacket of one pastor refusing to go down when he stands up and forming a hump on his back. Just the awkwardness of old preachers trying to keep us occupied made us laugh our lungs out. Another incident would be chewing gum and trying hard to hide it from the matron. This one was our pastimes. We would share the gum even though we knew that we were not allowed to chew it inside the church. Another incident would be the presence of a bat squeaking and flying all over. Not to say that the bats were a blessing because they would defecate all over the floor. When they decided to disturb the service, they would be some little creatures that knew how to keep little girls entertained. Just looking at a bat flying up there and squeaking would attract our attention and start us giggling forever as we watched the adults and wondered what they were thinking since they could not control this one thing. It was good to anticipate the frustration of adults at that age.

Once in a while a missionary who was arriving or bidding the church good-bye would stand up and bid his farewell. We would listen as we wondered what the United States of England was like. We would feel bad if it was a high school teacher we liked. There were times when we felt sad because we had come to like some families even though it was from a distance because nobody among the missionaries really interacted that closely with us.

I remember a family that had lost their child to leukemia saying good-bye to us. We were very sad because they had been in the country for a long time. We were happy when some of the strict and nosy missionaries left. We would rejoice because we would feel freer. We felt that they took us for very naughty children, yet our naughtiness was not beyond the usual naughtiness of kids our age.

After church we would go and look for Makhosi's grandmother and take whatever she had brought for us and then run and join the other girls before the matron saw us. We would then walk back to the hostel. It was always nice to watch the cars on the road on our way back to the hostel. Seeing cars on the road made us feel what it would be like to go home. When those thoughts crossed our heads, we would feel as if we were in a prison at the hostel. This is because we never left the mission unless one had a dentist's or optician's appointment. This made us feel as if we were tied to one place. It made us wish that one day we would finish school and be able to feel what freedom was like. When we were free, we would do what we wanted.

It is when I look back that I realize how free I was as a child. The biggest freedom was the fact that somebody else thought for us, did things for us, planned the day for us. The very thing we detested was what we should have appreciated. Life is funny in that you always wish for what you don't know and fail to make the best of what you have. If I could go back to those days, I would cherish every minute of the freedom to be. I would be and be and be until I cannot be anymore. To be to me is to sit down and consider nothing but the emptiness in front of you and then see yourself able to do whatever it is that you have to do even before you do it. Instead of being those days, we spent time longing for a happiness that was elusive because it was not there. Even if we were not in the hostel, we would not have been happy because we would have longed for other things. This never ends unless you tame it by creating a state of being as you breathe and say, "This is it," because you are healthy and not hungry. It is hard to understand such things as a child.

We would get to the hostel and go straight to the dining hall after the bell rings. This was a big hall that had big tables that filled the whole center and just left two aisles on the sides. The matron would stand here and inspect how we are eating. On Sundays, she would be dressed in her Sunday best, and we would be wearing our black-and-white checkerboard-design skirts. The smell of chicken or beans would be all over. If it was chicken, we would be all smiles. If it was Bean Sunday, we would be very sad. We lived for Chicken Sunday.

After lunch, we would go and bask in the sun. We were not allowed to read books on Sundays. The Bible was the only book we could read. My friends Sisile and Makhosi and I would go out and lie on the grass near the flower beds. We would spread one blanket on the ground and cover ourselves with another. All three of us would fit under the blanket. One moment of selfishness would take hold of naughty Sisile, and she would pull the whole blanket to her side leaving our bare bottoms in the air. What is good about being in a girls' hostel is that you are away from the prying eyes of males. You can do anything you like. Even when the blanket was pulled, we would fight for it to be shared even when it meant pulling it toward you and leaving others uncovered until Makhosi said her usual "Hhayi phela yebonine," which meant "not that, you girls," and we would start to be considerate. Mean tricks are sometimes a fun thing with girls at thirteen. We would play April fool on each other and throw slices of bread over the walls of the dormitories in the dark of night because they did not reach up to the ceiling. Being a person meant fighting to be yourself. If you got angry quickly, you would have a tough time because there would be nobody to sympathize with you. It was better to enjoy the fun and join in whatever the girls were doing.

"You said the matron said we must go to her about the spookie," Makhosi said.

"Yes she did; she said the two of you have an explanation to give to her. I did my share of explaining. Go to the matron and talk to her," I said to the girls. I still wanted to get even with them for laughing at me over the hiding-and-not-going-for-prayers punishment. I watched as they started to show worry over their faces. Everybody dreaded going to the senior matron. She was a lady who had a big voice, and nobody wanted to cross her path. We had nicknamed her the "Koor," which was said with an American accent on the *or*.

Makhosi and Sisile went out, and I watched through the empty door and realized that they had fallen for my ruse. I went to the window to watch and see if I could see them when they descended down the dining room steps to go into the matron's door. You could see the entrance to the door from our dormitories. You could actually see the matron in her lounge. When I saw them appear on the other side, I waited to see what they would look like when they came out. They came out very quickly. They were carrying the big bowl of fat cakes. I knew that they had not got into any trouble. They were with the matron's niece. I made for the door and went to join them. Sometimes the matron gave us fat cakes. I did not want to miss the feast.

"You were lying, Rebel 2. The matron did not say anything. She just told us to go and help Mavis carry the fat cakes to the wall where we play," Makhosi said with a smile on her face.

"I think she forgot then. You are lucky, but don't think it is over," I said as I made for the wall. We were going to play galloping on an elastic string this day. I could see Makhosi pulling the elastic band out so that we can position it around our ankles for the first version of the galloping game. We held this elastic band up to the shoulders and the neck. Whoever was galloping had to jump and get it from up there and twist it down and then jump inside it and twist it and jump out. It was an interesting way to pass time. We would make noise as we watched that there was no cheating. If somebody made a mistake, they would lose a turn. This would go on until the bell for locking the doors rang. That meant we should go to the bathroom. We would run for the doors and take our bathroom towel, toothbrush, and soap and make for the bathroom. Even though the water in the shower was cold, we would take a shower because we were sweating. We would not feel the cold. We would play and laugh and sing. One day I fell down in the shower, and my friends laughed at me. I was embarrassed by this act, but I did not make much of it. I noticed that the fungus on the cement floor of the shower made it slippery. I was not paying attention to this because my friend was playing with me. That was how I ended up on the floor. I did not get hurt even though I did fall. The whole feeling was that of a slipperiness that was all over because I had soap all over my body.

The end of the day began with prayers in the chapel. We sang a song from our hymn book *Ezokudumisa* (praise hymns), and one of the student teachers or the junior matron would read from the Bible and preach. If there was a happening, like somebody who was pregnant among the students, the matron would then preach to us about how disappointed she was that one of us had fallen along the way. Some of the older girls understood the message. At that time, I did not understand what it meant. I had no clue about female reproduction when I got to the hostel. Even when I saw sanitary pads, I believed what the girls told me that they were soiled from stuff that came out of their ears. It was when the matron spelt out that those who were young must leave the chapel that I realized that there were things she wanted to talk about that we the Sisters Three did not know about. After prayers we would go to bed after three hours of studying. I still remember the sound of the fluorescent lights as they hummed on continuously when we were studying in the dining hall. I always made use of study time. I liked to sort out what I would learn for each day. I hated having work pile up until I cannot handle it anymore. I always studied every subject and made sure I was up to date with both my notes and my readings. It was subjects like Zulu that bored me stiff. Reading the Zulu book *Uhlelo* for grammar and reading lists on the noun and the pronoun made me go crazy. I discovered a way to do it and make it less boring. When we were chatting in the dorm, I would call out the words and the girls would answer. I would be looking at the book and lying on my back with my feet on the wall. It was a painless collective effort. Even for the Zulu proverbs book *Injula*, I used the same strategy. Going through the long list of Zulu proverbs was impossible to do without getting bored. Doing it together in the dormitory became a fun thing. We ended up misinterpreting some idioms for fun. They just became a part of our lingo, and we were the only ones who knew what we meant. *Ukuyihulula imfibinga* started to mean wasting somebody else's things just because they were not yours. It was fun to be with my friends and do what we thought was the most boring thing in the world, growing up in a mission school boarding school.

While there was not much adventure, we created interesting lives. Out of what would have been the most boring life for other kids became a very interesting life for us. The evenings ended with us switching off the lights at ten o'clock and whispering in the dark. If we failed to keep our voices low, the matron would come and switch on the lights, and we would know that Saturday meant that we would go and chop wood up on the "mountain."

"Rebel 2, you see what you have got us into," Sisile would say after the matron switched off the light.

"Sisile, it is not me. You were the one who started talking about boys. All I did was just to laugh," I would say in self-defense.

"What if the matron heard all we were talking about? Do you know how long she stood outside before she came in?" Makhosi would ask.

"I don't know, and I don't care. Let us keep quiet and go to sleep. We will be marked again, and that will be double punishment," I would say and get under my blankets. My thoughts would wonder, to my home, outside the hostel, what it was like in the moonlight, and I would eventually drift off to sleep.

That term I had mumps; and my cheeks, which are not on the small side, were swollen and even looked bigger than their normal size. I woke up one day and found that my cheeks were feeling funny. They had a tingling feeling that was halfway between pain and being well. I went to the matron, and she sent me to the hospital. At the hospital, they diagnosed me with mumps, and I was sent to a ward where I was all by myself for the whole week. It was terrible to be alone in the ward with no one. If I had thought being locked in the hostel was boring, this was worse. Once again I would go to sleep to the sound of the fluorescent lights. I was not allowed to go to other wards. I had to be in quarantine because mumps are contagious. I stayed in one place, and the only people who would come to my ward were the nurses. They had to cover their mouths with masks when coming to the ward. I sang and went to the window and watched when a car came to take a body from the mortuary. It was a scary thing to watch cars as they came and went and thought that if I died, that is what would happen to me. I would get bored from watching the world through the window and then go and lie on my bed. I would go back to the window in the evening when the men who lit up the boilers were at work. I would watch as they worked through the pile of coal at the back. I would see the laundry of the hospital as it was taken in because my ward was at the back, almost at the end of the Raleigh Fitkin Hospital.

I spent time thinking about school. I wondered what my friends were doing. I did not miss school that much. It was just being alone in the ward that made me feel bored. I would sing at the top of my voice. I was singing at the top of my voice when the door opened. I saw the head teacher at the door. He was followed by my uncle. I was surprised! I sat there and enjoyed the visit. I did not say much. To see the two men go was sad. I resumed my stay in the lonely ward. It was on Friday when I was pronounced free of mumps.

"How was your stay at the hospital, Rebel 2?" Sisile asked when I came out. "We missed you," my friend said as she hugged me.

"Twigza, it was boring. If we say being here at the hostel is boring, we don't know what we are talking about. Your only company is just the fluorescent lights droning on and on, especially at night. Of course I slept on the hospital bed, and the nurses came to change my sheets every day. That was the only luxury. The food, the same thin porridge and bread, Twigza," I said that and asked about the schoolwork. I was behind in my classes after a whole week of being away from school. I decided to go through the notes of my friends in order to catch up in my lessons. I studied science and math and geography from Sisile's books. She was very good at these subjects. I studied religious knowledge and English literature from Makhosi's book. She was good at these too. After that I made sure that I repeated the information. History gave me a problem. I remember going to the teacher to ask what I could do. He gave me a chapter to summarize. Eventually I caught up with my work. I took my studies more seriously than my friends. I studied faithfully and made sure I asked myself questions and answered them after my reading. This stood me in good stead when it was examinations time.

Our Zulu literature books were interesting. We read Sibusiso Nyembezi's version of Alan Paton's *Cry, the Beloved Country*. In English literature, we read Shakespeare's *Romeo and Juliet* and Cyprian Ekwensi's *Burning Grass*. It was good to think about faraway lands. We knew nothing about the Harmattan, but when we read the book, it became real even though we were living in southern Africa and had never been to West Africa. We read about young Rikku and imagined the cattle herders who were Fulanis taking their stock all over. Since our culture was also a culture of stock farmers, it was easy to see that African culture was more similar than different.

The year we were in Form II was also the year of the custom called *umcwasho*. Girls were supposed to wear tassels on their heads to show that they did not have sex before marriage. Young girls who had no boyfriends wore blue and yellow woolen tassels. Older girls who had boyfriends wore red woolen tassels. The tassels were made of wool that is bundled into a long skein and then tied with pom-poms on each side. It is hung around the head with a round beaded string. The day scholars wore these tassels everywhere except in school. When they got to school, they took the tassels off and hid them in their pockets because the missionaries would have none of the "pagan" practices on the school premises. When they left school, they wore them because there were guards outside the fence of our school who would beat them if they were not wearing the tassels. Our school was well known for not observing Swazi customs and traditions.

It is in Form II that I swallowed a drawing pin. I was watching another student pinning some obscene pictures on the board. I did not know how obscene they were until I got close to the board. She had drawn naked human beings, and she had words that were naughty attached to the pictures. I got close to the bulletin board and started reading. I could not believe that she could use such language. I picked the drawing pin that attached the paper to the wall and put it in between my lips and moved my hand to the next one. I did not realize that the girl who sat next to the wall had read the words on the paper. She bellowed the obscene words out, and I laughed out of embarrassment. I had forgotten that I had the pin in between my lips. I bent double as I laughed and the pin went down my throat. I tried to cough it out, but it did not come out. I was worried. I could imagine it tearing my intestines into two. I started crying. I was crying as I ran down the steps to the office. Little did I know that the boy I liked was also in the office. His name was Bobby. He looked at me as I walked into the office door with tears on my face. I lifted my hand to hide the tears. A feeling of shame overcame me. I think it was from the thought of seeing a boy I liked who did not even know I liked him. It was worse to think that he was seeing me in this situation. He looked at me, and I felt humiliated. At that time, I wanted him to think I was more mature than a thirteen-year-old. I told the secretary what had happened. She called the Raleigh Fitkin Memorial Hospital, and they told her that I should go back to the hostel. When I got to the hostel, I went to the matron. She had already been informed about my situation. That day I had to eat six slices of white bread. It was not fun to eat the slices of bread when other students were eating sandwiches that had fruit jam in them. I wanted to drink some tea out of a mug like the others. That was not on my diet that day.

"What happened, Rebel 2? We heard you swallowed a drawing pin?" It was Sisile who asked me after my meal of six slices of bread.

"Why do you ask?" I was pretending to be very angry when I asked this question.

"Twigza, I just want to know." She knew I would not be cross when she called me that. I also called her Twigs when she jumped over the high jump pole at school. Twigs and Twigza were names we had adopted from one of the books we read. They were good names for us because we were very thin. Makhosi's name was Bamboo Stick. She was tall and thin all over—long, to be honest—like a bamboo stick. There was no fat on her. I think my big head and fat cheeks made me look less of a stick than her long, thin legs. The thigh and the leg were just the same with Makhosi. We knew she did not like this, but we were not giving each other names we liked. She was just not there when we chose the names out of the book, so she got the worst side of our rough humor.

"Well, girl, as you might want to know I humiliated myself even to the Form Vs. I was seen by this guy," I said, talking about the boy who wore glasses in Form V, crying after this ordeal. "How do you like that for an end of the day story?"

"Shame," Makhosi said as she got closer to me.

"Don't shame me. You heard Mrs. Mururi. She said that is not English. Don't ever say that again." I was correcting my friend in order to save myself from the situation.

"But, friend, imagine being seen by this guy, crying in the office! I would have died," Makhosi said.

"I died a little, Twigza, but I came back to life in a minute. It wasn't going to help me in any way to die. I just had to brave it, my dear. Such things happen in this life. You just have to experience the mortifying moments of our existence." The story hushed a bit after I had told them about this one. That evening, I was the talk of the hostel. Everybody wanted to know what had happened. It was at such times that I hated having friends. They behaved like a real bush telephone. Everybody would claim that they heard from so-and-so and on and on the story would go. By the time I went to the bathroom to join the others in the afternoon bath, I was tired of hearing girls talking about me. I decided that I would do something to anybody I heard talking about me.

"Shut your mouth!" I shouted at one girl who was talking about me and the drawing pin. She backed off quickly because she could see that I was angry. I left the bathroom feeling triumphant that I had done something. It did not help to be shy with the girls when they were teasing you. You felt bad when you did not speak up for yourself. I learned this at that time.

"You did well by shouting at that girl," Sisile said when she saw the girl retreat.

"Sometimes you have to act out of character; some of these girls don't know when it is time for them to mind their own business." I was proud of myself as I reiterated what my friend had just said. It was good to be supported by one of your own.

There were many incidents that made me feel humiliated like the swallowing of the drawing pin. I remember playing with another girl and we fell on top of each other and my tunic came up to the middle of my back, exposing my whole behind. I felt very bad when the boys reacted and turned away as if I was doing something bad. Being in our school made us feel like girls, as if girls were different from boys and also that we were expected to behave differently. While the boys were rough, we were expected to be soft. Nobody really said we should be soft. It was just known that we were expected to be good girls, and good girls were soft. So my falling, yelling, and shouting were seen as out of character. I was classified among the naughty girls. That is why even when I got good grades, the matron was surprised. She did not expect much to come from me. I knew that she did not understand me.

I started improving my writing in Form II. I remember reading books on writing when I was in the library. I remember another girl lending me a book on composition writing. I read it and found that I understood a lot about how to write a composition. I learned that my composition had to have an introduction, a body, and a conclusion. This seemed to be easy for me. After this reading, my writing improved tremendously. It is in Form II that I improved and started to be one of the best students. In our school, being best meant that you were compared to others. We were given positions according to the points we had scored in the exams. When my marks improved, I got closer to leading the class.

I was excited when I got my results at the end of Form II. I could see that I had given my work my best shot, and it had paid off. I decided to keep working on improving. That year, I felt I had accomplished a lot. I had sewn a dress to fit, done some embroidery on a pillowcase that I took home to show my parents. I also started typing classes.

The sewing classes had been fun. The senior inspector for home economics would come to our school with her assistant, a white woman who was older, and they would teach the class once a week. The girls who were naughty would even wear their dresses to fit even as we were sewing them. I already knew the basics in sewing because I had done five years of it in primary school. I knew the jargon like placing on fold or sewing crossway strips. I also knew the basic stitches like running, hemming, and backstitch. What was good in high school was that we were now using sewing machines when in primary school, we had done everything by hand. I had sewn a floral baby's romper in primary school, and now it felt good to sew a dress to fit. My dress had a floral green color, and it had round collars. I remember how challenging fitting in the sleeves was. The top part of the sleeves had to be gathered, and the senior inspector helped me. She was a light-complexioned woman who was kind and gentle to all of us. We liked her very much.

On the Swaziland social scene, life was also interesting in 1971. This was also the year when Percy Sledge came to Swaziland. It was the first time we got to see an African American. We were very excited. There were gigs at the national stadium, and people paid a lot of money to go and see him and dance to his music. When we returned to school after his show, everybody was singing his songs. The girls who had songbooks wrote his songs in words. We joined together and sang "When a Man Loves a Woman" and "Take Time to Know Her." We had music talent shows at our school. One boy decided to sing the song "Take Time to Know Her." It was funny because his leg was in a cast and just watching him carrying the guitar and dangling his leg down the flight of stairs to get to the front of the auditorium was quite a sight. When he opened his mouth, we were hoping for the usual religious song such as a Jim Reeves piece or the other songs we sang in the school. The surprise turned to a roar of laughter when he started strumming his guitar and imitating Percy Sledge in a mission school where this was a taboo. "I found a woman," he sang, "I felt truly in love, but she was . . ." As he continued, we were laughing until our stomachs were painful. I laughed and laughed and cried because everybody in the hall was amused by the circus of a show that he was putting on. We knew that the principal would not be amused, but as high school talent shows go, we knew that they had to put up with this one. It was just sheer protest walking in a cast and telling everybody that we were not to be left to ourselves to choose songs. After that show, this boy was called "Take Time," and being the matchmakers that Sisile and Makhosi were, they found a girl to stick him with. I felt sorry for her because there was nothing she could do. She just laughed and took it easy.

Our boisterousness used to irk some of our teachers. There was just one teacher who could not stand us. She would shout at us and then give up. After that she would give us the silent treatment when she thought we were too naughty. She would sit in class and expect us to keep quiet. The punishment was for us to sit and just do absolutely nothing while she sat in front of us in order to show us that she was cross with us. This was very funny because we did not feel the punishment. Instead we laughed some more and hid under our desks. It was after Percy Sledge's show that another boy decided to break the silence by singing, "Come softly, darling, come to me," which was one of Percy Sledge's songs. The class was quiet when she came in. This was the fourth day, a Thursday, and we had been on the silent treatment for four days. It was in the quiet of that Form II class when my eyes were wandering and looking at the tall poplar tree that could be seen through the window that I heard the music. It came from the back in a soft, calm, determined voice.

> Come softly, darling,
> Come to me
> Early morning
> I want, want you to know me
> Your kisses—

He did not finish the line about kisses. The teacher, Ms. Maqeks, was so cross that she stood up from behind the table and walked about the classroom like a mad woman,

"Who is that great musician?" she asked as she walked around. "Who is the great musician?" She went over to the boys' side where the music had come from.

"It is Killer," one of the boys said, pointing at Killer.

"You go out and sing outside there," Ms. Maqeks said, pointing at the poplar tree that we could see through the window. "I want to hear you up there." She went to the window and pointed down at the tree, which meant that Killer had to go downstairs and sing so loud that we could hear him on the second floor where our class was. We were laughing as the whole drama unfolded. Killer walked out and went to sing. We watched as Ms. Maqeks waited for him to get downstairs and go to the back of the school and get under the poplar tree. Just to imagine him opening his mouth and bellowing so that he could be heard upstairs was enough to crack us up with laughter. We laughed our lungs out as Ms. Maqeks started instructing him on how to sing from upstairs. She was looking through the window and conducting the show as we watched. "Here. I mean stand here," she shouted. "Sing, you said you are a great musician." This incident was the funniest because Ms. Maqeks had been so cross that she had broken her code of silence. Now instead of us getting the silent treatment, we were being entertained by the fact that she had got frustration instead of straightening us out. Killer came back to class after Ms. Maqeks's class was over. He was dragging his legs on the floor in a naughty way that made us feel he did not care about the whole thing. We laughed at this incident for days, and Killer became the Great Musician. He had earned the name after the drama of upsetting Ms. Maqeks by singing like Percy Sledge.

There were other times when we enjoyed Ms. Maqeks's temper. She would come into class and react with outright annoyance when the boys at the back leaned their chairs against the wall and sat as if in readiness to watch her. She would not mince words in describing for them how annoying they looked with their backs to the wall, chairs tilted and feet dangling in the air. She would say, "YeKiller, uyateneka, umanti." (Killer, you are spreading yourself to dry, you are wet.) We would look at the back as the student she was talking to straightened himself reluctantly and laugh at the way she was describing what was happening. It was as if she was talking to the skin of a cow that was being dried out outside. Just the sequence of the words she used made it funny to think that a person could spread himself out as if wet.

When she taught us about the frogs in her favorite lesson about the plagues in Egypt, she would jump about when imitating the Egyptians walking where there were frogs all over the land of Egypt after Moses had requested Pharaoh to free the children of Israel. What made things funnier was that her ankles were a bit swollen compared to those of other people. Her legs did not show the muscle structure of the leg that everybody had. Hers were very long and even all the way, and then where the leg meets the ankle, there was a swelling that made you feel that her leg was turned upside down. Since she used to wear long dresses, this was the only part of her leg that we saw. In her usual flat shoes, all we saw was a thick ankle and a little bit of leg that left us wondering what the whole leg was like. We guessed that it was a thin, long mass that went right up her femur bone that is probably one of the longest bones on earth. We would laugh when she imitated these Egyptians because she thought such stories were real. We were not about to believe these were true. When she talked about "darkness that you can feel," we would imagine

WEEDING THE FLOWERBEDS

that type of darkness that was. We would imagine the feeling of darkness, and it would not register in the minds of the likes of us that such a thing could happen.

When she taught us about Potiphar's wife, the boys did not mince words in telling her that the guy was a fool. They were not going to run away from manna. She made the mistake of asking what manna was, and we all laughed. The more she insisted on her being told, the more the students laughed. She left the class angry that day, and we knew that the next time she came to our class, we might be in for another silent treatment.

When she came back the next time, she got yet another surprise. This time she was teaching us the stories in the New Testament. She had asked us to read about Jesus and all his teachings. As soon as she got into class, she paused the question, "Who came to Jesus at night?" Ms. Maqeks asked and looked at us to respond. She had asked us to read about Nicodemus, so anybody who had read should have answered. When nobody answered, I knew that the students were giving her a little bit of her own medicine. Everybody knew the answer to this question, yet nobody bothered to answer. There was silence in the classroom.

"Who came to Jesus at night?" she asked again and looked around, and there seemed to be nobody who was interested in answering.

Killer raised his hand lazily after some time. He seemed to be uninterested in his own answer and then lazily spoke softly and with determination and said, "Logodima." This was the Swazi way of saying Nicodemus, and we all knew that Killer was asking for trouble from Ms. Maqeks. We pretended as if we had not heard what he said while stifling laugher and looked on as the drama unfolded.

"I said Logodima," he repeated again with a softness that mirrored imbecility. I could not help laughing when he repeated the second time because he was as loud as ever and so languished in his reply that it became clear that he was giving an attention-seeking answer on purpose.

"Killer, stop fooling around. You know the name of Nicodemus in English," Ms. Maqeks said with a temper that we knew was going to render her powerless because the students were already laughing. "You know his name was Nicodemus; there is no Logodima in this class. We are not drunkards; we are serious. Your Logodimas are out there in the shebeens." The lesson continued after the laughter as if nothing had happened.

Listening to the stories of teachers in our class was fun. They made our lives interesting after the dreary days spent at the hostel. It was refreshing to be at school with different people. I think we felt too confined and even feared our own mischief would get us into trouble if we stayed at the hostel all the time and did nothing. It was better to be at school with the teachers even though they sometimes bored us.

Another teacher who made us enjoy our class was Ms. McClou. She had the structure of a human-sized doll. She also styled her short hair like a doll. She would always tiptoe silently into class with her stiletto heels as if she wanted to catch us being naughty. We would behave because she was the deputy of the school. She would read to us from *Burning Grass* or even read the poem by Longfellow called *Hiawatha*. Her voice was memorable because she sometimes sounded like a bird on a tree. One day she was reading a line from *Burning Grass*. I was absentminded when she blurted out the words of Rikku's father, "I foresaw it, I foresaw it." When I came to, I was so surprised that she had even pronounced what I had read with a lifelessness with such animation that the words created a clear picture of her in class in my mind. I would always imagine her wearing her white floral dress with the garters and the belt of cloth reading into the afternoon air these two lines, and laugh. We enjoyed reading about Hiawatha's wooing of Minnehaha. We loved to hear about old Nokomis. We imagined what it was like near the shores of the lakes in North America the way Nokomis and Hiawatha did. We would picture the wigwams of the American Indians. It was amazing to imagine a life in a country that was far away from where we lived and connect with what the old woman and the boy were experiencing in Longfellow's poems. While the wigwams were different from the African huts, the story of a young man and her grandmother sounded like a typical life story that we could understand. It was interesting to know that people in other countries liked their grandmothers the way we liked ours. It was also interesting that Nokomis was interested in the love life of Hiawatha so much that she took interest and told about his wooing.

Ms. McClou also taught us "The Ballad of Semmerwater." I just remember in a hollow voice saying, "Deep asleep, Deep asleep, Deep Asleep it lies. The poem is by Sir William Watson (1858-1935).

I would watch her mouth as she read the lines and wonder if she realized that we were more interested in her performance than in the content of the ballad. We would read about the ship that lay wrecked in Semmerwater even though we did not know where Semmerwater was until the bell rang. After class, Ms. McClou would tap on the floor with her stilettos as she left for the staff room. We nicknamed Ms. McClou "Cilo" because she was nosy. I also think the other meaning was *ciligotshwa*, which refers to a small sharp knife. She was as sharp as the knife when she wanted to know what the students were doing that was contrary to the rules. If we painted our nails, she would punish us. After Ms. McClou left, the students would relax and start making noise again. It is amazing how students are expected to keep quiet and behave when their lives are boring because they are doing the same thing every day. If school life was as interesting as watching television or dancing, I don't think students would be as bored.

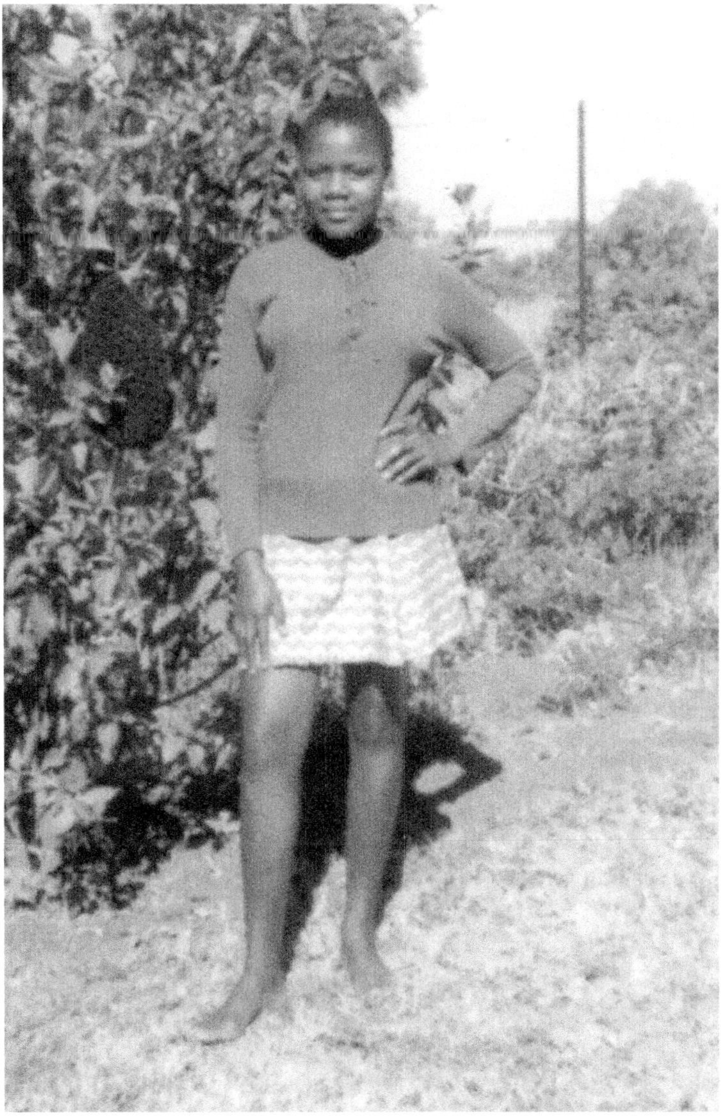

Chapter Three

"What happened?" Sisile kept asking me as I giggled away.

"You mean Cilo? She is mad," I said, taking my side even before she knew what had happened.

"You should have seen her," I said, talking about Ms. McClou who had just displayed one of the cleverest stunts I could imagine. "She jumped up and landed on her stilettos on the other side of the pool of oil," I said with tears in my eyes.

"Why was there oil on the floor?" Sisile asked.

"I don't know. I think the girls who work in the kitchen left it there by mistake," I explained. "I was sure she was going to slip and fall into the fat. She didn't. She sprang up and jumped a distance of about two feet and landed far from the pool of oil. It was something far better than any long jumper has ever done."

"Poor woman. Did she get hurt?" Sisile asked, concerned.

"She did not, like I tell you, she landed on the other side on the high heels. It was quite a stunt. After she landed, she asked, 'Is it fat?' I was already laughing, so I hid behind the big pot. I did not know how to respond. She continued on her way. I think she was going to the senior matron's house." I think that day I retold the story of Ms. McClou about ten times. All the students wanted to know what had happened. While they did not particularly sympathize with Ms. McClou, they wanted to hear everything about her problems. Most of the curiosity was due to the fact that students felt that she was nosy. She was not somebody who would get their sympathies if anything happened to her.

The missionaries were a part of our lives while we were in boarding school. They seemed to be there as supervisors. When we were in Form I, the head of the school was a female missionary. She lasted for only two years. The end of the sixties had ushered in a period where the Swazi people wanted to take the course of their lives into their own hands. We were experiencing the very last years of the missionary era. In almost everything, the country had to show that it had come of age. That is why our generation did not have much respect for people who were not African when they treated us as if there was something wrong with us. The apartheid regime in South Africa with a slavelike manner of governance was another reason why we did not particularly take to structures that were based on race. In order to protest this, we had subtle resentment that showed itself in excessive ridicule of the missionaries and the oppressive manner in which we thought they governed our lives. In all the positions that they occupied, we were sure that we wanted Africans. My laughing at Ms. McClou that Monday morning had a lot to do with the fact that I did not even want her tiptoeing in our kitchen. I was glad that there was fat on the floor. I was also happy that she had almost fallen because she had been mean to me when she was a library teacher. Ms. McClou had fined me a five-cent piece for a charge that was falsely laid against me. She accused me of writing in the book that I had checked out. Days after I had dropped the book in the library, she came to me and said I should pay for the book.

"You were the last one to use the book," she said after calling me into the library.

"I read this book, but I never wrote those words, even the handwriting is not my handwriting," I kept on protesting.

"You will pay five cents for this," she insisted.

"I will just give you the money, but you must know that I did not write in that book," I said as I took five cents out of the pocket of my shirt. I put the five cents into the palm of her small hand. Ms. McClou took the money and put it in a tin. I was angry when I left her office. I did not like the way she had treated me over this incident. It is one thing to be accused of doing something you have not done, but to part with money for such a thing is quite another.

I did not like to go to the library after this incident. I read books that my friends were reading. It was not because of the five cents. It was just the thought that such a thing could happen again. I started to exchange books with my friends. We collected James Hadley Chase mysteries and read them in turns. I think in those years, we read over twelve of those books. I asked the day scholars to bring us forms from the Swaziland National Library in town, and we enrolled there as members. We would borrow the books from the library or buy them at the bookstore in town. They were always fun to read. They also did not take long to finish.

The first term of school took long as we prepared for athletic competitions. We would do a lot of training on our own and then hold the school's interhouse competition. There were four houses in our school. There were the Zebras, Cheetahs, Kangaroos, and Tigers. Each team would select the best athletes and field event participants, and we would then go and compete for the trophies that were in the school. The events were fun to watch. The male hundred meters was the best event to watch. The stampede of the boys as they run toward the finishing line would be the most interesting part. They would run amidst shouts from the different corners of the field as students called out to them by "Zebras! Zebra!" and "Kanga! Up the Kangas!" The winner would hit the finish line, and the disappointed cheerers would go back to prepare for another shout as another sprinter took over the positions for other races. There were relay races that were just as interesting as the shorter races. It was seeing the ability of the students to create teamwork to a winning position that was interesting. We would jump up and down as we watch each race. Both the male relay races and the female relays were interesting. The girls who were sprinters were as popular as the boys. Of course throughout my high school days, nobody interested me as my friend Sisile's high jump skills. The Tigers always knew that the high jump points for the girls would come to them. After the interhouse sports, the school would select the students who would represent us in the national athletics competition.

It was usually in the month of April that we would compete with other schools in the Manzini region and compete either at the show grounds or at the Matsapha High School playground. It was quite an outing for us because we never went anywhere. We would watch the drum majorettes from Saint Michael's High School. They were interesting to watch because they would swing up and down the sports field before the games began. The girls would wear the shortest dresses and swing batons as they walked about with big caps on their heads. We did not know the intricacies of this sport, but it was good to watch. The Salesian High School band would play, and the girls would follow the band. When they had circled the sports ground, the races would begin. All sprinters would line up on their lanes when their race was announced. Those who ran the hundred meters would take their place according to the lane that their school had been given, and then they would take off at the bang of the gun. We would shoulder the colors of the school. Our school was "the Reds"; Salesian High School and Saint Theresa's joined forces under the banner of "the Blues." The main competition was among a few schools. The other schools were insignificant because very few of their students won. The field events would take place at the center of the field. At the end of the day, we would listen to the results. If we had won, we would run to our buses and sing as the buses drove to school. We would shout the "Up the Reds" all the way to our school.

The adventures of the competition would end with stories of which boys the girls met at the competition. These stories would make the gossip at the hostel. It was a good thing to have a boyfriend. There was something heroic about it. Even at the age of thirteen or fourteen, I knew that the girls who had boyfriends received their letters at a different box number from the one that all the students used. The letters that were not supposed to be seen by the matron would come from PO Box 315 Manzini. The day scholars would pick them up and give them to their owners. If a letter from a boyfriend happened to land in the matron's box, the girls would have a tough time explaining how it happened that there was such a letter.

Strict though our rules were, some girls still got pregnant. The girl who was pregnant would be taken to the Raleigh Fitkin Memorial to be checked. The trunk box of that girl would be under the jacaranda tree when the khaki-colored van came to take the girl to the hospital. One lady always took the girls to the hospital. Her home was at a nearby farm. She would also accompany the matron on the way to the girl's home after the hospital has confirmed that the girl was pregnant. Our sermons at the evening chapel services would be about the girl who had fallen pregnant. The matron would begin by telling the story and say, "My children, I always feel very sad when one of you has to go home," and then she would expand on how we should behave in order to get out of such trouble. Her solution was always to tell us to get Jesus and put him in the seat of our hearts.

The second term was the winter term. This term was the music season. Schools would practice songs in Zulu and English and then compete for the best rendering of the chosen pieces. Songs such as *"Uponi"* (pony in Xhosa), *"Sylvia Mntakwethu"* (Sylvia my dear), and many others would be sung at these competitions. Our school was good at singing. The four years that I sang in the choir were years of victory in the vernacular song. We did not often win the English songs as much as we did the Zulu songs. Some of these included Handel's Messiah songs such as "For unto Us a Child Is Born" and "Worthy Is the Lamb" and many others that were not necessarily religious songs.

Our music teacher was a very interesting teacher. He was a good motivator and yet not personally gifted in voice. He sang with a nasal twang that all the students imitated. It was fun to hear him tell us how to strike a note. We would struggle with the notes and listen more to the harmonica rather than him. Even though this was the case, we won and brought home many trophies. The mixed choirs had to have sixty voices.

There were also girls' and boys' choirs. The boys' choir was the most melodious to listen to. Songs like "Come Bounteous May" still ring in my head from those days. It was very good to listen to the music as the boys glided through their stanzas. Even though we did not know their lines, we would bellow their music in the hostel with my friends. We knew the chromatics and staccatos in the songs. We sang the crescendos at the top our voices and kept practicing voice until we achieved the standard choral voice.

On the last days when we were preparing for the competitions, we would sing outside the school in the open air. This practice was done in the front of the school near the steps that were overlooking the teachers' parking lot. We would stand outside overlooking the school garden that was landscaped into steps in order to even out the ground. Standing there, you would see the beautiful poinsettias, the aloes, and the other shrubs that I could not name. The bigger trees would also be in bloom on that side of the school. When we started singing, it would be as if the sky and the whole surroundings could hear our music. The conductor would give us the key on the harmonica and then hand it to one of the students and then begin to conduct the song. I always thought that he wanted to hear how strong our choir was and also to give the other conductors a chance to pick up some of our notes that were out of tune. After correcting a few wrongs, we would go back to the auditorium and practice some more. Since we put a lot into our practice, we were ready for the competitions when the time for meeting the other schools came. They all knew that we were a force to be reckoned with.

The eliminations for the Manzini region would serve as a preliminary competition to eliminate some of the poorer choirs. Only the best choirs went to the finals. The final competitions were often held at William Pitcher Training College or Mjingo High School. They were adventurous activities. It was good to meet students from other schools in the Manzini region. We would meet with students from as far as Mahamba and Franson Christian High School and other places. The day would be filled with listening to each choir through the windows for students. We would go in when our school was called and render our piece in front of the row of judges who sat just below the stage where we sang. "Come on, girls and boys, now it is time for us to go and sing," our conductor would say, and we would stand in a line and enter the stage from the side of the hall. We already knew our positions, and each person would follow the person they always sing near as we filed onto the stage. Our girls were looking beautiful in their short hair and red and white shirts. The boys would stand at the back. They were also looking smart in their striped ties and white shirts. We would wait as the choirmaster takes his position. He would bow to the judges and then turn to give us the key by blowing the main notes on the harmonica. We would connect with the tune in our heads and wait for the clue to strike the notes and sing on. He would raise his arms and start off with a hard stroke and then float in a way that indicates the beat of the song. He would show us the crescendos by raising his shoulders and pulling the song up in his beat as his hands went higher and higher. Our voices would rise and follow his guidance, and when we come to the solo, he would focus on our main voice. The soloist would lead the song as we hum the melody, blending with the melodious single voice that leads the song until we join in, in harmony and take the song to the end. After that the conductor would bow and then show us the way out, and we would file out of the stage. It seemed as if the most important thing was blending the song and hitting correct notes together and creating a melody that carries consistently to the end. The judges would listen and look on as we continue. Our focus was on the conductor and making sure that we do our best for the sake of our school. We would be so focused that even if somebody caused any disturbance in the hall, we would not have heard it. After the singing, we would go out and wait for the conductor to tell us how our singing was.

We had women conductors in the girls' choirs, and they were equally good in teaching us music. We would split into two choirs for the English song and have a different group for the Zulu song. I was in the English song, and I remember how our teacher led us through "Which Is the Properest Day to Sing?" It has a beautiful melody, and we would say which of the seven days of the week was the most proper day to sing. The pronunciation of the days of the week was important for this song. She put a lot of work into making sure that our words were very clear, and when we went to the competitions, we won. One reason why we won was that there were not many schools that entered for the girls' and boys' choirs. Salesian and Saint Christopher's sang these pieces because they were boys' schools, and Saint Michael's and Saint Theresa's sang the girls' pieces because they were the only few girls' schools in the Manzini region. It was good logic for us to go and compete because these schools might have been winning because there was very little competition, and as fate would have it, we entered and brought home most of the trophies. Such was the power of the melodies at Manzini Nazarene High School.

Some teachers would act up and make the audience laugh. I remember a teacher who lifted his legs at the end of the song and ended the song by saluting the judges. I also heard of a drunken teacher who kept receding until he fell off the stage while his choir was in the middle of the song.

The day would end with us in the bus on the way to our school. We would go through our routines and wait for the head teacher's car as he came back with the big trophy. He would drive to the school around eight o'clock. His car would hoot all the way when we had won, and all the girls would go to the dining room to hear how we had been victorious. My friends and I would enjoy the "sounds" of happiness as we looked at the happy girls running up and down, throwing nighties in the air, and laugh our lungs out. I have never seen people as happy as we were when we had won the music trophy. It would be an evening of happiness like no other. "Up the Reds! The Reds! The Reds!" we would say this over and over. In the songs in which we had a soloist, we would go on forever shouting and shaking hands with our soloist because we would know that she had fought it out all alone in that part of the song and had to be congratulated for doing a good job. Such was the joy of the collective spirit that we had as young Swazi girls growing up in a mission school.

We lived for the Monday after the music competitions. The trophies would be brought to the morning assembly, and the results of the competitions would be announced. This would be the first time for us to hear the exact points that we got and also to know how far ahead we were in terms of points against our opponents. We would shout "Up the Reds" once again, but our second part of celebration would be nothing like Saturday night at the girls' hostel. We would take pictures in front of the school for the *Nuntius*. Everybody wanted to touch the trophy. It was good to feel what victory was like when it was in the form of a big silver trophy. After all the hours of standing and repeating notes, we needed something to celebrate our success. The music teacher would sometimes serve a meal to all the students who were in the choir. We enjoyed those meals at his house because they were different from our usual diet. We did not know at the time how important music was to our lives. We just sang because it was required of us, and also because doing something together was fun. It is today that one realizes how important it is in the lives of all southern Africans. When someone is bereaved, we sing; when we have parties at home, we sing. In adulthood, you just sing to bring back the days gone by. We sing all the songs. We sing the song about "Della" and remember that the best soloist in our school had that name. We sing about the Zulu Kingdom in "Emasangweni AkwaDukuza" (In the gates of Dukuza). This song recounted a visit to the kingdom of King Shaka. There was a soprano solo in this song. The best soprano was chosen to sing this part. She would sing on while the other members of the choir hummed beautifully as she punctuated the song with her words.

> Namhla ngikwazi ukuthula,
> (Today I know the peace and quiet)
> Noma ngilele ngikwesikabhadakazi,
> (Even when I am asleep at twelve o'clock)
> Ngiphupha umKabayi ethi kimi, ethi kimi
> (I dream of Mkabayi saying to me.
> Saying to me.)

The choir would then join the solo.

> Vuka wena kaMancinza
> (Wake up son of Mancinza)
> Vuka wena kaMancinza,
> (Wake up son of Mancinza)
> Vuka wena KaMancinza,
> (Wake up son of Mancinza)
> Vuka wena kaMancinza
> (Wake up son of Mancinza)
> Awuzalelwanga ukulalubuthongo
> (You were not born to sleep only)

> Vukubonge ndaba yemikhonto
> (Wake up and praise the story of the spears)
> Nankumthwal' engakwethwesa wona.
> (Here is the load that I made you carry)
> Nangu umthwalo lwengakwethesa wona.
> (Here is the load that I made you to carry.)

We would finish the song and go on to sing other songs about how the Americans Armstrong, Aldrin, and Collins landed on the moon. And when I got to the solo, I would sing it as if I was the soloist in our choir when she bade the astronauts farewell.

> Hamba nabo bawo wethu osemazulwini,
> (Go with them Our Father who is in the heavens)
> Mdali wezulu nomhlaba.
> (Creator of heaven and earth.)
> Naloku kungumsebenzi wezandla zakho.
> (Even though it is the work of your hands.)
> Nalapho beya khona isekwa nguwe.
> (Even where they are going you are the one who supports it.)
> Hamba nabo, hamba, themba limi alikho
> (Go with them, go with them, hope is not there)
> Ngaphandle kwakho.
> (Without you)
> Uzubalondoloze, bawo osemazulwini
> (Keep them Father who is in the heavens)

The rest of the choir would join and sing.

> Ngunaphakade Amen.
> (Forever and ever, amen)
> Zafika indaba ngomoya
> (The stories came in the air)
> Zafika indaba ngomoya
> (The stories came in the air)
> Zisithi, bayisile o Amstrong, Aldrin, noCollins.
> (Saying they have been, Armstrong, Aldrin, and Collins)
> Halala, Halala, Halala.
> (Hurray, hurray, hurray)
> Siyiqhayisa ngoApollo weshum'elinomvo.
> (We are proud of *Apollo 11*.)

We celebrated *Apollo 11* when this song was sung. We would repeat the solo over and over, and every one of my friends would take a turn, wanting to make sure that they pull the longest at the end. There was nothing like music at our school.

It was in Form III that mathematics started to make sense to me. Throughout the other years, I was in the dark as to what I was being taught. I was not good at this subject. I felt bad that even when I tried hardest, I still did not make the best marks. I would go through my book and try hard to learn. The teacher we had in Form III was very good. He tried his best to teach us even though we did not understand. It paid that year to try hard and practice the exercises over and over again. I ended up getting a good grade overall in the Junior Certificate examinations. My worst subjects were typing and Zulu. I got a G in both. I could not explain how I did so poorly in these two.

I had felt that I was doing well in typing especially in the speed test because I had occupied the seat for the highest scorer twice. I was very disappointed with my grade. I knew that I was poor in setting the grid for the statement and invoices that were required in the examination. I am grateful that I did all the work in typing when I was in high school. Today I whiz through my work. I know that my education paid off. Even though we did not know that there would be computers, we persevered in typing; and when computers came around, we found that we had acquired one of the most important skills, for nobody can say they are educated in today's world if they have no knowledge of computers. High school had given us one of the most important skills, the knowledge of the keyboard.

I remember the typing lessons and the teacher and the songs that were played in the tape recorder in order to make our fingers follow a rhythm as they went from note to note. It was interesting music, and we would all go at once when he shouts, "Start typing," and then he would stop at the end of the line and say, "Carriage return." We would make sure our carriage goes back to the beginning of the line. "Nisutile?" he would ask in broken SiSwati, and we would laugh. He meant to ask if we were happy or if we did not need any more help. We would just laugh and not even answer to his SiSwati, which was so wrong as to be near an insult. We enjoyed the typing lesson. Even though the typing machines were old, they were not as old as most of the typewriters I found in the schools when I started teaching. I look back and appreciate the education we got because there was a lot of foresight into what our futures were going to be. It was as if our teachers knew that the world ahead of us would be a world that would be navigated through computers, and it was a must that we should learn how to use a typewriter since without this skill, it would be difficult for us to live in a modern world.

It was in the area of self-esteem that I felt that effort was too lax. Nobody seemed to realize that we would have to face a very cruel world. We were not taught the important issues about presenting ourselves powerfully through the word in a world where people want to put down others. Today I wish teachers could teach a lot of psychology so that students would know that it is important to have a strong sense of self. We were not told that God does not like a person who has a low self-esteem. We were just taught how to be obedient to the orders that were given to us. Life demands that people learn to choose carefully what they will do and why they are doing it. It demands that people set goals and pursue them. It is hard to set goals and pursue them when you listen to everything around you. A sense of strength in being an individual means being very strong inside yourself and holding your head up all the time. Students need to be taught about the ego and how they portray it in everyday life. They need to learn how to be strong without harming others or allowing them to harm them.

Some of my friends were good in this area, but others were not. I was very weak. I just enjoyed being naughty and laughing with my friends. Not to say that there was something wrong with this. I just felt that school could have imparted some life skills because life after all was going to be about life skills and not just singing and reading the Bible alone. We needed a lot of grilling in the importance of self-confidence, creating a sense of personal dignity and independence of mind.

Being in a coed school had its own challenges. The boys were freer and learning better life skills in their tough male world. They would play jokes on us and laugh at us. We did not know that we were giving in to their teasing by being unhappy. It was much later when we were older that we realized how we had hurt ourselves by reacting in such an emotional way.

It is in Form III that we started to be interested in boys. My friends would get letters from boys, and we would read them aloud in the dormitory. We would all contribute to the reply to the letter. One of the letters read like this.

> Manzini Nazarene High
> PO Box 14
> Manzini
> Date is Love
>
> Dear Sisile,
>
> I have been thinking about making this request ever since you came to the school. I have always found you beautiful. I think that you were meant for me. I know that you might not like what I have to say. I am thinking about you always.
>
> Anyways, what I want to tell you is that I love you very much. You are the most beautiful girl that I ever saw. You are more beautiful than any princess here on earth. Could you please be my princess by

accepting my love? I mean, I love you dearly. I will not sleep these days while I await your reply.

Please don't think that I am saying this because it is easy for boys of my age to say. This is a very special letter. It is the honest truth from the bottom of my heart. I will keep thinking about you, beautiful rose. Keep blooming for me.

Your loving sweetheart,
Mfundo Mdluli

It was fun to come up with the words that would be in the letter. Everybody felt that they should say something if the girl did not like the boy. The boys who were liked were never discussed in front of everybody. Only a few friends knew the truth about what went on in the relationships. While none of the relationships were serious, they were a way of letting us understand what happened to people when they fall for each other. Even though we did not know much, we felt that we knew a lot. We did not want our parents to know about these boys. The letters were often short.

I remember Sisile's letter to one boy named Patrick. He was from Johannesburg. He looked smart. I think she did not like him because he looked worldly wise. The letter we wrote was like this.

PO Box 14
Manzini
Date is nothing doing

Dear Bra Solly,

I am not sure if I understand what you are saying in your letter. I just want to tell you that I am not in love with you. I am not interested in you sending me other letters. Please stop looking at me in church. It will not change anything.

Yours faithfully,
S. Dlamini

When the letter from the boy came, we all read it. It was about how the boy's heart was pining for Sisile. He claimed that he could no longer sleep from thinking about her. Even though this was a lie, we believed it. We did think that people would love others and even fail to fall asleep. Such was our innocence in those days. They were days when everything we saw in films and heard in the love songs that were broadcast on Lourenco Marques Radio were true. Everybody listened to the pop songs on LM Radio. We even copied the songs down so that we would sing them in school. We would sing, "I hear the sound of distant drums, far away." We would sing Elvis Presley's "I Just Can't Help Believing." We would imagine the woman whispering her magic to a man and see her cheeks "shining honey sweet with love." For us, love was real. It was something that dripped down like honey. It was somewhere inside a person's heart. We knew that we would find it someday. Nobody felt that they would not find it. If they did not feel it, they were not looking hard enough.

On Saturdays, we would look out the window hoping that somebody from home would come and visit us. It was nice to peep through the windows and look down the road when the poinsettias were in bloom. Once in a while we would see someone from home, and we would be happy. When you saw your parents appearing behind the poplar trees, you would go to the dining hall and wait to be called. We knew that the matron would send someone to call us, and we would be there waiting. It was a moment where you sat down with your parents, and they got a chance to hear how things were going with you. If you were giving the matron a difficult time, you knew that she would tell them. I never gave the matron a difficult time except when I stole peaches from the peach tree.

"Twigza," I said, relating to my friend how the matron had caught me stealing peaches from the tree. "I was caught red-handed," I said, laughing at myself.

"Twigza, you should stop this nonsense honestly. Just recently you were caught hiding and not going for prayers. You are fast becoming a seasoned rebel. We made rules about stealing. How could you break them first thing before the term even gets quarter way to the end?" Makhosi was feigning seriousness as she chastised me. I talked to her in seriousness and explained about how ashamed I was when I was caught. I reflected on the incident of stealing as I was talking to her.

"I thought she was asleep on the couch, yet she was watching me through the window." I tried to explain my way out of the situation in vain. There was the pain of being caught doing something wrong and the pain of being one of the leaders of the "no-stealing brigade." The pain in this was in having to face the person whom you have offended face-to-face. There is a sense of shame that makes you want to hide your face. Even though I knew that the matron was not very cross with me from calling me by my nickname, I was full of shame at what I had done. I walked to her house, and she told me never to eat the peaches again because she was not sure if they were healthy. I walked on to school feeling sheepish like a real naughty young person that day.

It was good to walk back to school after lunch. The school, with red paint, stood in front of us. Some of the day scholars were still finishing their lunch when we sauntered down the dirt road that led to the school. There were trees along the road, and once in a while the car of a missionary would pass by and leave a lot of dust behind it. We would shake off the dust and walk on to school. Going down the rough steps that led to the main building of the school was such a routine that we never thought that we would ever leave the school. The feeling of school life being forever is caused by the boredom of the everyday routine. You feel as if you have done something for years even if it is just one year. You always look forward to the future and not realize that life is always about looking forward to the future. Failing to make use of the present always leads to a bad future. Yet even today I still have to talk to myself and discipline myself by saying it aloud that I must take care of today so that the future can take care of itself. Most people who lack discipline do not know this rule. They shuffle through life doing one wrong after another and hope that the wrongs will add up and turn into a form of success. I realized from the few wrong things that I did that you can never correct a mistake by making another mistake. Mistakes have to be undone, and a new foundation of correctness has to follow or else what you do is doomed to fail.

We would go back to our classes and go through the last lesson of the day with lethargy. Lunchtime is a time for relaxing. After lunch, it is even worse because everybody is working on their last bit of energy. The consolation of the day coming to an end is always in every bit of the after-lunch session. We would be happy if the last session was music. We would go to the assembly hall and wait for the music teacher. Everybody carried the copy of the song in their hands. We would listen carefully as each note was taught and sung after the teacher had explained what we were supposed to sing. Time and again, we would make a mess of our lines. It was usual for girls to be told that they were screaming the notes and not singing out melodiously. The tenors were always giving problems. Most of the time would be spent correcting them. Once all the members understood the song, we would sail smoothly through it. There were areas where some songs were tricky. This was when a song went up by a note. We would spend a lot of time polishing those areas because the teachers knew that this was where the judges would catch us. Most of us sopranos were always good. We were a good team together.

Once in a while a coach would come from another school or even from South Africa to help us polish our songs. We would enjoy working with these coaches because they had better voices than our choirmaster. The change was also good for us. We would sing until it was almost suppertime at the girls' hostel in the music season. The sun also went down much earlier at this time because it was winter. It was also very cold. We would walk toward the hostel and find that we just have to go straight to the dining hall without resting. Eating supper while still wearing the school uniform was not the usual thing to do, so we tried to be extra careful when eating so that the food does not get on the uniform. This also meant that we would not have much time to rest. It would be bath time and then time for the evening chapel service.

There were days when we would not sleep much. This happened when there was a book that needed to be read at night. These were the books that we did not want the matron to see. Since we took turns in reading them, we would spend time in the bathroom reading because when the lights were turned out, this was the only place that would be left with the lights on. I would read fast so that the next reader could get the book. Some books we were reading fast because the owners wanted them back. Some we were hiding because we were not allowed to have them. I cannot even mention the dirty books we read at this hour. Sitting on the toilet seat, with the lid down, each one of us would take turns to read; and then it would be another's turn. It is funny how all the things that happen in adulthood are of interest when we are young. When we are old, we wish we were young and did not have all the responsibilities. When we are young, we see our lives as restrictions; and yet when we are old, we feel there is too much responsibility. It is important for people to know that happiness is more about making good choices at the time when you have the choice and then being happy that you have chosen to do the right thing.

Friday night at the hostel was the day when we washed our uniforms. We would go to the outside sinks with metal buckets. The buckets were used for fetching water from the two taps that were at the edge of the two lines of the sinks. The first bucketful was for washing the sinks and rinsing them out before we poured the water that we would use to do the washing. We would pour powdered soap into the water and then dip the shirts. The uniforms we washed with a bar of Sunlight soap or even blue soap. The shirts were always rinsed with Reckitt's Blue to keep them looking bluish white. Somehow this made them look whiter, and the armpits did not look brownish white. We would hang our uniforms on the clothesline to dry. At night, we would take them in and take them out again the following morning

Saturday was the day for ironing. We took turns ironing on ironing boards in the dining hall. Each group had its own ironing board. We had to work out who would iron first, and then each person would call the next person after finishing with the ironing. The Sunday uniform was also ironed on this day because there would be absolutely no work on Sunday except polishing shoes.

The routines of boarding school were many and boring. The jobs would vary when we were the group that was washing dishes. It was only in the evening that we washed dishes. We did not like doing this task. The only job we liked was cleaning our dormitory. The person cleaning the dormitory would not work outside in the garden. She would just go straight to the dorm after morning chapel and sweep the floor and then scrub it. Red wax polish was applied on Saturday. The rest of the week was for shining the wax polish off the floor.

The second term in high school was also the term when we went for trips. We looked forward to the trips each and every year. In Form I, we only went as far as the factories in Matsapha. We would make special preparations for this day. We would buy biscuits and fruit and carry big cake tins on our trip. Even though we had food, we still wanted to have something to nibble along the way. Since we were not allowed to go and buy food in town, most of the students asked the day scholars to buy the goodies that we needed.

We went to school at eight. The bus that had been hired to take us on the trip would be waiting for us below the steps on the south end of the high school. We would file into the bus and take seats of our choice. It was just good to be going somewhere together with the members of our class. Our teachers were also with us in the bus.

We did not take long on the road since Matsapha is very close. We got to our destination in less than thirty minutes. We envied the senior students because they were going even farther. For us, Matsapha was all there was. The bus would pass KaKhoza, and we would look out of the window and see the small disorganized settlement. It looked very different from our school and the other sections of town such as Fairview and Coates Valley. The poverty of KaKhoza made one feel a little bit of embarrassment about the way people lived in our country.

As we neared Matsapha, we began to feel the difference in the layout of the land. It is gently undulating slopes that are broad. They are very different from the view of Manzini because the town is in a river valley. The Umzimnene River seems to bend toward the east coursing through the town as if it meant to circle the center and divide it from the nearby suburbs. Entering Matsapha near the Ndlunganye and going past the police college gives you a good view of the whole industrial sites. From near the police college and casting one's view toward the road to Mbabane, one sees all the factories. The bus would wind down toward the bottom of the sloppy expanse of land because we were going to start at the lower end of the industrial sites and come back toward the college in our sightseeing. We went to the meat factory, and the guides took us throughout the factory. We saw the workers wearing all white. They were wearing white overalls, white boots, and white helmets. It was interesting to see the cows when they were readied for slaughter. We also watched when they had been skinned and they were dangling on hooks. The hooks were relaying them on a cable that took them to the huge refrigerated sections of the factory. We learned that almost everything that came from a cow was useful. Apart from the meat, which we ate, the skins were used to make leather goods, the horns were used to make glue, and the bones were used to make bone meal, which was used in fertilizers.

After the beef factory, we went to Matola to see how cement is made. It was interesting to see the big mixers and bags of cement being relayed by a conveyor belt. While we enjoyed Matola, we also noticed that it was very dusty. The powder from the cement was everywhere. We had to walk carefully wherever we went. We also went to the sweet factory. The smell of that place was very interesting. It was fun to be out of the boarding school and learning things that we would not have learned in the classroom.

In the late afternoon, we went back to the bus and drove to the Matsapha Airport. The Matsapha Airport is the only airport in Swaziland. We went to the tower, and they showed us how the operator of the tower watches the airplanes that are coming into Swaziland. It was nice to be up in the tower and get to see more of the land around Matsapha from the level of the tower. From there, we would see as far as Lobamba and even Sidvokokvo. After the airport, we went back to the bus. It was already late in the afternoon. We got into the bus and drove back to school. For us who were in boarding school, it was back to the hostel. We were happy to get back to our dorms and talk to other students about our trip. Day scholars made their way home together because it was already late. The day of the trip was one of the only adventures we enjoyed because there would be no other outing until we went or would go back to our homes.

In Form II, we went to Mlilwane Game Reserve and the Houses of Parliament for our trip. We started at the Houses of Parliament and saw the two houses, the House of Senate and the House of Assembly. We imagined that one day we would know what these seats were for. We went to the side of the parliament that is a museum and saw the old cars that King Sobhuza used to drive when he was young. We liked our king. He was a wise man. After that we drove to Mlilwane and went to see the animals. It was nice to see the land around Mlilwane. There were a lot of wattle trees and gum trees. The surrounding mountains were interesting. It was interesting to pass the railway line. I had been on the train several times because my parents worked for the Swaziland Railways. When we got to Mlilwane and the animals we enjoyed ourselves. We saw hippos, giraffes, zebras, and buffaloes.

In Form III, we went to Mhlume Sugar and the Sand River Dam. It was nice to see the process of making sugar. We saw first the liquid syrup and then saw the molasses and eventually got to the last stage where the sugar actually becomes granulated. All these were fascinating trips where we enjoyed ourselves. We would shout and sing in the bus. There was a boy who was the school photographer. He would take photos of us and charge us money. At the end of the day, we would return to school and feel good that we had learned new things on the trip.

After the trip, our lessons would touch on some of the things we had seen, especially in geography. In the other subjects, there was not much to discuss that related to these trips. The excitement about the trips died slowly, and life resumed its usual pace of going to school in the morning and back to the hostel after school.

We would sometimes play volleyball in the two courts that were on the west side of the school. I enjoyed this sport very much. I found it very relaxing. There was no running around like in the other sports, yet one had to pay attention to the ball and be ready to volley it back. I had never played volleyball before I came to Manzini Nazarene High School. I had always seen girls play netball, and boys play only soccer. At Manzini, Nazarene girls also played soccer. Some also played softball. All these were new sports to me.

Thursday afternoon was time for the Student Christian Movement. The students would hold prayers in the auditorium after school by themselves. They would talk about Jesus among themselves. Once in a while they would invite teachers to give talks, but on the whole, this was their time to talk about Christianity themselves. They would sing songs

> When I was but a little child how well I recollect
> How I would grieve my mother with my folly and neglect
> One day a message came and now I miss her tender care
> Oh, Savior, tell my mother, I will be there.
> Tell mother I will be there, in answer to her prayer
> This message blessed Savior to her bear
> Tell mother I will be there, in answer to her prayer
> Oh, Savior, tell my mother I will be there

It was interesting to listen to this song especially because Makhosi and another girl had lost their mothers while we were in Form II. I listened to it with them in mind because my mother was still alive. The thought of going to hell and not being with your mother in heaven used to haunt everybody when this song was sung. We listened to the beautiful rendering of music as the students sang songs of their choice and thought about our behaviors. We already knew some students to be devout Christians. There were those of us who were trying, but not really there. I think at that time most of us did not think that Christianity was a good idea. There was something like being a "goody-goody" and selling out the course about it. I think it was because it was the expected behavior, and very few people who portray the expected behavior are seen as clever by students. It is the naughty ones who are seen as clever because they are willing to break the code. Being young is about not being what the adults want. I am not sure what we wanted to be as young people. I think we were not present inside ourselves enough to even know which version of ourselves we wanted to be seen as. To see ourselves as ourselves and be truly committed to what we were was hard. I think the fact that there was so much teaching about sin, we felt that we were never going to be good anyway, so it made sense to just be and not even try to be anything. Only those who could make it to heaven could try. Some of us seemed to be bent for hell even though we had not made that choice.

The end of term was a lot of fun because the daily routine would change. Things would work down to a relaxed pace toward exams. We would write one subject in the morning and another in the afternoon. There was plenty of time to read in between. It was nice to know that we had struggled all term, and now the time to show what we were struggling for had come. Apart from the relaxed schedule of the exam period, there were end-of-the-term competitions. In these, we would try to win points for our houses. There was the cleaning competition where the school was divided according to the houses. The Kangaroos would get the north side of the school, which meant the auditorium and the volleyball courts; and the Tigers would get the west wing of the school, which meant the classrooms downstairs. The Cheetahs would get the upstairs east wing of the school and the grounds behind it. The Zebras would get the downstairs east wing of the school including the flower garden outside the toilets. It was fun to scrub and polish the school with the students whom we just knew in class such as the day scholars. We would throw water all over and then clean and polish everything so that when the judges come, everything would be clean. The Cheetahs used to win most of the competitions. Their purple banner, which was painted on a grass mat, would be lifted by the leaders of this house to the envy of everybody.

We also held the music competition where students would sing in smaller groups. We would sing all kinds of songs trying to impress a judge who had come from outside the school. The teachers all belonged to a house and would not have been good judges for our teams since they were already affiliated with one of the houses. Sisile and her housemates would sing songs, and I would also find friends and sing with them. I remember singing with one of my friends the song "Swing Low, Sweet Chariot." We did not win, but the older girls were impressed with our singing. They said we had good "voice production." I did not know much about voice production except what I had learned in primary school. Our primary school had been very good in music, and we had won the music competitions for primary schools more than once. When I got to the Nazarene High School, I knew most of what I had to do. It was not as easy to sing in the small groups because each voice had to be heard and the focus of the students was on us at this time.

The other competition would be the debate competition. Four students would be chosen from every house, and the houses would compete and eliminate each other until there were champions. The Tigers always won this one because there was a girl who was a champion. I only remember chairing the debate competition, and I think I did a bad job of it because I was too soft. I think the Zebras won that one. My house, the Kangas, as the Kangaroos were known in those days, always lost. We lost in music, lost in the athletics competition, and then lost the end-of-term competitions.

The last competition we would have would be the Bible quiz competition. This competition was fun because the students sat on boards that indicated the person who stood up first by showing a red light. It was fun to see students stand when another one has already stood and then brush their hands in their hair when they have to sit down after losing. Of course when the results were announced, it would be any house but the Kangas, which was my house. I used to be disappointed that we did not win.

Throughout the last days of the end of each term, we were looking forward to the last day when we would go home. This was the time when we would dress up in the best clothes we had. It was a time when everybody wanted to look their best. This was when we saw the latest in shoes, dresses, and all that is fashionable. This was also a time when we got a chance to see the boyfriends that the girls were pining for while they were in the hostel. Boys from Saint Christopher's and Salesian High School were the most popular. Even the boys from our high school were also popular, but not like the ones from the other schools. The girls from Saint Michael's were also liked by all of us because we thought that theirs was the best school in Manzini. Even Saint Theresa's was respected. Most of this kind of ordering also depended on how schools fared in the international examinations that were taken after Form III and Form V. Our school was starting to pick up at the time when we were going there. I think our group was one of the most significant groups in producing good results for Manzini Nazarene High School. This is why you are reading this book. We had some very good teachers who were dedicated to teaching us.

We left school after good sermons from the matron about how we were supposed to behave ourselves. We took our suitcases, which had been packed for the whole week, in preparation for this day, and set off on the road home. It was a joyful walk because we went to the buses with our friends. We did not catch buses when going to town. We would take our suitcases and walk with the other students on the road past Lewis Store. Walking toward the Umzimnene River with our suitcases held firmly in one hand was not that tough because the suitcases were half empty. It was only going to be a three-week vacation, and we would come back to school.

We would go straight to the bus station and wait for the buses that went to our homes. When we saw the buses, we would ask the conductors to load the suitcases, and then we would go for a walk around town. Once in a while we would see a girl from our school standing with a boy from Salesian or even Saint Christopher's, and we would put two and two together and come up with all kinds of conclusions. It was nice to watch the young Romeos and their Juliets. These sights would make up our stories when schools opened. We discussed whom we saw with whom but always did so under hushed tones because we were young, and since the matron relied on us for information, we knew that the bigger girls would not like to know that we knew about their boyfriends. This was the time we got to know where the letters that were posted to PO Box 315 came from.

My friends Sisile and Makhosi had received letters from boys; but since the replies had been very negative, I knew that even when the boys approached them, they would not even talk for long. Nobody liked to talk to a boy they did not like. I am not sure what it was that we did not like. Sometimes it was just the fact that we made fun of some of the boys. Sometimes we would sing the school band songs about the boys and how they like a particular person and matchmake against the person's will. To see that person in town drew a lot of laughter from the other girls because we knew that our friend did not even want to see this fellow. We would go to the cheap stores like Jet and buy cheap clothes. Mostly what we bought were just cheap things because we did not have much money. It was good to be out of the hostel and walking around town and window-shopping even though we did not have much money. It was nice to be free. I am not sure if we understood that freedom comes with responsibility. We just wanted freedom so much and felt that we were entitled to it. Since this was immediately after colonialism, we were enjoying being ourselves in a country that was marching to the freedom march that had been hard earned from the colonialists. As the future citizens of the continent, it was good to use the word even though we had been too young to understand what colonialism really meant. At that age, we just read history books, and most of them had not started to bring to our understanding where we had come from and where we were going. Such concepts as freedom were sometimes likened to just being free to dance to pop music and understand ourselves as we wanted to. Even the teachings of the mission sometimes felt like something we really needed to free ourselves from. Who wanted to be at the place where we were always told about hell? It was hard for us to live since it was as if all people thought teenagers were these bad people who always want what is bad for them. I am not sure how life came to be conceived like this, but walking through the streets of Manzini on "home go" day felt like a time to do whatever life did not want us to do when we were inside the four walls of the hostel.

We were not thinking about school when we were in town. We were tired of the piercing glances of teachers like Ms. McClou. We were looking forward to another world, the world of our parents and their rules. We liked going home. We were tired of routine and regulations about what to wear and what to eat. Home was the place where we felt most welcome. It was the place where everything surprised you. Every meal was something to look forward to because we did not know what to expect. It was a place where we were special. Something about being in boarding school was like being in a kraal like cattle. Something about filing into the chapels was like cattle at the deep. Getting on the bus on the way home felt unique because for once you were doing something alone, taking your own decisions, and not following suit after another person. For once you were your own prefect and not guarded by other students. For once you had the chance to see if you could survive without rules. School had tried to teach us how to be. We were supposed to be the citizens of the future. Had we been equipped to make the right choices? It was when you were alone that life came and sat on your lap and said, "Hello, live me the best way you know how."

For some of us it felt like Christmas Day. Standing with boys in the park and talking about a hidden future that we were looking at far ahead of us was something we were now leaving behind as the day we called "home go" began to end. It meant walking to the bus station and taking a seat and thinking about life and learning that freedom is not free. Whether we had learned enough to last us till the following term was something that every one of us would answer to when the schools opened.

That was how I felt when I parted with my friend Sisile. My friend would get into Impala bus or Morning Star and go to her home. I tried to make her out inside the crowded bus as it turned to take the road to Siteki and heard her call me, "Twigza, bye-bye." She was waving at me and smiling. She was still waving when the bus turned and pulled out of the bus rank.

Something inside me fell as the loneliness of my own life became reality. I took steps toward the bus that would take me toward the lowveld. It was now past two o'clock. Most of my friends were gone because their buses left around two o'clock. All the other bus conductors for buses like Phathaphatha, Ocean Current, and Sukumani Maswati were running the engines because it was now time for them to leave. Bus conductors were shouting, "Siteh five, Mzilikazi four, this side, Siteki! Siteki!" The conductors of buses that go to Hlatikulu like Sondundu were also calling for people to get on because it was a long way to the south of Swaziland. Some bus conductors were writing out tickets and handing them to the people as they came in. Women carrying loads on their heads and some dragging little girls and boys were also walking fast toward the buses. An ice cream vendor here and there would shout lazily, "Ice cream! Ice cream! Ice cream!" Some vendors were sitting under the shade of an umbrella and leaning on a Coca-Cola bicycle that carried tins of Coke in a refrigerated box. A man over there would be talking to a young woman, and there was laughter everywhere. It was good to be immersed in this hustle and bustle of the bus rank after months of being shut in at boarding school. My mind took in everything with a relaxed nonchalance.

I went to my bus and sat down. There was quiet in the bus. Apart from a woman who was pushing in her two children, everything looked calm. The bus driver was standing outside the bus. The bus conductor was quiet.

The quiet was broken by a man who came in with a suitcase. "*Ingcam ngcam bomake* [mother], *siyadla* [we are eating], sweets, biscuits, and even this," he said, lifting a brush and mirror combo made out of plastic. "With your two rand, you look at yourself as you brush your hair. Let us eat Malangeni. As we go to Big Bend, we eat. What will you give the children when you get home?" He was smiling at the woman next to the door. She took out some money and bought bananas. Afterward the man came up to the seats and went toward the back. Since nobody paid attention, he closed his box and walked out. I watched him as he got out. Looking at the front of the bus, my eyes focused on the words that were written in the front: "Ayikho inkhokhelo yemtfhwalo lolahleke uhamba nemnikati." (There is no compensation for baggage that gets lost when the owner is in the bus.) I wondered why this disclaimer was there. The words staring at us seemed to have a power of their own. I thought about my suitcase at the top and wondered what would happen if anybody took the wrong suitcase. It was unfair for bus owners to get out of compensating passengers so easily. I wondered what incidents had led to such a disclaimer. My thoughts wondered to each and every passenger and then went back to the last hours with my friends. I wondered about my home and my brother. I was glad that I was going home to see him.

We sat in the bus and waited, and at quarter to three, the bus conductor started announcing, "Inyatsi YaMswati Bus Service, Big Bend, Big Bend in here." He would shout and gesticulate while holding the door of the bus. He would whistle after each phrase and swing the door of the bus. He would raise his voice even louder and show passengers in when they neared the bus. It was not that passengers did not know where they were going. As the time got close to the hour, the vendor who had come to be called "Ngcam Ngcam" would come back and tell the men and women that they should buy something for the children. He would walk up and down the aisle of the bus, and once in a while a woman would buy sweets or even the plastic brush and mirror combo. It was at exactly three o'clock that the bus pulled out of the bus station toward my home. At that time, my mother, who was a teacher, was teaching at Gilgal Primary School, which is one of the primary schools that are close to Phonjwane, where I had done my primary education.

The bus would start off and go past Nkoseluhlaza Street and turn into Ngwane Street full of passengers. If there were adults in the bus, I would stand up. If there were seats, I would sit down. I would watch as it went round the circle near the Manzini Club and up past the golf course and upper Courts Valley toward Moneni. The water tank on the left was the only thing that attracted the viewer's eyes. The slums of Moneni would come into our view like slides in a movie. They were a sharp contrast from the beautiful suburb, with bougainvillea fences, of Courts Valley. The slums were made of stick and mud and even offcuts, and looking at them, you knew that this was poverty looking at you. The thorny bushes that never flowered except in the summer separated the lush suburb and the shanty town of Moneni. There was one sizeable grocery store that faced the road. The bus would go uphill and come down near Shangri-la, and the mountains would come into view. I would sit in the bus and watch as it went winding down the road toward the southeast of Swaziland. I would look at the beautiful landscape as the bus wound its way toward Gilgal.

"Joy Mission, Joy Mission, is there anybody who is getting off at Joy Mission?" The bus conductor would ask impatiently as he wrote tickets from a dirty receipt book. "Where are you going?" the bus conductor asked me.

"I am going to Gilgal," I answered. He winked at me, and then I said, "I would pay half the money because I am standing up."

"All the schoolchildren who are sitting down will pay full amount. If you know that you are a schoolchild and you have no respect for the old people, you will just have to pay the full amount," he said, looking at some of the girls who were wearing uniforms from Saint Theresa's High School who were sitting down.

Once in a while a woman would shout, "I get off at Joy Mission, my child," and the bus conductor would whistle to the bus driver so that he can stop the bus.

"Move back and let the woman out. Move back," the bus conductor would shout at the passengers who are standing in the aisle of the bus, and they would shuffle about as they let out the passenger. If you were standing, you would feel squashed as a mother and baby pass near you. A waft of the smell of a young baby and sweat would envelop the space, and we would feel even more squashed as the woman passed. Some passenger would hand her the bag, and the bus conductor would yell at her for not having the baby on a sling as she works her way down.

"This baby will fall. If it was my baby, I can fix you up. Next time I will not let you out if the baby is not on a sling and on your back. I mean, a baby sling, not a blanket. This thing gets undone easily, and the baby can fall. We don't want accidents here. You hear me all you mothers? If you stand up and your baby is not secure on your back, you are not going out of this bus." The bus conductor would let off even when the woman had got off so that other women cannot make the mistake. If a baby cried, all the men in the bus would react, *"Mnikingono* [Give her the nipple], make, *sekuyahela lakimi* [Woman, I feel the birth pangs myself]." The people in the bus would laugh and the woman would breast-feed the baby and the noise would hush down.

I am not sure how this treatment of women felt to me at the time. I felt that women were people whom people could just say what they wanted to without them saying anything back. I thought this was not proper even though I did not know why it was wrong. I have grown up to hate being told by somebody else. But just being on the bus made me feel bus conductors felt that they could do anything to people who are on the bus. They would tease women and frustrate them when they throw their luggage down. It was only much later that I saw kind and honest women in Malangeni Bus Service. They were decent and calm. This was a big change from the male bus conductors who dominated the bus world during the seventies and eighties.

I got off the bus and took my suitcase and made my way home. When I got home, my brother would come and meet me. I would carry my suitcase into the house and check if there was any food. I would change into my home clothes. It was nice to be back from a town school. All people asked you about school as if you were a superior person and knew a lot. You knew that people respected you for your knowledge. For a few days, I would walk to familiar places in Gilgal and prepare for our trip to the Railways where my father worked. Having a mother who was a teacher in the eastern part of the country meant that I had to go toward the east and then make a trip to the north within two days of closing.

"Are you going to pass?" my mother would ask me.

"I am going to pass. I may not be sure how well, but pass I will," I answered, very sure of myself. After that I went round the primary school and greeted the other teachers.

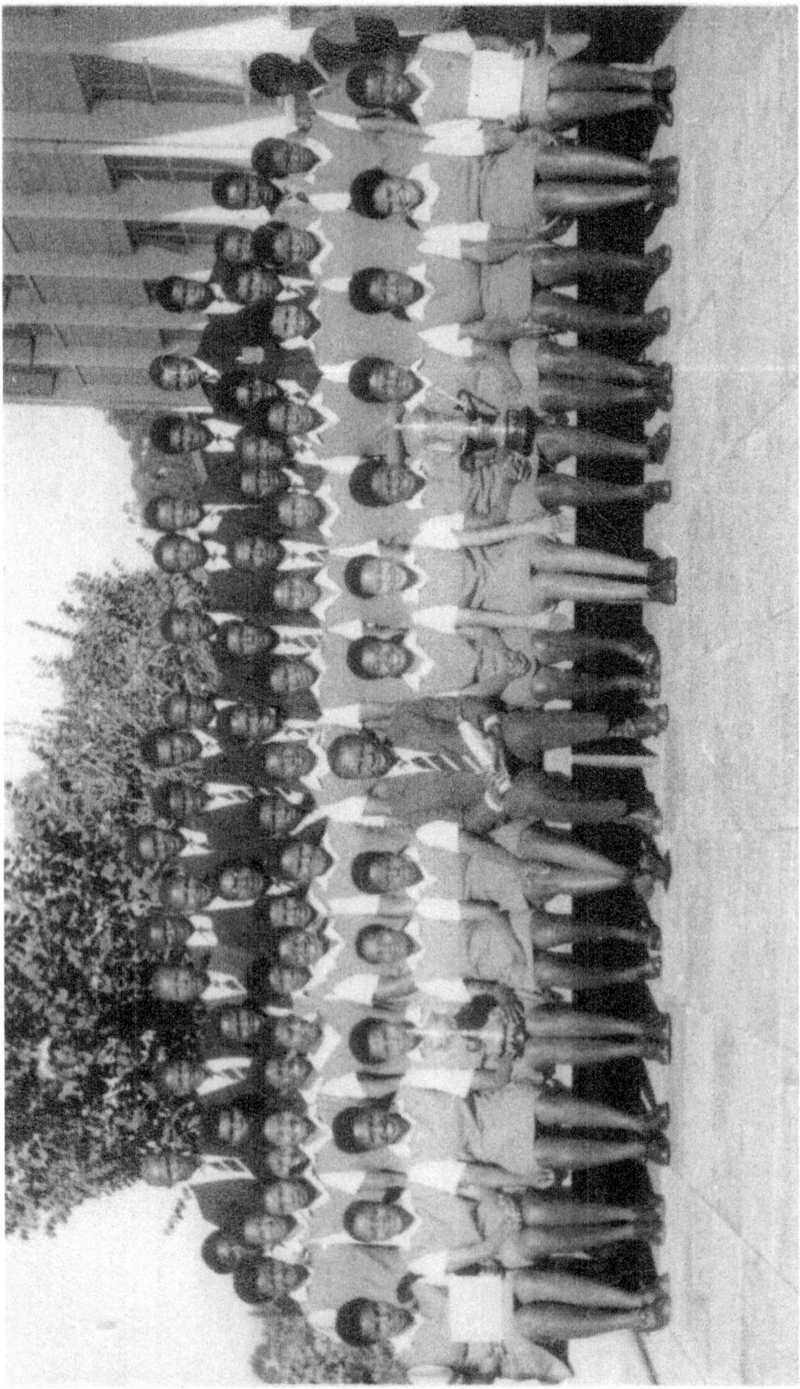

Chapter Four

I did not spend much time at Gilgal. My mother would wind up school, and then we would pack and get ready to go to Ngwenya where my father worked. We would wake up early on the day when we were supposed to leave. Half past eight had to find us at the bus stop so that when Inyatsi Bus Service is on its way to Manzini, we would be waiting for it.

We would get on the bus and drive to Manzini where my mother would go and do her shopping while I waited with my brother. My brother was young at the time, and he would be excited about everything that was bought at the store. When my mother came back with a box of oats, he would sing loud in the bus about "my oats" and say in childish Swazi, "Nayi iOthi yami," which means "here is my oats." He would jump up and down in excitement.

We would take the special bus service or Inhlavu Bus Service and go to Mbabane. At Mahlanya, the buses would stop so that the passengers could buy fruits. We would buy all kinds of fruits—pineapples, apples, peaches, and even sweet potatoes. Mahlanya is the biggest market in Swaziland. All the fruits and vegetables can be found there. The bus would start moving while a passenger was taking a plastic bag of fruit from a vendor, and the passenger would have to throw the money to the vendor through the window.

We would get to Mbabane and wait for the Zeeman's Bus Service and go all the way to Ngwenya, where the iron-ore mine was. Mbabane was a fascinating town with its three-story buildings. Nowhere in Swaziland were there buildings that were as high as the ones I saw in Mbabane. Seeing all the electricity and the cars and the people was all new to me when I first went to the capital town of Swaziland. Things seemed to be different here.

We would get to Ngwenya in the evening and get home when it was dark. Life in our three-bedroom mine house was slow and boring. I lived to listen to the radio and play with the other children in the mine village. The village had one store and two churches, and all the people worked at the mine. The mine buses would come for the workers and take them to the mine and bring them back. On the first few days of our arrival, we would be greeted by the neighbors who were surprised that we were back. I would tell them that schools are closed for about three weeks. Life would be working at home and going to the store, to the church, and maybe to the border gate. Apart from that, I visited my friends who went to Saint Theresa's High School. We would exchange notes about school, and then I would tell them about my friends Makhosi and Sisile.

Once in a while I would get a letter from my friend Sisile. She would be telling me what life was like at her home in Siteki. She would talk about the lowveld and the family home and her father and mother. You could tell that Sisile loved her family and did a lot at home. She would talk about how they visited her grandmother in Hhohho and her aunt who was a nurse.

I would prepare for school by listening to new pop songs and reading the novels on my father's bookshelf. I knew that my friends would be doing the same in their homes. We were preparing for school. We wanted to come back having learned new words and new pop songs. Part of our learning pop songs had to do with loneliness. If we knew the pop songs, we could be radios and pass time singing at school. We would sing Elvis Prestley's "I Just Can't Help Believing" and learn the words because we knew that we had to do as much listening to the radio as we could since this was the last time we hear pop music. We would listen to Lourenco Marques Radio and hear songs like "I Don't Wanna Play House" and "Guitar Man." Everything we did those years was about school. I would save every penny that I got in preparation for school because we knew those were days when we would have no money. The last week of the holiday went very fast. I would spend it at the Ephesus House with students from Saint Theresa's, Waterford, Our Lady of Sorrows, and Mater Dolorosa. We would spend the week with the Lutheran sponsors who paid for my high school education. I think they were from Sweden. This was where we saw the first African American. She was volunteering at the Ephesus House. She was one Mrs. McLinton, a stately tall lady who would enjoy talking to us. We did not know much about African Americans at that time. Even the American missionaries who were at the Nazarene mission were all white. The only African American we knew about was Percy Sledge because he had come to sing at the stadium. We spent the week weeding the fields and putting grass around strawberry plants. In the evening, we would watch as the students enjoyed themselves with the guys from Waterford Kamhlaba while playing records and dancing to music. Most of the guys were doing A levels, and they were from Zimbabwe, which was Rhodesia then. We knew that there was a war in Rhodesia, but we did not know why.

I returned home and did not spend much time, since we had to start preparing for school again. I would wash my clothes and iron them and pack them in my suitcase. On the day when we returned to Gilgal, I would be looking forward to going back to school because I missed my friends. My little brother was the only person I would miss. He would be excited to be going on the bus and to be with me. We loved each other and taught each other a lot. I would give him a little bit of my money and ask him to polish Father's shoes and help me when I go and look for firewood.

On the day when I took off for school, he would go with me to the station. We would wait for the bus and see it as it comes round the bend near Maphakane, and he would cross the road and prepare to go back home. I would wave to him and take off for school.

"School come," as the first day of school was known, would begin in town. I knew which buses my friends would be on. Makhosi lived in KaKhoza, so she would cross over the fence and be at school in a short while. Sisile came from Siteki, sometimes in her father's car or by bus. I would get off the bus and go to the hostel to drop my suitcase. We would leave our suitcases under the jacaranda tree and make our way back to town. This was the fun part of our lives because if I was lucky, Sisile's parents would drop her at the hostel at the same time as I arrived to drop my suitcase. The fun would be in walking to town again and going to see the students and their boyfriends. School come was a busy time in town. The buses would be full, and the shops would also be full as parents did their last-minute shopping before schools started. We did not mind the hustle and bustle in town; but we walked about and went to stores like Jazz and bought fruits, biscuits, soap, and toiletries, knowing that this was our last day in town since we would go back to the hostel for three months and not come out until the schools closed.

We would walk down the road to town and walk about into each and every store. We would catch up with other friends and go wherever they were going until a boy would interrupt us because he wanted to talk to one of our friends. We would continue walking and leave the two alone. I remember one of the girls saying one thing that had a lot of wisdom. She said we should not bring shame to our parents by behaving badly with boys. That had a lot of influence on me. I knew that school was very important and had to be taken seriously. Even though I did not look serious to many people, I did not play with schoolwork. I worked hard and did my level best. I always knew that I would do well if I worked hard. Even with boys, I knew that there was something shameful about being with them, but I did not understand what it was. I knew that they kiss girls, but I was not so sure what was wrong with that.

It was when we were going back to the hostel and seeing girls alone in the park with a boy that we felt a bit uncomfortable. We knew that some of the girls had boyfriends, and we knew that they were not allowed to be in the park with the boys holding them so close. We were considered too young to have boyfriends in the lower forms, and we knew that we were not allowed to have them. We also knew that there was something dangerous about concentrating on boys. They affected how one performed since the thoughts of the boy would linger in the mind of the girl. Therefore, there would not be enough time for the studies. However, since we had been taught reproduction, we did not feel that having a boyfriend was that bad. We did pass shyly at the park when we saw girls from our school sitting in a compromising position with a boy. We looked and yet did not look.

We would walk fast at this time because it was time to go back to the hostel. We were supposed to get there at five o'clock. Nobody wanted to be late because that would mean going to chop wood up on the mountain. We would walk past Lewis Store and know that this was the last time we saw the inside of a store. We would stop and buy a packet of chips and just look around, taking in the last minutes of freedom. Getting over the cement fence at Sharpe Memorial Church meant that we were back in the mission, and freedom had to remain where it belonged. Life now was being handed over to those who had been given permission by our parents to teach us about heaven. That is how our journey to a new term began. We would look at buses like Uhambe Uze Ukhule Ngwane Bus Service that goes to Mankayane through the trees and know that we would be inside a bus after we have been inside for three months. We would rush as we walked under the boulevard of the flamboyant trees that lined the road that was near the Practicing Primary schools and take the long stretch to the hostel at a fast pace because we knew that time was against us. Anything that was bad behavior had to be cut off. We were like Moses when he saw the burning bush. No "shoes" from the world out there were allowed where we were going. We would go to the jacaranda tree and pick up our suitcases and go to greet the senior matron. She would be happy to see us and always say, "You are back, my children. Go to your dorm." We would go up the steps of the dining hall and look at the fine-polished steps that had specs of red and blue paint and open the grey double door of the dining hall and look at the long tables that we would eat off for the next three months, and life would have begun. If Makhosi and Sisile were not in the dormitory, I would go back and look through the window of the dining hall. When I saw Sisile's father's car pulling in under the jacaranda tree, I would run out and help her. I would take her suitcase as she went to the matron. She would step over the bricks that lined the flower bed near the matron's door and jump over the small shrublike reddish plants that were the only plants that were in the shady part of the entrance to the matron's door. The student teachers would be peeping through the open brick fence as if they wanted to note everything that was happening outside the matron's door. I would wait on the steps, and when Sisile came out, we would walk to the dormitories. She always came back with a big cake tin that was full of goodies. We would go to the dorm, and she would start making her bed.

"Twigza, no untidy locker above my locker," she would say as she lined her locker with gift-wrap paper.

"I don't care how my locker looks," I would say as I pushed my belongings into mine. "As long as my soap, toothbrush, and the few toiletries are within easy reach, I am all right." I would push in my clothes into the locker anyhow. I could see that Sisile's clothes were ironed and straightened out as they came out of the suitcase. Mine had been thrown in, and they were going into the locker as they were crushed and crumpled as if I had somewhere more important to go.

"What is this?" Sisile would say as she pulls out my locker. "You are not serious. I am going to do it myself this time," she would say as she fixed my locker. "I know, two days from today and everything will be upside down," she would say when she was done. It was good to have a friend who cared about me. I envied her neatness and prayed that one day it would rub off on to me.

"Let us go and wait for Makhosi." We would go back to the dining hall because even though Makhosi lived in KaKhoza, she also had to go to the front of the hostel and greet the matron. When she was late, she would take the path that went past the big pit and come down toward the sinks and then go round to the front to the matron's house. We would wait near the windows in the dining hall hoping that any minute she would appear.

"Bulelo, come here," we would hear Makhosi as she shouted. "I hid food over there," she would say, pointing at the guava trees. We were not allowed to take meat to the dorms because of cockroaches. If we had chicken, we would have to eat it outside until it is finished. That is why the girls would hide the meat and go to the matron and then pick it up after they have talked to her. On the first day of school, we would feast on the provision. I would eat a lot even though I did not have any provision. My friends knew that I would not have much. I would eat peanuts, avocado pears, chicken, steamed mealie bread, maize, and all the perishable foods because we did not want any of it to spoil. The peanuts, sweets, biscuits, and fruit would be hidden in the locker under the clothes so that the matron would not see it. If by any chance she saw it, she would take it outside, and the owners would have to go and eat it there. Once in a while a student would have a birthday party, and we would go and celebrate by eating together up on the mountain. It was not that we were not allowed to eat it in the dining hall. It was just that it was easier to hide some of the cake and take it into the dormitories if we eat it away from the prying eyes of the student teachers and the matron. We did not like the attitude of the student teachers because they saw us as if we were naughty children, and they reported us to the matron. There were those whom we liked. Some of them washed our uniforms and called us their "babies" and we called them "mommies." It was nice to have a mommy because she gave you money and washed and ironed for you. This kind of game did not last. By the time I left high school, it had petered out.

The third term was a serious term. We arrived and found that all the bunk beds had been sold to a man who lived near Sukumani Grocery Store. It was interesting to watch as he dismantled and carried the steel frames home. We got new single beds and felt much better not having to sleep on the bunk beds. I was afraid of the bunk beds when there was a girl who walked in her sleep. I remember a girl jumping from the bed and running away in her sleep, and I was amazed. I could tell that she was asleep when they called her to come back.

The third term was nice and warm. When we arrived, we found the tree inside the ring that was on the way to the chapel in bloom. Its purple flowers were all over the circle. It was obvious that we had not been around because the grass on the path to the chapel was green again. The sand showed that it had rained. I looked out the door toward the chapel and knew that soon we would be sweeping the grounds again in our morning duties. The pawpaw trees and the leaves that had fallen on the ground added to my picture of what our morning duties would be like as we weeded the flower beds near the resident missionary's house. Most of the years, it was Ms. McClou who lived in the resident missionary's house. She would preach to us on Sunday morning. After taking in the first day of our arrival, I would watch how all of a sudden all the short floral curtains on the windows were open. The curtains were made of blue floral material that had tiny squares that were pasted onto it. We would open the windows and push the curtain out of the open panes because there was nothing to tie them back with. The dormitories would soon be alive with noise as girls shouted and laughed. We were not marked for making noise during the day unless we were too loud. Girls who visited other dorms were marked. If you were found in a dormitory that was not assigned to you, you were marked. On these days when we were sharing food with our friends, it was common for the matron to sneak in on us; and seeing her at the door, we would look at a visitor in our dorm and try to hide her by having her lie down behind us on the bed. Sometimes the visitors would hide where we hung our clothes. If the matron suspected something, she would check everywhere. If we were hiding one of the girls under the bed, it would be quite a situation to watch as the person was marked. We were not allowed to share beds with other girls. Some girls would visit their friends and share a bed with them even though it was against the rules. This was because we were used to sharing blankets at home with our siblings. We had grown up in poverty fighting over the four corners of the blanket at home with our brothers and sisters, and that is why we were a bit amazed at the regulations of the hostel because we felt that this was an unnecessary rule. It is in today's world that I have come to understand that girls can be attracted to each other in the way a girl is attracted to a boy. When we grew up, this was not heard of.

The first event when we would meet together was in the dining hall. Girls who had new clothes showed them off there. We would go back to our routines, and chapel time would be the event that would really make us feel that we were back at school. We would sit on the benches and wait for the leader of the chapel service. By the time we were in Form III, the girl who preached about Much Afraid was gone. The junior matron would conduct most services because this seemed to be her duty. I think she had been to the Bible school. She preached well, and she also led the music in the services at Sharpe Memorial Church. We liked her, and we had shortened her long last name to a single syllable that was a nickname that only we students knew. She loved to carry her Bible. She was also very friendly, though strict when we made noise. Most of the time when we had to go to town, she was the one who went with us. The big girls were escorted by us when they had to go to the optician or dentist. I think they did not realize that we would not report if the girls spoke to a boy on the way to and from town. The matrons thought we were little angels.

The senior matron started to be unwell around my third year of boarding school. When we heard about this, we were sympathetic. Even though we were sympathetic, she did not escape our sharp tongues. One day Sisile was talking about her. I think she had been marked for being noisy after lights-out. She was shouting about how she can deal with the matron if she had her way.

"I can just jump and kick her heart," she said, demonstrating with her high jump skills how she would deal with the matron. "She doesn't know me. I can just kick her heart, and it can stop right now," she said, not aware that she could be heard from outside because the walls of the dormitory did not reach up to the roof. As she went about protesting, a stick was thrown into the dorm, and it landed on the blue table. Sisile pushed the bench that she had been holding in readiness to sit down, and the old rickety table squeaked as she made for the door. Her red flip-flops were left under the bench as she hurried to catch the assailant. She opened the door, and lo and behold! Who did she find at the door, but the matron. She stood there like a mummy in her beautiful blue coat and short crimplene hat. Her head looked as if it was going to sink into the collar of her coat as she stared quietly and peacefully at Sisile. Sisile was shocked! She lifted her arms into the air and ended up putting both hands on her mouth as if to shut it and stop it from saying things it should not say. Nobody needed to ask her what she had seen. We knew that whatever it was, it was something we did not wish to see. "IKooooor," she whispered as she tiptoed to where she had been sitting behind the table. She was holding her chest. I could see that she was afraid.

"What did she say," I whispered.

"Nothing," she whispered. I knew that I should not continue to ask questions. The other girls were holding back the laughter because they thought it was funny that we should be caught saying such horrible things.

We were quiet until we heard the door that led into the kitchen close and knew that the matron had gone before we laughed. Makhosi went to peep on the door to make sure that there was no one who could hear us. We laughed sheepishly as we talked about the matron's heart. A part of us believed that it was because of our naughtiness that she was suffering. We also just thought that she had always had a weak heart. We could not imagine what life would be like if she should no longer be able to work. We would have been devastated even though we did not like her and the strict rules of the hostel. It think it was the rules that we did not like and not her, personally. I think authority is something that people detest no matter what form it comes in. I think she was the symbol of our being shut in at the boarding school, and since it was she whom we identified as our oppressor, she had to take the brunt.

When the bell for going to supper rang, we went out, wondering how we would face the matron now that we knew that she knew that we were teasing her about her weak heart. When we went to table 10 for our supper, our "mother" was there. Our mother was from Johannesburg. She was a sweet girl who had a soft-spoken voice. She did not know that we had been caught red-handed by the matron, uttering "unutterables." Everything went on as normal. When the matron came to our table, she wanted to see if we had enough food. She offered us a second helping that day, and we began to relax. We felt that even though we had been naughty and insolent, our naughtiness was of no consequence since she was nice to us. We were relieved, and like all other cases of our usual naughtiness, this one was also forgotten.

Weeding the flower beds began again as we cleaned the hostel grounds. Our duty was to sweep the area between the dorms and the tuckshop where the tree that grew inside the ring was located. We would go to fetch brushes of green leafy plants called *umsutane* that had a funny pungent smell. It was available all over. Sometimes we would go to the big gum tree near the student teachers' dorms and get it from there. We would break the branches of this tree and go and sweep. Our leader would be waiting for us. She would sweep with us, and then when we had a pile of leaves, we would carry it to the big pit up on the mountain. This is where the big girls used to burn all the dirt from the bathrooms including sanitary pads. They had a bucket near the pit that was quite old. I did not envy this job. I was glad that I was not a "mother" when I got to know why they were always burning something over there when we went for breakfast.

We would pick up the pawpaw leaves from the flower beds and rake them into a pile and then carry them to the big pit. We would enjoy ourselves as we walk up the steps that made it easy to scale the donga and get to the top. After throwing the rubbish in the pit, we would walk back to clean up some more until we were done with all the work.

Wednesday evening was time for NYPS (Nazarene Young People's Society). We went to the big church and had a service. There was something interesting in walking all the way to Sharpe Memorial Church in the dark. The church was about half a mile away from the hostel. We would walk together, the student teachers in front and we high school students behind. The matrons would follow us at the back. When we got to the church, we would take our position on the left-hand side of the chapel. The ground around Sharpe Memorial Church was soggy and moldy. The storm drains were always showing signs of a strange algae that was always there. The weeds would grow in the months that we were gone. We would step on them as we enter the church. We would take our positions on the benches, and the leader of the service would start choruses. We would sing songs like "I have the wonderful love of Jesus, where, down in the depths of my heart" and keep repeating where the love was and answering to confirm that it was there in the depths of the cockles of our hearts. Whether it was really there or not was another story. After that a quartet of male student teachers would stand up and sing. They would sing songs like "I hear the words that Jesus spake to them of Galilee, to fishermen besides the lake, he said come follow me." This song was our favorite in the hostel. We would imitate these guys and tap on the floor and point at the sky. When we were in the shower, we would sing, and I would laugh and throw my legs in the air as Sisile imitated the baritone.

"Follow me, follow me fishers of men, always to be," we would sing in the shower, and all the students would watch our naked quartet, which was made up of Sisile, Makhosi, me, and one girl from Botswana called Mantho. We would sing until it was time for us to go to the chapel when we are really possessed by the spirit of the girls of the "Koor." This is why we listened so carefully when the quartet took its position. The leader of the boys would use a harmonica to get the tune, and then the guys would hum their parts and then sing on. Sometimes the quartet would imitate the King's Messengers, a South African quartet that was popular at the time. They harmonized very well.

After the boys, a girls quartet would stand up and "render an item." They would sing songs like "Precious Lord, take my hand, lead me home to the light, I am tired, I am weak, I am worn. Through the storm, through the light, lead me on to the light, take my hand, take me home, precious Lord." They would also sing, "Little is much when God is in it," and tell us not to labor for wealth or fame for "there is a crown and you can win it, if you will labor in Jesus's name." We would wait for the lesson of the day. Sometimes the lesson would be taught by a woman preacher who used to make us laugh. She would talk to us about praying for our partners of the future. She would teach us that we have to pray for partners that we will marry and not just go out with boys for fun. She would say we should not close one eye and pray for someone that we like and say, "God, I am praying for Jonah." She taught us that God listens to sincere prayers where we close our eyes and pray for whoever he wants us to have in our lives. She would also say that we should not look at the bell-bottoms of the boys, especially the swollen part in front, and think that that is what marriage or love was about. We would laugh and giggle when that woman was preaching. She would then sing and call the altar call. Some girls who wanted to repent would go to the altar. If they had boyfriends, their boyfriends would think that they were no longer going to go out with them. Ms. McClou would go to the altar and talk to them in her broken

Swazi, asking them about what they thought about Jesus. I think that she wanted to show that she was there for them if they changed and came to Jesus. I would go to the altar sometimes even though I knew that Sisile and Makhosi would laugh at my attempt to repent. They knew that one minute I would be back to the life we loved, which was not necessarily evil. We thought that religion was a "halo" of something. When you went to the altar, you had to come out with a sign that showed that you were "saved." Many people still believe this. Many people fail to realize that being saved is just committing to love all people and connect with the bigger power that has all the goodness of who you are meant to be. We did not know that about God. We just thought that he was big up there and did not know how difficult life was for us if he should demand that we be different. After the altar call, I would try to consider everything I did and change. For a few days I would remember, and memory would lapse when the usual life set in. Routine and boredom are two companions that never part. Spicing them up is what made life for us. I think our naughtiness was our own way of spicing life up.

We would return to the hostel after NYPS and go to sleep immediately after studying. Since the service took two hours, we had one hour of study before lights-out. We would go through all the essential work quickly and get ready for the following day, which would be Thursday.

The third term was short in Form III because we were preparing for the external exam called the Junior Certificate. This was an examination that was organized by the BOLESWA (Botswana, Lesotho, and Swaziland) examination board. We had to respond to questions that required us to reflect on all that we had learned in the past three years of school. It was difficult to have to review everything in every subject. We had vowed that we would pass these examinations. We would set questions on all the subjects and review everything that we knew. Makhosi was the one who helped us with science. Her cousin who was at Salesian High School would teach her some of the things we needed to know during the holidays, and she would teach us when we were back in school. I don't think we would have passed as well as we did without her help in science.

Everything we did in the last term was like getting ready for a grand finale. We went back to practicing the songs in the choir so that our performance at the last biggest event of the year, Speech and Prize-Giving Day, would be at its best. We looked forward to this day. It was a day when those who had been doing well would be honored.

It is hard to set a goal for an examination when you are writing it for the first time. I just decided that it would be best to know everything that we had been taught. When we went to class, I would concentrate on studying even when the other students were making noise. The boys would file into class like policemen. They had removed the rubber from their chairs. They would take the chairs and bring them to the door and slide on them until they got to their seats. While they did that, one of them would watch the stairs to see if there was any teacher who would come up to our class and disturb their fun. If the boy saw Ms. McClou, he would indicate by circling his hand on his hair that the woman with the doll-like hairstyle was coming, and the boys would rush to their seats and put their heads on the desks as if they had never done anything except keep quiet. It was easy for teachers to hear noise in our classroom because our classroom was right above the staff room. Ms. McClou would come up the steps and tiptoe to the door in her stilettos and stand there and look at us. I could smell her perfume from where she stood. It was a subtle scent that was just so much a part of her that it had or had become a symbol of her personality. She would wink at the students whom she suspected and tell them to follow her.

We would keep quiet and read our books when all this was going on. The boy who was a prefect had a tough time in Form III because all the naughty boys were his friends. He would quarrel with them when they did naughty things. One time one of the boys took a broken chair and put it where Ms. McClou would sit when she came in to teach us English literature. The chair did not look broken to an onlooker. It was the students in the class who knew that when one sat on it, the back legs folded inward and the person sitting on it would crash to the floor. This trick had been tried on many of us. Seeing the boy put the chair in Ms. McClou's place and take the chair that was behind the table caused a stir in the class. The prefect jumped and took the chair away, and there was a squabble over this as the other boy wanted it to be there. That day we grew to respect the prefect because he had fought for what he believed by removing the broken chair and replacing it with the correct one. We all wondered what it would have been like to see Ms. McClou fall. When she came into class, we were relieved. She led us through the literature lesson by reading to us *Romeo and Juliet*. Since we're now going through the book for the second time, we were now ready to ask questions. Our literature classes were fun because Ms. McClou would be too shy to answer some questions and blush in front of us. We asked questions about love that we knew would embarrass her.

At lunchtime, the siren that announced one o'clock for the whole mission would sound, and we would hear commotion throughout the building as students prepared to get out of class and go for lunch. The pushing of desks and pulling of chairs on the floor was heard throughout the building. We would walk out of the classroom and make our way to the stairs. There would be a jam in the square that led to the stairs as students waited to go downstairs. There was a boy who would hide at the bottom of the stairs and kiss any girl who was not alert as she stepped off the corner of the stairs. We would then go up the hill and head for the hostel. We would walk slowly at the edge of the narrow road that was behind the hall as a long car belonging to one of the American missionaries passed, raising dust as the missionary hurried home for lunch. The student teachers would also make the walk up to the hostel in their blue pleated skirts and white shirts. We would pass the dining hall and see the workers putting the bowls of food on our tables. We would all go to the dormitories and wait for the bell that would announce mealtime. When it rang, we would walk to the dining hall. There would be commotion in the dining hall as we walked in. The pulling of benches as students sat down could be heard here and there. The final *klink, klink* of the bell would mean it was time to say grace. We would sing a song about asking God to bless our food and then sit down to eat. The mothers would dish the food, and it would be passed on to all the students. If it was summer and the pawpaw trees had yielded some pawpaws, we would alternate in having pawpaws with our food. The same thing would

WEEDING THE FLOWERBEDS

apply to boiled corn. When the gardens had some corn, we would have it with our meal. This meant that we would have extra food from the usual meal of mealie rice and meat.

On lucky days, I would walk out of the dining hall and see my uncle's truck as he came to deliver fruit at the hostel. He would give us pears and other goodies in the truck. I would be very happy on those days. My friends and I looked forward to these treats. As soon as we finished eating, I would go back to the dormitory, comb my hair, and take my copy of *Romeo and Juliet* and head for the cement block where we waited for the bell to ring so that we could leave the hostel for school. This is when I would read Shakespeare. I did not like studying Shakespeare seriously. I enjoyed spending this time reading one speech and reflecting on it. That way I did not feel that I was doing the hard work of trying to study a whole play. I would look at the notes on the side and reflect on life.

Sitting on that cement wall, I could see the rest of the mission very well. To my left was a house that belonged to one of the missionaries. I could see clothes hanging on the line, and one short woman who had a hump on her back would come out and pick the clothes. Beyond that house was the Nazarene Primary School, which we called "UmPra." The students who were in the Nazarene Primary School could be seen outside the school in their navy blue uniforms that had yellow collars.

Beyond the high school buildings were the blue buildings of the teacher training college. Just below me were the gum trees that were between the school and the boys' hostel. They were separated from the jacarandas that were to my right and the football field of the high school. That field seemed to be down in a donga-like plain because of the slope of the terrain. There were reedlike plants that we called *khontoyi*. To my right was the house of the head of the mission station. It was a big house that was made of red bricks. It seemed to be a three-story house. I wondered why one family that had three girls needed to have such a big house. It was also lined by jacaranda trees beyond which were more guava, gum trees, and flamboyants. The poplars and conifers were just below the hostel. It was intriguing that there were no indigenous trees on the grounds of the Nazarene mission. It was as if somebody had come and planted foreign trees only. The trees were as foreign as the education we were getting there. Very little that was African was taught except in the Zulu class. From where I sat, I could see the boys leaving the boys' hostel and coming back to school. The day scholars were the ones who were milling around the school. Some were still standing at the window where they received their lunch. I would watch as the cars of missionaries passed on the road. One or two student teachers would come down the steps from the hostel. They were carrying teaching aids in their hands. When the bell rang, I would take a few steps and walk slowly toward the school. Once in a while my friends would join me.

We would walk down to school together as the other students made their way to the grounds of the school. We would see buses on the road far away beyond the Nazarene Primary School. They were moving slowly going uphill on their way toward Mbabane. The cars that were moving fast were the ones that were going downhill toward the main part of town. Whenever we saw the buses and cars on the road, we would feel the nostalgia of home go and wish we were out there on the road. We would walk to school and make sure that when the electric bell rang, we would be ready to go to class. If there was still time, we would stand outside the office or even move to the front of the school and bask in the sun.

When the bell rang, we would go to class. Sometimes it would be time for the science class, and we would go to the lab. Our lab had long lab tables that were made out of hard dark wood. There were tall lab stools that had a hole in the middle. The bottles of chemicals and beakers were neatly stacked in shelves on the wall. Glass cylinders and pipettes could be seen lying near the white sinks that were near the wall just below the windows. The black plastic taps created a feeling of difference that we associated with the lab. We knew the rules of the lab. We were not supposed to touch any of the chemicals when the teacher was not there. Going into the lab meant waiting for the teacher until she came in. She would then light up the Bunsen burners and set up the experiment of the day. The smell of gas would irritate my nostrils as we waited for the experiment to yield the results. It was a long wait to the end of the experiment. When we came out, we would be ready to write our notes on the observation. The last bell that announced the end of the day came at a time when we really expected it. The shadows of the trees would indicate that it was time to go back to the hostel. We would take our books and go because yet another day was over. Passing near the auditorium with its blue-tinted glasses gave our having gone to school its own reality, for this was where the day had started with prayer, and now we were leaving for whence we had come.

Our studies became more serious as the year got closer to its end. After school I would leave my friends in the dormitory and go and read behind a small brick house that was near the big pit. It was small and square, and only the big axe for chopping wood as punishment and the bucket that measured the chopped wood were the only things that I knew to be there. I would sit there and read my notes and wait for the bell for going to the chapel to ring. It felt good to have my own spot. It was nice to look down at the ants and watch them busy and remember the sermons about learning from the ant. I would read and take time to look at the land around me. There were big gum trees up here on the mountain. Once in a while I would see a car passing outside the fence. It felt funny to look at the outside world and see so little of it. The undergrowth obstructed my vision. It is the top of the cars that I would see. I would wonder how the people lived out there in the world.

After I felt that I had done justice to my work, I would go back to the dorm and find my friends eating the last bits of the provision from home. I would join in and eat the peanuts and lemon creams, and then we would sit astride on the benches and start talking about the events of the day. We would recount how the day was and laugh at its happenings.

My friends who had taken the music class with the recorders would play the instruments, and we would listen as they played on. It was interesting to listen to instruments because it was different from the usual singing that relied mostly on voice.

Afterward the bell for supper would ring, and we would make our way to the dining room. On a hot day, we would come in and smell the sweet smell of Kool-Aid. The wet droplets on the big white enamel jugs would indicate that something cold was inside. While the drinks changed, the bread did not change. Three slices of bread that were the regular supper meal and thin porridge would be there in the big white enamel bowls come rain, sunshine, or winter. We would sit down to our meal and enjoy the cold Kool-Aid.

If our table was responsible for washing dishes, we would go to the sinks inside the kitchen and get ready to wash the dishes. The plates would be brought by the students from the different tables, and we would wash them and stack them on racks that were kept inside the kitchen close to the hatch that was used for passing the food to the students. One student would wash the dishes while another rinsed them. Another would stack them. Leftovers of thin, sour porridge and tea were thrown outside in a bucket. A woman would come and pick the bucket and go and feed her pigs.

We would leave the kitchen clean when we were done. The stainless steel sinks would be shining. All the dishes and plates would be stacked in their place. After this we would head out and know that we did not have much time before chapel. We would head for the bathroom and wash quickly. When we saw the student teacher who locks the door, we would know that it was almost time to go to chapel. The bell would ring immediately after she locks the door, and we would file out for the chapel.

Chapter Five

Our food supplies dwindled, and we would have to send the day scholars to buy us biscuits and other goodies in town. Since we were not allowed to have any food in the lockers, we would hide the goodies under our jerseys when we passed near the matron's house. We did not carry backpacks and schoolbags. We carried our books in our hands and stored everything in our desks at school. We would pass quietly, feigning extra confidence whenever we knew that we were hiding something. We would share the supplies in a guarded manner since we were now spending our meager gifts of pocket money that our parents had given us to use for school supplies.

When we were waiting for the service to start on Sundays, we would watch the buses and long for home. We would send some of the day scholars who attended our school to Lewis Store to go and buy us goodies like chewing gum and creamy sweets called Toff-o-Luxe. We would share the chewing gum, and it would help us through the three-hour ordeal of church. We would look at the matron through the corner of the eye to see if she did not see that we were chewing gum. If she had already seen us, she would give us "the look," and we would know that we should spit out the gum. It is amazing how we always got into trouble for chewing in church. There was a time when the senior matron moved me, Sisile, and Makhosi to sit near her. Some of this was done because Makhosi would bend down and show that she was not into what is being preached about. Sometimes she would hide a novel inside her Bible and read while the service was going on. When we were in Form III, we had mastered the habit of reading for pleasure and self-improvement. We preferred reading to sitting and listening to sermons and watching Ms. McClou sitting with her forefinger on her lips and watching us from the far end where the missionaries sat as if she wished to punish us for offences that she was imagining in her mind. I think she thought we were the naughtiest people on earth, and even when we were in the service, she wished nothing for us except the worst punishment that the school could give. Since she did not have children of her own, I was not sure how she could even be so sure that we were badly behaved.

That year Ms. McClou became the resident missionary in the teacher's house that was attached to our dorms. We would peep to see if her red Volkswagen was in the parking lot outside her house, and then we would go to the back of the chapel and sit there and read or even take photos if we had a camera. We did not want her to see us and then go and say we were planning to run away. Such was the level of suspicion between us and Ms. McClou. She would report us for the slightest offenses. If she saw us talking to boys, she would come close and listen. One day another girl gave me a letter to give to the prefect in my class. I knew that this was a love letter. She made the mistake of giving me the letter outside the assembly hall. From where she stood, Ms. McClou could see that we were exchanging something. The girl was older than me even though she was behind me by a year. We shared the same dormitory because I was always with students who were a year behind me. When she gave me the letter, I placed it in my Bible. We had hard-covered maroon Revised Standard Version Bibles that we used in class and carried to the assembly hall in the morning. As soon as I saw Ms. McClou tiptoe out of the hall in her stilettos, I knew that we were in trouble. Ms. McClou came in between us and looked at the girl in the eyes. Since she had her back to me, I knew that if I did not run away, we would be in serious trouble. I backed off slowly and turned and ran. I got into the nearest classroom and saw a girl who was in our dorm and told her to hide the letter. She understood what I was saying, and then I went back to the hall. Ms. McClou was still questioning the girl. I passed them and went into the hall. That was when I realized that my heart was beating hard. We had been very close to getting into serious trouble.

Such incidents made life interesting for us because their passing meant that the events of our lives were also developing their own time line. We were in school for a number of years, and we would soon leave and go back to our homes. We were not angels, so we were bound to get into trouble at what we called the "place of no!" When were we going to learn to use our own minds? I think this question was also in the minds of the teachers because things started changing. Wednesday morning started to be a day for life skills. We did not go to the assembly hall. We met in our classes, and teachers came to the class to teach us about life. They talked to us about etiquette and how boys should treat girls when they take them out. They demonstrated how they should pull out the chair for a girl to sit. Since the boys in our class were naughty and they had broken the back legs on one of the chairs, we regretted why they had been taught this one. They started to play the stunt of the "falling chair" on us. If you fell for the idea that Killer, one boy in our class, would pull a chair for you, you were in for a high jump. He would take the chair that had the back legs that were broken, and with a friend, they would pretend to pull the chair for you, and you would land on your back on the floor with your legs in the air and be the laughingstock of all the students.

In the Wednesday morning life talks, we were allowed to ask any questions we wanted to ask our teachers. One question I asked was why we were not allowed to wear sleeveless clothes. I remember the deputy head teacher, a tall man whom the students had nicknamed about his nose, shying away from my question. I felt that he found my question offensive. It was as if I was questioning the policy of the school. I did not get any answer to my question. I guess nobody wanted to say that they thought maybe that the boys would peep at our breasts or whatever the answer was or even that it was a rule and rules were just rules.

Our lessons in etiquette were also in effect at the boardinghouse. We would go to the dining hall and find that there were no spoons on one of the Sundays. There would be rice and fork and knife. We were afraid of using a fork and knife. Some of us did not know which hand the fork was to be held and which hand the knife was to be held. We learned there on the spot and used the cutlery accordingly. We had come from Swazi homes where we used our hands to eat. In some of the homes, spoons were reserved for adults. In homes where there were plenty of children, members did not use spoons. I can say in my home, we had always eaten using spoons. This was a sign of affluence because there were homes where even a spoon was a very expensive piece of cutlery that only the father used. The same thing applied to china. In some homes, there was china that was never used. In my home, there was china that was used by adults only. Even today I know that it is never used. We use all the other utensils, but not the china "of the home." I guess it is decorative and just there to show that we have it.

The third term like all terms would have its own incidences with girls who would be expelled for pregnancy. Toward the middle of the term, those girls who had "eaten of the fruit of life" would start showing. I remember mentioning to one girl how she did not have a figure like her sister. Little did I know that I was the predictor of things to come. One day we saw the trunk box under the jacaranda tree, and the girl was waiting under the tree when we were passing and going to school. We all knew what this meant because the trunk boxes were only taken out of the storeroom in December when we were going home at the end of each year. We would see the cream white van with the wired windows and the fat light-skinned woman whose duty was to take students home when they had "eaten of the fruit of life." We would be sad and whisper to our friends that "it" had happened. The evenings after that would be lessons on how we should not go under the guava trees with boys. The woman who took the girl home would ask her in front of her parents how she had got into this mess, and she would have to tell all the details. This is how the "rotten figs" were weeded out before they spoiled the whole crop. It was in the evening chapel services that the senior matron would begin her warning with *bantfwabami*, which means "my children." Her neck would look as if it was sinking into her coat as she began the lesson of the day. She would preach from the Zulu Bible. We would all turn to our Bibles and listen as she read the scripture of the day. It was after the lesson that she would elaborate about our behavior and tell us that one of us had got into this trouble. She would say how she did not wish this for us. I think we listened, but we were a bit rebellious, and the more sex was mystified like this, the more we wanted to know what it was about. The only thing we did not want to happen was to drop out of school and be humiliated inside the van and stand under the jacaranda tree when all the students were going home. If having boyfriends meant not finishing school, we were prepared to forgo the fun.

The letters from boys would come pouring in during the term. The day scholars would bring them from PO Box 315 Manzini. We would read them quietly. One day I was called by one of the older girls. She said she wanted to show me something. I went to her, and I was surprised. She had the picture of my uncle who worked in a nearby town in her jersey. She did not explain to me why she had the picture, but I knew that she must be his girlfriend. After that she was nice to me. One day when my uncle came to visit me, the girls all went to the dining hall. They wanted to see whom he had come to visit. My uncle was popular because he played soccer for Manzini Wanderers, one of the football teams in town. I think the girls were surprised that he was my uncle. He gave me ten rands, which I used to buy my dress for home go. Since I was in Form III, I was expected to dress especially well on home go. After his visit, a lot of the girls from Mbabane who were student teachers talked to me. They asked me about him, and I told them what I knew. At that time, my uncle had also been to Malawi to the polytechnic college to learn about computers. He was obviously one of the upcoming young men in the country and definitely among the most sought-after young men of his time since he played football for Manzini Wanderers.

The real problems with peer pressure started in Form III. This is the year when we had the revival with the preacher whom we called "the Verse" because of the way he pronounced the word *verse* in SiSwati. We found it funny that on this one word, he should use a "very" American accent when everything else was in our language. I don't think I remember what he preached about. I remember that I did not go to the altar the day most of the girls went to the altar. I got into class and opened my desk and put my head inside my desk and read my novel. I heard the boys coming in. They were marching like policemen or soldiers as usual. "Even this heathen called Bulelo has gone to the altar today," I heard one boy saying. I pulled down my desk and looked at him in the face.

"Who is a heathen and who has not gone to the altar?" I asked as he turned to look at the others. "I mean you."

"I thought you had gone to the altar and thought that this was a really good sermon," he said.

"You should mind your own business." I was fuming when I said that. He went to sit down and wished that he had not said what he said. We waited for the morning class to start. Things would be delayed on these days since the teachers had to wait for the students who were in the hall and praying after the sermon.

Sometimes they would start the lessons ten minutes after the morning service. The first class of the day was always dreaded. We would go through it slowly and be glad when we heard the electric bell ringing and knew that we were done with that teacher and waited for the next.

There were many revivals at our school. These were conducted by visiting pastors. I do not remember what they were about. I just remember that there was hysteria at the girls' hostel as all the girls were praying long after the service. Obviously everybody must have been touched by the Word and wanted to repent. Why it should be all the people at the same time made me think that this was transferable psychology. Ms. McClou had to come to the dorms and try to quiet the Holy Spirit that had spilt all over, even on myself. Sisile was the one who remained untouched even by this deluge of the Holy Spirit. The only sad thing is that the main leader of this revival was the one who described the guys and what they do when we were washing in the bathroom. It was ironic that when the Holy Spirit descends as in the days of the apostles, it should fill this one girl to overflow and spill over on everybody. Even her other buddies became saved. Since they were not as hysterical, we can just say they had got sprinklings of the "wind from above." After these services, the girls who had been most repentant would go to the altar during the main service and the NYPS service and pray. They would also stand up to testify at church. Since they had boyfriends who were not saved, these boys had to expect letters of rejection since the girls had now "chosen a new path."

The writing of rejection letters was communal. Everybody threw in a word. These were very common in the last term, especially toward the end. It seemed as if it was easy for girls to say the simple "I love you" to boys if they knew that they had nothing to risk. As soon as the time for home go got closer, the fear of meeting the boys face-to-face and not knowing what to say became real. After the matron's sermons and the risk of everything that came with going out with boys, the girls would reconsider the friendships. That is why we all joined in writing rejection letters. Many a letter was tossed into the brown dustbin that stood in the corner of each dormitory.

The gist of the message was "I don't love you, full stop." There was no room for explanations. It is the other girls in the dormitory who would fashion excuses. Of course the letter would be written in the handwriting of the girl who had the best handwriting. It was nice to share in this exercise of rejecting a young man. I was always a part of these letters until some of the girls thought they were older than us and started to exclude us from their letters. Since I did not receive any letters, I did not care what happened to the whole letter-reading syndicate. I just remained in the reading syndicate that passed all the unwanted books that were read in the bathroom at night.

The first examination was written in the month of October, toward the end. We were looking forward to these examinations. We had reviewed everything. I had made sure that I was going to pass no matter what. We had one old female reverend supervising us for this examination. She would come into the classroom and put an examination pad on each and every desk. We would go and sit behind the desks when we came in. After that she would take the examination paper and open it in front of us. We were supposed to ensure that it is sealed. When the long, thin examination papers were passed out, I was sitting quietly waiting for my own paper. I opened my English language and literature examination paper and chose my questions. I sat down and waited for the invigilator to say we could start writing. When it was time to write, I started with the easiest questions and drafted my points for them. I was drafting the sequence in which I was going to write the paragraphs in pencil first. After that I went to the language section of the paper and chose the composition that I was going to write and drafted it. I wanted to write a powerful introduction and then leave the rest to my power of storytelling. I looked around and noticed that every student was working. There was total silence in the classroom. Even the boys who were always making noise were quiet. I turned to my work and started answering question after question. I would stop here and there and think and also look at my watch to make sure that I had allocated enough time for each question. Even though there was a watch on the wall, I still looked at my watch. It was a round black Wilson that had a black leather belt that encircled my wrist daintily. I would poke the holes of the black leather wristband of my watch when I was thinking about the question. This had become a habit since most of the time I found myself thinking about life in class instead of living it. I would continue to write when I realized that time was not on my side. I attempted all the questions and then went back to review what I had written after rereading the question paper and once again underlining the key words of the question. I did this to make sure that I had answered the question as best I could. I was sure that I would pass this examination when I went to put my paper in the pile. The confidence that I had in myself was not usual. I had no doubt about what the outcome would be. I just had the usual fear that came from the uncertainty that examinations always bring. It is an anxiety that makes you wish you did not have to write the examination. It goes away after you have finished it and accepted that whatever will be will be.

After the first paper, which was taken in the morning, we went out to rest and prepare for the second paper, which would be after lunch at two o'clock. We would go to the assembly hall in groups and play there. We would also huddle in groups as we looked over the notes we had made during the course of the year. Some of us who had made up questions would ask the questions, and the other students would answer. Some students who accepted that they were not smart would not even try to join the groups and learn together with the rest of us. They seemed to have accepted their fate that they were not made for schoolwork.

We were supposed to have learned that fear, jealousy, and anger were negative emotions that yielded nothing at this time. Yet as Speech Day neared, I would hear signs of jealousy from some of the students who were not sure what the classroom was about. We did not have a teacher for physical science. One teacher came from Saint Theresa's to teach us after school. He used to walk as if there were springs in his heels. He was also very slender and influential because the boys started walking like him. I did not think boys were as impressionable until he came. I did not understand him very well even though I thought he was trying hard to teach. He just used to look interesting in his white lab coat. The truth of the matter is that science and math did not make much sense to me. I was more fascinated with words. The science fair started around this time. We would enter a few projects. I was never a part of the team that had winning projects, nor did I remember what they were about. I just was not made up of the stuff that scientists are made of.

As the term got closer to its end, I started to focus on creating better beginnings for my compositions. I paid attention to how each book I read started in the very first paragraph. I felt that this was the paragraph that made the reader pay attention to the whole chapter and wanted to make my writing very interesting. I wrote long and short pieces. I described women and thought that my writing, though sensuous, should make it into the *Nuntius*. We were all preparing short pieces for the *Nuntius* because being published in our school magazine meant a lot to us. In my story, I described a woman called Susannah, who was a hooker. I described her long legs and her slim body. She was very seductive on my page. Small wonder my story did not make it into the *Nuntius*. I think when Ms. McClou, the teacher who was in charge of compiling the articles that would be published, read my seductive story, she threw it away. It did not impart the values such as being good and godly that the mission school expected of us. I was disappointed when the magazine came out because nobody had told me that the stuff I wrote was only good for the dustbin. There were students who had written short thoughtless pieces about lugubrious laughter. I thought these were just displays of big words and not much sense. I had wanted to see something that made students stand up and wonder what they are made of when they pick up the reading. It just did not work out that way. The only picture I liked that was in the *Nuntius* was the picture of the mascot of the school, little Douglas Graham. This was the son of the secretary. He has always been there, running up and down behind his mother when school was on.

The teacher who taught piano would teach students how to play now that it was examination time and there were no lessons. He would sit with some of the boys and play some keys, and they would play way into the late hours toward the end of the school day. We would go into the assembly hall to listen to the music. Sisile thought that it sounded like jazz. Her impression of jazz was that somebody just sits on the keys with their bums and whatever sound comes out is music. I knew that I did not like or even understand this music, but I felt that it was an art of some sort. Since we were just beginning to learn about African Americans, we were fascinated by it.

    Life became very slow because it seemed we took each and every examination one day at a time. It was rare to have two examinations in a row. It became clear that we were very well prepared for all our exams. I did not panic in any of them. I just went in to do the best I could. As each day passed, I knew that we were getting closer to the end of term. We were very short of food supplies at this time, and we relied on the peanuts that were sold by the little girls who came to sit up on the mountain. We would buy these, and they would be the only thing we shared among ourselves. Apart from the rare pawpaws, life was down to the regular three fruit jam sandwiches and Kool-Aid. It was a routine that we had mastered as we got closer to the end of the year. I would look down from dormitory 35 and look at the school. In the afternoon, when we were waiting for the bell to ring for supper, life seemed to slow down. The shadows of the tall poplar trees were long, and they could be seen on the walls of the high school buildings. Looking out of the window, one could see the sewerage dams far away. The grass was very green all the way from where I was standing. I looked up at the gum trees way ahead of me. I looked at the treetops. All seemed quiet on this day. Life seemed to be moving at a slow pace. Everywhere the shadow of the trees was cast in a way that made one think life comes together somewhere somehow. I could see that we had a future out there, and things would come together like the tall shadows of the trees at the time when the sun was out in the west. They were cast toward the east. They were very long, so long that you wondered why things were long and demanding in the waiting that accompanies life when one is expecting a future to come and declare a form of success. That is how I thought about the end of Form III examinations. I thought that they had come to demand of me if I knew where I was going or not. They had come to demand of me what I had done in the three years of life that I had been given to live in a place where I was sheltered from all harm so that I could learn. I did not know how to answer these questions. I just felt that there was success way ahead of me, and it would come to me in the same way that I faced all things in life. It would come to me with the eagerness that I would reach for it. I was thinking about the future but not specific about what it was I wanted from it. I knew I wanted success. I wanted an education. I was happy that school meant focus, and then later you find that what you have been doing is what will make the future meaningful. Even though I was not that sure of what it was I was doing, I could see a future unfolding. Three years had passed with me inside this place. They were a meaningful three years. I had learned a lot. I knew I was not ready yet because two years still lay ahead of me.

It was during these exams that Ms. McClou went to the head teacher to report that we had violated a rule. We had gone out to drink at the tap when we were supposed to be in class. Ms. McClou said we should go to the office. We knew that this meant a real hiding. People who were sent to the office were those who had committed serious offenses. We knew that Ms. McClou did not like us. Even if we had not committed serious offenses, she just wanted us to be punished. We went to the office of the head teacher shaking because we knew he would beat us. When he took his stick from behind the chair, I was shivering. I stretched out my hand, and I was already anticipating how painful it would be. I was surprised when he just tapped on us lightly. This was my first-ever beating in Manzini Nazarene High School and the very last. We were smiling when we got here in high school. We walked back to class and sat down and read our books.

The end of term was a time when we liked to mix with all other groups. It was nice to go to the dormitories of the Form Vs and see what dresses they were going to wear when they leave. We saw beautiful crepe dresses with buttons in front. They were designer clothes that were very expensive. The platforms had come into fashion that year. Most girls who wanted to be seen as fashionable were wearing those. The best designer names were Crazy Horse and Delswaa Sweaters; skirts of the best crimplene were by these designers. Stockings by Arwa were the in thing. All the senior girls wanted to make sure that they left the hostel in style. It was as if there was competition between them the way everybody wanted to be seen in their best clothes. I would go to the dormitories of the Form Vs on Saturday when everything was quiet. I would sneak in quietly knowing that the matron was not there. If she came, I would go into the private bathroom. Only the Form Vs had a private bathroom. The rest of us shared the big main bathroom that was made out of two rows of sinks, a bath, and five showers. The boredom of the weekend was always a challenge so that sneaking into other people's dormitories became a fun thing for us.

As the term drew to a close, cleaning was more about trying to leave the school looking clean after we left. We would clean the square outside the dormitories that was behind the sinks for washing clothes. We were expected to pull out the weeds that grew into the fine lawn of the thick grass we called *ngwengane*. This was difficult to do because the ground was hard. We would then make a big pile of the weeds and eventually take them up to the big pit.

Our next task would be to clean the cement sinks that were for washing the clothes. We would pick up the covers of Sunlight soap, a green bar of soap that was popular at the time. There would also be boxes of powdered soap like Omo and Surf. We would take the empty boxes and throw them in a bucket that we had ready for the rubbish that would come out of the sinks. We would rub the drain with our sweeping branches and then go and get a bucket of water and pour the water into the drain so as to clear any sand that was in it. The algae in the trenches were a challenge. Some of it would have dried onto the sides of the cement. It would give us a hard time when we tried to remove it. It was slimy, and it felt and looked extremely unclean when we poked it with our stick. We would also find one or two white pieces of cloth with Reckitt's Blue in them. The girls would forget these after doing their final rinse of the white shirts. I don't remember spending money on Reckitt's Blue. I always used what was left over from the others. When Makhosi and Sisile rinsed the shirts, I would go and dip mine in with them.

We would collect all the dirt and then go for the big scrubbing brush that was in the cement courtyard that was outside the kitchen and brush the sinks. We would take turns brushing the sinks with this big broomlike brush because it was heavy. In the holes on the wall that was near the sinks, we would find more pieces of cloth with Rekitt's Blue and sometimes even cakes of soap. One could tell that these were forgotten by the girls when they were washing the uniforms. Cleaning this area was like reliving Friday afternoon and washing time. We were the scavengers who were supposed to pick everything up and clear the place for the girls.

There was an avocado tree that was just outside the bathrooms. In the three years I had been there, I had never thought that it would grow to the window levels of the bathroom. Now that it was so tall, the girls were throwing things through the windows with a clear conscience because this tree hid all the toilet paper and other ablution-related dirt that I need not mention. Since we're the cleaners, we did our best to pick up the papers and clean the drain so that the minor blockages would be taken care of.

There was a flamboyant tree that grew near the sinks that was a nuisance. It had beautiful red flowers that would fall into the sinks. They were pretty on the tree and on the floor, but when they fell into the sinks, they frustrated us when it was cleaning time. I wished that some wind would come and cause it to fall because it grew right over the cliff and hung over the sinks, and its leaves would fall into the trench between the sinks. It was tiring to clean the leaves in the windy season because we knew that they would be falling into the sinks the next minute. The branches of this tree would also break and fall into the sinks. The big flat pods of the tree would also fall into the sinks. All this was rubbish that we would sweep away and pile into an old bucket that had holes in the bottom and then carry it up the cement steps all the way to the big pit. During the week, we only spent about thirty minutes on doing grounds. Saturday was the day when all this cleaning was on us because we had to put in two hours into making sure that this part of the hostel was clean. The easiest and noblest of these tasks was weeding the flower beds. I think it is because we knelt on the grass to do this task. It was not backbreaking like bending to sweep.

We would work way into midmorning and keep going up the mountain to throw away the rubbish from the flower beds. Around midmorning, the poor people from KaKhoza, the slum right above the hostel, would start coming. They came with big buckets that they would use to carry leftovers after lunch. The lunch meal was always made up of mealie rice and meat. They would spend time around the pit, and we would greet them and laugh with them as we went about our chores.

There was an old woman who always came with the group that came for leftovers of our meals. She used to wait near the big pit so that when we went to throw away the food, we would pour it in her bucket. She was tiny and dark in complexion. She was small in stature and looked as if she smoked snuff and drank a little bit. It was always fun to see her. It was like seeing the real outside world and all the things that we were being kept from. A colored young girl would also come with her. She also represented the unfortunate in that one could see that some white man had fathered her and abandoned her. She would also wait there with the others for the time when we go and dump the remains of our supper. There was also thin porridge to dump. We mixed it with the tea. I think the people who took the remains fed them to their pigs. I am not sure what they gave the pigs when we were on holiday because the place would be deserted.

After all the Saturday morning work, the matron would come to check if we have done the work to her satisfaction, and she would tell us to go back to the dormitory and take our bath things and go and wash. We would go and play and wash after playing. We would play high jump by tying a rope onto the poles that supported the thin wire that was for drying clothes. We would take turns trying to jump as high as we could. I enjoyed playing with my friends, but I never dreamt that I could improve in lifting myself up and jumping to a height that was as high as Sisile's. Makhosi would try harder and make a few inches above what I did. When we were tired of high jump, we would go and get the ball and divide ourselves into two teams. We would play a simple game of netball where we threw the ball and did not score. Winning was making sure that the opponents didn't get the ball. We would run around as the bigger girls and student teachers watched us with looks that showed that they thought young girls have a lot of energy.

If any of our parents arrived to check on us on a Saturday, the matron's niece would come and tell us. That would be the climax of the morning because we knew that we would have food from home and have a taste of what the outside world was about. We would go to the dining hall to peep through the windows in order to see which one of the parents had come. If it was Sisile's mother and father, we would be pleased because we would know that we would have scones, peanuts, biscuits, and what have you. We would once in a while also have a whole chicken. It was important to go out and spy to see if there was a chicken so that we would take it in while she went to show the matron what was in the cake tin. We would then go and hide the food in the dormitory and make sure that we put it way up where our suitcases were so that nobody would ever see it. The person who was in charge of cleaning the dormitory knew that the windows had to be closed so that there would be no smell of food because that would cause the whole place to be searched and we would lose our chicken. There were times when we did not get to eat any meat that was brought by our parents. Sometimes the matron would keep it in her fridge and tell us to come for it and eat it out where she could see us, or she would throw it away and tell us that we should tell our parents not to bring meat to the hostel because it brought insects.

The health of the senior matron started to fail toward the end of Form III. She was admitted at the Raleigh Fitkin Hospital several times. This is the time when Big Nkosiyami came to substitute as senior matron. It was strange to have a woman of such crude homeliness looking after us. This was when we realized how the senior matron meant to us. We realized how much she loved us. When we went to visit the student teachers, she did not beat us. Big Nkosiyami had a scorpion. She had a leather belt that had four prongs; if you've seen the prongs of a fork, imagine a belt with the four whips that are a continuation of the other end of it. We would be made to lie down, and she would go all over our buttocks with the belt. When we left, we would be red with welts. We had never been beaten like this in all our lives. What was happening to us was a nightmare.

The feeling of what it was like to be in boarding school changed. She would walk with her hand on her chest as if she was trying to stop her voluptuous bosom from falling. When she spoke at the chapel, we did not take much note of her. She would stand in front of us, a small shawl wrapped around her waist with the fringe covering her skirt. It is not that she was as awkward as she was out of place. She would walk about the place with her knitting, and we would wonder who wore the jerseys that she was always, always knitting in dull colors of yarn that looked as if it had been donated.

I think what bothered me with Big Nkosiyami was the cruelty to our group. Some said she believed that those of us whom she felt were not from the Swazi countryside were from South Africa, and she believed that we brought cooties and lice from the trains to the hostel. Since she did not know who was from where, this meant she generalized and just put everybody she suspected of not being a countryside person under the cruelty of her scorpion. I would cry and shout when she was beating us. We were glad when she left and Senior Matron Koor came back. Things went back to normal.

The climax of the third term in Form III was writing the last paper of the Junior Certificate examination. We would rejoice, and there would be noise in the dormitories of the Form IIIs. We would sing and shout because we were now free to relax. It was funny how we all felt relieved now that we were done with this grueling task. We were now ready to enjoy ourselves. I think the greatest excitement was more about going home and Speech Day.

All through the term, we had known that Speech and Prize-Giving Day was coming. There were many preparations for this day. We sang new songs because the Form IIIs would also be asked to render an item. Our special song was "Cry Out and Shout Ye Inhabitants of Zion." We practiced this song everywhere. We sang it in the bathroom and in the dormitories. Each one of us had yellow sheets for this song. We would sing about the "beautiful fore situation" even though we did not know what that meant. The staccato in "mark well her bulwarks, consider her palaces" was the climax. When we got to "tell it to the generation following thee," we vowed that we would tell it to the generations that would follow that it was important to "cry out and shout." As things drew to the peak of the action with Speech Day, it would be clear that whoever produced the *Nuntius* should work even harder. The school magazine had to be there during Speech Day. We had taken photos in the winter with our class teachers in preparation for this day. We wanted to see this on the day of the Speech and Prize Giving.

We would wash our uniforms on the day before Speech Day and iron them early on Saturday morning. Students would buy Inecto Rapid, a type of hair dye, and tint their hair. Around eleven o'clock in the morning, things would start moving. We had to wash and polish our shoes and get ready to go to the big day. We were excited because we knew that our parents would be there. This was the only day where we did not have to be peering through windows. We would file out of the hostel and walk downhill past the high school on the dusty road and wish we did not have to walk on the stony, dusty road on this day because our shoes and shirts would show the dust. Walking to the Sharpe Memorial Church took us about fifteen minutes. We would get to the church and go and sit in our section of the church. Things would slow down after we arrive in the church. We would watch as all the people came in. If we were lucky, we would see our parents. This meant straining our necks to view the people coming into the church through the main door.

The events would start with the head teacher's school report for the year. He would go through how the school had performed in the Form III results and the Form V results of the previous year and then get into how we had performed in the athletics competition. The parents would be shown the trophies that were displayed on a table in front, near the podium. He would talk about our performance in the music competition and show the parents the big trophy for the Zulu song and the English song of the boys' choir. For a long time, we dominated in these two areas. Sometimes the girls' choir won the English song. Our conductors for the different songs would stand up, and the parents would see them.

After the head teacher's speech, we would hear the speech of the main guest speaker for the occasion. Sometimes it was a missionary who was the head of the Siteki Bible School. At times it was Sisile's father. When Sisile's father was speaking, her mother would give us the prizes. Sisile's father would highlight the role of our school in the nation and state that our school was counted among the best schools in the nation. Almost every speaker would talk to the school-leavers about going out to the outside world. They would talk about the place where no bell would ring, no prefect would mark you, or no teacher would chastise you for doing wrong. They would talk about life being the thing that looks after you if you look after it. They would talk about jobs and unemployment. They would urge the school-leavers not to leave behind what they had learned about Jesus. They would tell them to go out and be the light of the world.

After the speeches, it would be time for the songs. We would go through the songs of the main choirs of the school. Since these were choirs that were made up of sixty voices, there would be commotion in the church as the girls moved to take their position in the space up front behind the podium. The boys would also stand up and go and take their place behind the girls. The choirmaster would come walking lazily with his harmonica in the hand. He would blow the tune, and the choristers would get ready to sing the song. "Worthy is the Lamb, that was slain . . . ," they would go as they sang a song that was in Handel's *Messiah*. We would listen and clap at the end. We would wait quietly for the Zulu song as they got ready, and we would hear "Uponi lihhashi lami endilithandayo," a Xhosa song about a pony that the owner loved. As the song went on, we would listen as the students sang about how the pony galloped. The song would imitate the galloping with click sounds. All people loved this song. Since our parents enjoyed music, we would know that this was a treat for them. After the main choirs, the girls' and boys' choirs would sing.

The next event would be the giving out of the prizes. The Form Is would start. Prizes were given for each subject. Most of the prizes were books that would have the names of the students written neatly in calligraphy by one of the teachers. It was good to be called and go up to receive a prize. I started getting prizes from Form II. Sometimes I would get the geography prize, and at other times I would get the English prize. There would be a prize for the best sports student. Usually this prize consisted of a sports bag and a racket or similar stuff. Some of the athletic boys would get it. I wished that even the girls got prizes because they performed very well in sports. I felt that my friend Sisile should have got a prize because I did not think the school would ever have a high jumper like her. She had gone to jump in Botswana and Lesotho, literally becoming an international athlete. I do not remember her being given the honor that this level of achievement deserved.

After the prizes were given out, we would go to school where the students and parents would be treated to cakes and soft drinks. There would be huge trays of sponge cakes that came from the missionaries. We would eat a lot of cake that day and then get an opportunity to talk to our parents. We would show them our prizes and ask them for pocket money even though it was close to going home. My mother would come with my brother. My little brother would tell me about the bats in Sharpe Memorial Church. Instead of saying "Nazarene," he would say "Mazarene." He would say that he saw their "poopoo" at the back where they were sitting. They would say good-bye and head for the buses because the last bus left around four o'clock. I would then go and mingle with my friends.

We would walk back to the hostel and talk about the events of the day. It was one of those days we wished would never end at Nazarene High School. We would talk about the prizes and the singing, and the excitement would die down when the bell for supper rang, announcing that our lives were back to routine. The matron would be there watching over our supper with familiar regularity. We would throw away the food and take the slices of bread and hide them so that we can eat them as a nightcap when we were hungry.

Since we were done with the examinations, it was time to get ready for the last day when we would leave and go home. We would try on the clothes we would wear on the last day and imagine ourselves in the outside world. On the night before we left, we would pack our suitcases. Even the toiletries and the sheets would be packed as if we would not need them the following morning. We would dive into our beds and say good-bye to them. Diving meant standing far from the bed and getting into it the way a frog jumps into a swimming pool. The springs would squeak as each person dived in. We would use our suitcases as pillows on that day because the pillow slips were already packed. We just wanted to pick up the suitcase and go on the following day, no more fiddling with things in the place of no.

We would hear the bell ring for the last time at half past five in the morning and know that this was the last time we were woken up by the bell in that year. We would go to the chapel and finish the other daily routines and not even feel what we were doing because our minds were on going home. After breakfast, we would go and dress up and take our suitcases and then go and say good-bye to the matron. We walked away from the hostel and did not look back, knowing that the life ahead of us was a life we had long been waiting for.

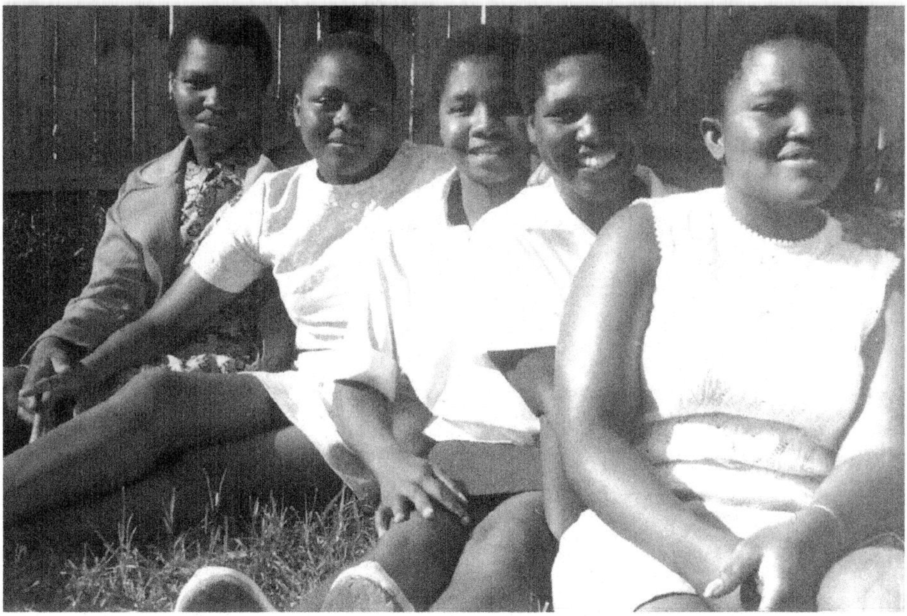

Chapter Six

Going home after Form III was not as much fun as the regular home go. We were few at the bus station, and the hustle and bustle of the national school closing commotion was not there. It was just quiet. You got home and found that everybody was going to school since schools were not closed. I spent a few weeks of my Christmas holiday at Ephesus that year in 1972. I remember packing my red-and-black striped suitcase and going to the bus the morning I was due to report at the Ezulwini Valley home where the Lutherans who administered our scholarships were waiting for us. I made a lot of friends that year. I met girls from Our Lady of Sorrows, a Catholic school that is in the south of Swaziland. I also met girls from Saint Theresa's and Mater Dolorosa. We had fun with my friends from Nazarene High School because we were out with other students who did not do things the same way as we did. The girls from Mater Dolorosa spoke English all the time. It was as if they wanted to imitate the few A-level students from Waterford Kamhlaba who did not speak SiSwati because they were from Zimbabwe and Uganda. We enjoyed listening to the radio and sang along with the girls to "She Is a Lovely Woman in a Black Dress." We picked strawberries and took walks to nearby stores. We also weeded the field of maize. I had never weeded in my life. I thought it was fun because we were given a line to take care of. We would speed with the girl from Saint Theresa's who became my friend. I envied the girls that they were allowed to braid their hair. They braided my hair while we were there. We were fascinated by the hair and the rollers of the girl from our Lady of Sorrows. She had long black hair. We had never used rollers or even seen them that close.

When the week for going home came, we were sad to leave our friends. The only fun thing that happened when I went home that day was that the boy whom I liked was in the bus to Ngwenya with his mother. I was excited. He introduced me to his mother and spoke nicely to me. I still felt the pain in my heart when I remembered that when I had seen him at the Raleigh Fitkin Memorial Hospital on the day I was sick, he had told me that he wanted me to tell another girl that he wanted to talk "substance" with her. It was funny that in the dorm, everybody liked this guy for me; and Makhosi, the biggest matchmaker, had paired us up. I had even prayed that one day he would consider me, especially after eying him in the long services at the Sharpe Memorial Church. I always wished that I would sit where I would see him, and most of the time I was very lucky because I was able to steal a glance at him once in a while. Anyway, it does not help to cry over spilt milk. This heartthrob was from Jozi, and he was going back to Jozi. He was going to wait for the railway bus, and he would go back to the big city, never to return because he was in Form V. I remember seeing him once a year later, and that was the last time. I have never seen him up to this day. I heard he works in Johannesburg for the record company called BMG Records. It was fun to get off the bus and think about this guy. It was intriguing that I had changed my attitude and started thinking about boys differently than I had done when I was in Form I. If you had asked me about them ten years earlier, I would have cried and sworn that I hated these crazy creatures. They seemed to be little creatures that were always teasing people.

I got home and read a book about the Sahara Desert. I do not remember what the title was, but it was on our bookshelf. I enjoyed reading this book. I also read the book I had got for the English prize on Speech Day. It was a poetry book entitled a *Choice of Poets*.

My life started to change as I grew older. I started to think about clothes and Paris and modeling that year. In my mind, I always told myself that Paris is just nearby. I had to see it and live as if I were from there. I am not sure why Paris and not London or other cities. In my world, I was going to go to Paris and be a model. I am not surprised that I have never been to Paris even today.

It was a long time to the time when schools would close and my mother and my brother would come and join me at Ngwenya. It was not nice to be with my father and the maid alone. Our maid that year was from Gilgal, and she liked working at our home. I had a strong suspicion that my father liked her. I think one night he sneaked into our room because I remember him walking out when I woke up. I did not ask what he was doing in our room. I figured it out much later when I asked the maid and realized that he was sneaking into our room to try to do stuff. I was embarrassed.

The maid liked it when I imitated old women who had no teeth. She would laugh whenever I spoke to her as if I was her grandmother. I would come up with different reasons to make her laugh. We would go and gather wood in the forest of wattle trees. We would also pick some green mopani worms with shiny silver thorns and roast them and give them to the children of the Portuguese employees who worked with my father. I enjoyed making fire in the boiler that was attached to the hot water system of the house. Sometimes we made fire on the brazier and cooked outside. Sometimes we would make fire on the stove in the kitchen. I liked to make fire on the brazier and then face it to the windward side so that it could burn the coal and make a red-hot fire.

Schools closed, and my mother and brother came home. Christmas came and went. I would watch the dahlias in bloom and enjoy walking under the wattle trees and eating berries in the forest. Apart from that, I listened to the radio. The main pop song that year was Johnny Nash's "Cream Puff." We would sing on and on so that when I got to school, I would pick up the song with my friends. When schools opened in January, I was still waiting for the results. When they finally came, it was way into February. I took the radio to the sitting room on the day the results were announced. I listened to all the names that were called. I waited anxiously to hear the name of my school. When the first name was called, I leaned my head even closer to the radio. When I heard my name, I ran to the bedroom where my father was sleeping. I flew into the room and threw myself in the bed. "I got a First Class! I got a First Class!" I was shouting and happy. Everybody was very happy. I celebrated with Marie biscuits and Kool-Aid and a cake that had been baked by a cousin of mine who was a Simelane who lived at the village in Ngwenya.

I packed my clothes and returned to school that year. I was welcomed by the head teacher. He was very happy that we had passed so well. My Zulu teacher who happened to also teach religious knowledge did not even want to see me. I had got the worst grade in Zulu. I was sure that this was a mistake because I was one of the best Zulu students. He must have felt disrespected because while I had got the best score in other subjects, I had failed his subject when it was the only subject in the indigenous language.

The fact that there was more responsibility in Form IV was shown by the number of books that I had to pick up from the bookstore. The *Bible Commentary* was the biggest of the books. This time in geography, I had to buy a bigger book entitled *Geography for Senior Studies* while in the junior forms, we had only used *Man's Environment: Geography for Secondary Schools* and notes from the teacher. In literature, we had to buy *Macbeth*, Chaucer's "Pardoner's Tale" in the original and the translation, and William Golding's *Lord of the Flies*. In Zulu, we bought Inkinsela Yase Mgungundlovu, Lemuka iZwe Elihle *by Imvu Yolahleko, which is a translation of* Cry, the Beloved Country *by Alan Paton*. We had new books in math, physical science, and English language. The Zulu grammar, the Bible, and the Alexander's hymns were the books that were a carryover from the junior years.

I did not notice how tall I grew that year until I got to school. All the students did not believe that I had become so tall. I also got more sophisticated because I had the Boot Joyce with a red sole. The real shoe of the year that year was the Boot Joyce. Every student who was from a family that was well-off wore that shoe. It was just a leather shoe with a wedge sole and shoelaces. Why it was so popular, I am not sure. I think it was because it was expensive. It definitely cost more than twenty rands. Form IV was the year that all students had to stay in the boardinghouse. There were no day scholars in the senior forms.

WEEDING THE FLOWERBEDS

It is in this year that we went to the big dormitory called "Enqabeni," which means "the fort." The dormitory had two large rooms that were partitioned with a cement wall that had about three feet of flat space where the suitcases were kept. It was farthest from the junior matron's room, and it is because of this that all the noise came from there. My bed was near a very funny girl's in that year. She would step on my shoes and put her shoes on my shoes, and I would be frustrated. I just felt tired down to the pit of my soul by this girl.

Coming back to school after the Form III results was like coming back to a new world. There were new faces from other schools in our class. Among these new faces was a girl named Praisy from my primary school Phonjwane. Some of the students were from other Nazarene schools like Endzingeni Nazarene and Siteki Nazarene. There were also students from Saint Michael's and Saint Theresa's. The new boys were interesting characters. One of them called himself "Sweet Saliva." On the whole, they were not much to write home about.

Since this was the sports season, it was good to have the new girls in our class. It was good to have a new crowd so that we could strengthen our athletics team. The term would have progressed well in sports if it had not been for the incident with the javelin. One student threw the javelin, and it went right into the knee of the sports teacher when she was running to go and mark where it had fallen. This was sad because we liked this teacher. Blood came out of the knee as if it was coming out of a tap, and the teacher had to be rushed to hospital.

I also started to throw the discus that year. It was my first time to perform well in a sport. I was the second best thrower in the school, and I made it into the athletics team.

Classes started off on a different rhythm. We were enthusiastic because we knew that we were no longer juniors but beginning the last two years of school. We knew that we were going to spend the two years preparing for the Examinations Syndicate of Cambridge University, and this was serious work. This was a big step in our lives because it would determine what would happen to us. We were either going to make the ranks of the educated and employable or the ranks of the unemployed. We were determined to pass and break into the world of the haves as new vibrant citizens of a country after its first few years of independence. That is why we worked hard and read even more books. We would ask the boys to check out books for us in town. One of the boys would refuse and say that we were not studying for him but for our children and our husbands. This was a harsh answer coming from a classmate who did not have much in his head but sheer audacity and a naughtiness that was typical at that time.

Despite the determination, we could see a number of obstacles in our way. We did not have science teachers. We would sit in the assembly hall and waste time during the time for science, and then later in the day two teachers would come from Salesian High School to teach us. We used to laugh when one of them talked about sulphuric acid because when he said the formula for sulphuric acid, he would say H_2SO_4 with an accent that brought laughter because it was not what we expected. The 2 and the 4 had a thing about them that had us all giggling when he talked. Since we took science classes in the evening, it meant that we would arrive at the hostel at suppertime. We did not mind that since we would have been bored in our rooms if we had come earlier. This continued for one and a half years, which meant that we only had a teacher for eight months in the two years.

The head teacher taught us geography. For English, Zulu, and literature, we had UBaba, the teacher who called every schoolchild an idiot. "Yes, idiot," he would say as we walk into the staff room. "How are you, idiot? What do you want?" We no longer thought that the word was a bad word. It was such a part of his everyday language that we could easily have interpreted it as his own way of saying, "Yes, my child." Even though he used it so many times, students would still laugh at you if he used the word to you.

He would begin a lesson on Shakespeare's *Macbeth* in Zulu and say, "Mina ngithi uMacbeth wayeyisilima," which means "I say Macbeth was a fool," and the debate about *Macbeth* would carry on in Zulu and then change to English here and there. It was not the debate that bothered us as much as the lack of structure in the class. It was not clear what we had come to do.

When it was time for *Lord of the Flies*, this teacher did not even know the title of the book. He would call it *The Flies of the Lord*. Since we did not know what good teaching was at the time, we were happy with these classes. In the Zulu class, we would read the words one after the other and do word calling instead of getting explanations on the concepts.

In English, we had the same teacher for two weeks. He gave us his classic composition, "Reading Maketh a Man." We were supposed to write and argue that this was true in an essay that was about two full-length pages. I remember that I barely made over 50 percent of the marks, which was probably the best mark in that class. After a few weeks, we got another teacher for English. She was nice because she told us that she had never taught. She used to like our work and give us good feedback. I remember that for her class, I wrote a composition on Jamaica entitled "Let It Be Jamaica." I was supposed to write about a country of my choice and argue why I wanted to visit it.

For mathematics, we had a young teacher from Zimbabwe. He was said to have topped the whole of Southern Africa in A levels. He had been a student at Waterford Kamhlaba. He used to make us laugh because he found the Nazarene mission a very strange place. He used to tell us that there were bats in his house. He used to say that his house was near the nurses' college, and the nurses were afraid of him. He used to say that in this place, "people fear each other." He would say we should imagine the cross of Christ when he was teaching us about the x-axis and the y-axis. It was interesting to have a young man for a teacher.

That math teacher left, and then we had the teacher who had a limp and a cleft on his upper lip, which was attributed to his service in the American army. This mathematics teacher was also an interesting character in his own way. He would write the problems sitting down, and then after explaining a problem to himself, he would ask, "Who does not?" He ended up being called "Who does not."

We did write examinations during the first term because our results came. I remember that for mathematics, we were studying matrices, and I had got a very good book in the library. The rest of the students were furious after the math examination. They said we should call the teacher and ask him when he had taught us what he was talking about. When we called him, he said the students failed because they did not understand English, and that made the students even more furious. We did pass that first term because I remember getting my results when we were on holiday.

We returned to school the following term and found that there was a new teacher, Mr. Fields from England. He was a young graduate, fresh from York University; and he taught us English language, English literature, and religious knowledge. For the first time, we got to understand that teaching and learning was about organizing information so that it is accessible to the student. We read Shakespeare and understood that drama was organized in acts and scenes and that the development of these meant that we should follow each character as she is revealed in the dialogues and that we could follow a pattern of development in the psychology of the person as a particular state of mind develops into a persona of some sort. That is how we began to understand the role of the witches in *Macbeth* and in society in general.

In English language, we were given compositions to write. I remember that I wrote about how I broke my aunt's china. The teacher was very happy with my work and commented that "I told the story with feeling." All this interaction with the teacher as marker was new to us. This teacher would make a small tick against good expressions, and he would put a NO in capitals with an exclamation mark against wrong spellings and other inaccuracies that were typical to students like us. He would then explain how a particular idiom was used.

In one composition, Mr. Fields had us walk out to experience the breeze of a May morning. We walked past the head of the mission's house all the way toward the farm. We would stand to observe as the meadow that lay in front of us created waves from the wind that was blowing toward the south. We observed how the sky looked and took in everything with accuracy because we knew that we would have to describe how it felt to walk out on a Monday morning in May. We returned to the classroom and worked on planning what we would write about. Mr. Fields helped us discuss the content of our composition and then left us to do the writing. It was our first time to learn that a composition had to have the kind of description and telling that was like in real life. We wrote that composition with a lot of confidence because we understood the assignment very well.

In religious knowledge, we were studying the synoptic gospels, Matthew, Mark, Luke, and John. We would read stories in all the accounts of these gospels and then mark the differences and know how one writer accounts differently for each incident from the other. The way, our notes were organized, making it easy to remember details about each story in the Bible. We would use the Bible commentary as we felt like. I don't think that the teachers realized that we did not open this book.

Our interest in our subjects increased after Mr. Fields, the teacher from York University, came to our school. He seemed to like his work. Even though he would spend an hour writing notes on the board, we were happy to take the notes and follow what he was teaching us. While he was writing on the board, his shirt would slip out; and when he faced the class to teach, his navel would be in the open. This tickled the students even though they did not comment about it. We would just laugh knowingly, and if it became too obvious that we were laughing, we would raise the lids of our desks and pretend that we were trying to find something in them. Whenever the desks went up simultaneously, my friend and I would be communicating unmentionables under the desk that we did not want the teacher to know. Praisy was a funny girl, and she was always making me laugh. As a pair and being ex-Phonjwane girls, we had a lot to laugh about from how I used to cry when they beat me in primary school to stories about boys in Manzini Wanderers football club. We would laugh at anything that was funny. I remember one day when Praisy bought sweets from the woman who used to clean the corridors. The woman came to the class during Mr. Fields's literature lesson and called Praisy because she did not pay her. Just the thought of her not paying the woman and being followed like a real thug made me laugh so much that she had to explain why she had not paid the woman during break. I was not satisfied with her explanation and thought that she was just up for mischief and wanted to cheat the old lady and disappear among the students thinking she would not know how to find her. It made complete sense to suspect Praisy because of her usual relaxed nonchalance. She was one who could do such a thing. Since Praisy and a few of my classmates did history, they called themselves "the women of history," and we became the geographers. This meant that they had to put up with being taught by UBaba and his ideas on apartheid. It was interesting to hear them talk about UBismark and wonder if they knew anything about what was going on in that class. I think what I learned there was that if teachers do not organize information well for students to learn, or teach students to organize information such that it is easy to learn, there would be little success in the learning of those students.

The second term of Form IV was an important term for us because we were going to undertake the longest trip in the school. All the Form IVs and Form Vs went to Durban by bus. This was important because it was the first time for us to see the ocean since Swaziland is landlocked. We all wanted to go. I remember that I was the last student to get a passport, and the head teacher had to phone my father to come to the school and take the passport for me. He went to town with us and helped me get the passport. Because the officer was and an exstudent of the school, and had a lot of respect for the head teacher, it was easy to get the passport. What would have been a difficult task was made easy by the presence of the head teacher mainly because the officer had gone through his hands.

We did not have problems in Durban because one of our teachers had moved to teach in a Durban high school. He would make all the arrangements for our trip. We would stay at Umgababa Resort in Durban, the only beach that was open to black people in South Africa's apartheid days. All the beautiful beaches were not open to us. We would go by train to the downtown area of Durban and go to Mini Town, the snake park, and the botanical gardens. We would have carry-on lunches in the bus since it would have been difficult to find restaurants that catered for black people in town. South Africa was a nightmare for us since our country was independent. While there was racism in Swaziland, it was covert and not government policy like in South Africa. It was a clandestine type, subtle, and only practiced by white people who were uncouth. In South Africa, racism was government policy. It was the harsh policy of apartheid, the state of being that was practiced in South Africa. I remember that I did not have much money when we went to Durban. I only had two rands. I bought a James Hadley Chase with my money.

Our duties at the hostel changed from being those of little girls now that we were bigger. We would cut grass or clean the drains. One of my biggest problems with cleaning drains was the frogs that we would find trapped in the drains. Sisile and Makhosi did not fear frogs. I feared a frog even more than a snake. They would grab the frogs by hand and throw them in the buckets that were full of water. We were supposed to use these for cleaning water, but because I wanted to learn to hold frogs, we would make the frogs swim in the water. I would get close, and they would encourage me to lay my hands on the frog.

"You can do it. Just close your eyes and get your hand close to the bucket and there," she would say as she threw a frog into the bucket.

"I will hold it now," I would say hopefully. I would bring my hand next to the bucket, and when my hand was close to the frog, I would jump back and land on my bottom two feet away from the bucket. My heart would be beating hard as I anticipated the softness of the frog in my hand. It was an ugly softness that was so real that I could faint that very moment.

"You are afraid of nothing," Makhosi would say and then throw the frog out of the water and go and pour the water in the storm drain so that the leaves and dirt can be washed out. We had to pour the water in the drains at school and even the ones at the hostel. We would clean the drains until there was not a single blade of grass or stone left.

"Let us go," Makhosi would say when she felt that there is nobody watching us. On Saturday, it was clear that we could clean the drains way after ten o'clock if nobody came to tell us to stop. I think the matron forgot to check our work because we were not going to school. We would walk away from our work and go to the matron's house to tell her that we were done with cleaning and then go and join the matron's niece in selling fat cakes. Sometimes she would give us one or two fat cakes and tell us that her aunt had given them to her. We ate fat cakes that were made with yeast and some that were baked with baking powder. The baking powder ones were nicer and more golden than brown. We would look at them and salivate as they filled the base of the big blue enamel bowl. Some had hard burnt edges, and some were soft and cakey in a way that showed that they had been in the cooking oil for too long. Their oily smell was inviting as we stood there wondering how we were going to pay for them. If we had a few cents, we would buy the fat cakes and then share them among ourselves. The smell of the fat cakes would linger in our mouths, and the oil would show on our fingers. We would sit on the wall outside the dining hall and wait for our parents to come. Sometimes we would go to the dorm and wash. We would make noise in the bathroom because we had the whole place to ourselves. We enjoyed pouring water all over our bodies from a bucket or just showering with the cold water. After this shower, we would take blankets and go and spread them outside and sleep in the sun. In winter, this was the best pastime. We would lie out there until suppertime.

One of the events that students looked forward to in the holiday of the second term was the Manzini Show. They would talk about whom they saw during the holidays and what was happening at the show. I never went to the show. I used to listen with envy as I heard the stories about how the girls had met this and that boy at the show. It became clear that the attitude toward boys was changing now that we were older. We no longer made fun of the letters of the boys in the same manner as we did when we were in the junior classes. We seemed to have developed a deeper understanding of what happens between girls and boys, and we each wanted it to happen to us as well even though the rules of the school were against it.

When we returned to school for the third term, one girl had to be sent home because she was pregnant. Since she was going out with one of the boys in our class, we felt that we should ask him why he had done such a bad thing. He laughed at us and told us point-blank that he had never "even tried." That girl was one dropout that caused us a lot of pain because she was our friend. The fact that she eventually died hurt us a lot. It was as if life did not have much in store for her.

It became clear that Mr. Fields was impressed with my work. This was evident during one time when I was going to the office. He stopped me and talked about my performance in the exam. After that he became my friend and asked me to help him in the library. It was funny to have a friend who was a teacher, young, British, and twenty-three years old. He acted like a brother, uncle, teacher, father, and even a real friend because he would offer advice on spiritual issues until I became convinced that Christianity was worth it after all. I still did not understand why it was wrong to just live as we were living. We did not steal or do wrong things. It became clear that he wanted us to pronounce with our mouths that we were Christians, "saved and believed in Jesus Christ as our Savior." It was also clear that there was a difference in the Christianity he was talking about because he did not see anything wrong with having boyfriends. He told us that he was a Christian, and he had a girlfriend and later gave me her address. I wrote to her in Holland and got a reply. He also gave me the address of his brother, and I wrote to him, and he replied and sent me his picture. We did not have television in Swaziland those days, so the content of the letters was about asking people in Europe to explain what television was and how it worked.

This relationship with Mr. Fields became very important to me in that I became the library prefect in the school. This meant that I would have access to all the books since I dusted the library and opened it for the students. I also worked with Mr. Fields and processed books so that they were ready for the students to take out and read. We would work endlessly putting new cards in books and putting new pockets inside the books. Mr. Fields bought a lot of books for the library and also requested books from abroad. He introduced the *African Writers Series* by Heinemann to our school. We enjoyed reading these books, and something more than the love of literature and story developed in us. We wanted to write like these writers. Seeing their books made us feel that we could also write. While in the junior forms we had read Cyprian Ekwensi's *Burning Grass*, we did not know that there were so many books by African writers. We were surprised, and when the library in town also started to have the series, we were pleased and read each book we could lay our hands on. We read almost all of them, and it strengthened the syndicate of the Sisters Three.

Rumors started to circulate about me and Mr. Fields. I remember Sisile asking me if there was *inhlasana* ("spark") between me and Mr. Fields. Just because we spent hours in the library my classmates were sure that there was something going on.

We were studying Chaucer's "Pardoner's Tale," and the boys soon started to call themselves "lordyings" and us girls they called "fruitesters." Mr. Fields became "Chaucer" after the first lecture on the life of Geoffrey Chaucer. When he returned our exercise books and gave them to me to distribute in class, they would whisper, "Lady Chaucer." I had to live with this name because there was nothing you could do with students in my class. So many of us had nicknames. There was "Triple V," "Umfazi womKristi" (the Christian's wife) from John Bunyan's *Pilgrim's Progress*, and other general nicknames that applied to all of us like "Diya." While we used this one between us girls, the boy who was a photographer also joined and became "Diya." I do not know how some of these names came to be. I just know that the "Rebel" came from one of the stories in Heinemann's *African Writers Series* and "Diya" came from the Zulu books.

We would also sing the pop songs in the hostel when we were bored. The favorite song for Sisile was "Distant Drums."

> I hear the sound,
> Thu thu thu
> Of distant drums
> Thu, thu, thu,
> Far away thu, thu, thu
> Far away, thu, thu, thu

Sisile would sing when we were bored. She had written the songs in her songbook. After that we would sing "Cream Puff" by Johnny Nash.

> We' been together
> A long, long, time
> I know her ways
> And she knows mine
> But be careful how you hold her
> Please don't ever scold her
> She's my cream puff.

We would sing on and on and enjoy ourselves while Sisile and Makhosi danced to the music we produced. I had heard Margaret Mcingana's "I'll Never Be the Same," and I sang that under my breath all the time. I was not as loud in doing things as Sisile and Makhosi. I was the loudest in laughing. I would even throw my leg in the air. I did not know that I did this until the girls made me aware of it.

"We think Mr. Fields has a special liking for you," Makhosi said when I told them that I had to go and work in the library on Saturday at two o'clock.

"That does not mean I am not going. I will see you when I come back," I said, giving them an answer that did not say whether Mr. Fields liked me or not. Sisile was jealous and soon asked one science teacher if she could work in the lab. She was allowed of course because I was allowed to work in the library. After that there was no more noise about my going to the library on Saturdays. It was fun to work with Mr. Fields. We would do a lot of work and even invite the librarian from town to come and check if we were doing the right thing in the way we were classifying the books. At that time, the librarian in town was a woman volunteer from England.

Sundays were the same except for the days when we went to the Sharpe Memorial Church and found that we had to sit through the report of *inhlanganisela*, the alabaster box service. The pastor's wife would stand up in her yellow jacket and black skirt and go through the lineup. This was the only service where women featured significantly in the church. Apart from leading songs or making a testimony and heading Sunday school, there was not much that they did. Most things were done by men. It was because of this that we would listen to the reports. It gave us a chance to assess the women who were the wives of pastors. We would hear report after report of how the money had been used in new sites that we did not know anything about. The reports about Ezindwendweni, a place in the south of Swaziland that we knew nothing about, did not interest us. If the reports had been short and to the point, I think we would have been interested.

Around two o'clock we would start fidgeting in our seats because we had been sitting since eleven o'clock. The lineup of activities was as boring as the reading of a report on a particular church, how many people there were and a few activities that had been done. This went on about each setting where new churches had been planted, and of course new alabaster boxes were given out. Some of the students were faithful in going to the altar to empty their alabaster boxes. I do not even remember ever putting money in the alabaster box. I do remember having one, and I think it would end up on the bookshelf until somebody found good use for it. If we had money, we would have used it to buy fat cakes. I doubt if any of it would have gone into those boxes and escaped being emptied to buy chewing gum and Toff-o-Lux. Such was our commitment to the alabaster box issue.

We would go to school, and Monday morning would begin with Mr. Fields's religious knowledge lesson. We were getting to the end of the gospel of Matthew, and Mr. Fields was agonizing about how he would teach us about the crucifixion. He made the mistake of speaking his thoughts aloud.

"I don't know how I can teach about the crucifixion of our Lord," he said, "because the crucifixion of the Son of God was a hard thing." I saw the hands go up.

"Yes, what do you want to say?" he asked, looking at the students.

"I just want to say that I don't know why you should have a problem. You are supposed to teach us the crucifixion and not preach to us. To us, you should not be having a problem with that. If you think you will preach about it, this is not the time. We are here to learn to critique this story and not moralize about it," one student said from the back.

Mr. Fields felt the hostility, and I felt sorry for him. I realized that he did not know that Mr. Nkonzo had taught us in the earlier forms that we should tell him if he was preaching. I realized that Mr. Fields would be hurt by this remark if he did not take what the students were saying in the perspective of the way it had been taught to the students. There was quiet in class, and he began teaching.

We graduated from weeding the flower beds when I was in Form IV. We started to do the chores that all the other students did. We would be assigned scrubbing the long corridors. This was a good chore in winter because while the other students were freezing outside, we would enjoy working indoors, and we finished early and got to be among the first to bathe in the bathroom. The girls used to book turns on the sinks by putting their washing towels on the sink. They would come as you washed and tell you that they were after you by pointing at their towels. After you finished, the girl who was after you would be standing near you, and you would pull out the stopper and see the water going down the porcelain drain that guided it into the grill that led it out to the plumbing system. The bathroom would be wet, and walking out in flip-flops meant that you had to be careful so as not to fall. There would be wet patches of mud that resulted from girls coming in and out. Whichever way, you were glad to be done with washing and the bathroom chattering and teasing. Some of the girls like Sisile did not mince words in laughing at people's behinds at washing time.

Grooming hair changed in our later years. We all wanted to have Afros because it was the time to be black and beautiful. After Percy Sledge, we all wanted to have big Afros like African Americans. The girls would use a plastic brush and push the hair backward so that when they combed in the morning the hair would easily shape up into an Afro.

The double-breasted, double-slash blazer was the in thing in the last years of school. The boys would swing into class in their double slashes, and the blazer would follow behind as they displayed marching antics that were typical of the youth of the day. Sometimes they wore peace sign emblems on their jackets. The peace sign was worn as a necklace as well those days. I am not sure if we understood the meaning of peace at that time. The Vietnam War was on, and the pop song "Vietnam" was popular. While we liked the song and saw the pictures of people who had died in the war in *Life* magazine, I do not think that the peace signs that were worn by the students were about that. I just think it was the craze of the day, and since older people were not doing it, the young people felt that they were different and smart to be doing something different.

While designer clothes were in, we still bought clothes that were sold in the mission. The matron would sell us shirts, and we would buy them for about fifty cents. Some of the students despised the clothes that were from America and called them *umphesheya* or *umdabualamanzi* (what has come from abroad.) Even though some of the clothes were nice, we still wanted designer clothes from Truworths, Edgars, and Square One. My uncle bought me a crepe dress from Square One, and I liked wearing it because it was one way of showing that I had class.

Makhosi's sister bought her clothes, and she was one of the best-dressed girls in the school. Sisile did not care much about clothes. Sometimes she would dress nicely, but clothes did not seem to mean a lot to her. It was only on Wednesday when we went for NYPS that we bothered to dress nicely. We would exchange clothes and try on this and that until we found something suitable.

We started to wear short dresses, and this annoyed the matron. She would call us and tell us to lengthen the hem of the dress. It seemed as if the more she asked us to lengthen the dress, the shorter the dresses became. We would wear short dresses and go and dance a style we called *kudiga*. It was the Mbabane girls who would dance in the dorms, and we would all watch and start to follow suit. They said they learned the styles at "The Place," in Mbabane.

I asked Makhosi to teach me how to dance to Swazi Reed Dance songs at this time. I would seriously imitate her as she danced, and she would say, "No, you are jiving. You are supposed to dance like this." She would show me how to dance and tap a little with the left foot and then land on the right foot with a stamp. It was very difficult for me. I would be discouraged because I did not see why my dancing was not acceptable.

"You dance as if you are in a disco. Don't dance like this, do like this." She would continue showing me how the hands should be when I am dancing. We would spend hours trying to learn the dances of Swaziland in the mission school where they were not considered as desirable. No matter how hard I tried, I could not get to the level of dancing Makhosi was at. She was a member of the royal family, and she always went to the Reed Dance.

Makhosi said to us one day, "Do you know that Mr. Fields called me and asked a question." She looked at us with surprise.

"What question?" we asked, wondering what the question could have been about.

"He asked me what it is like to dance seminaked at the Reed Dance," she continued.

"What a question! Why does he think it is nakedness?" Sisile asked.

"What did you say?" I asked.

"I told him that it feels the way it feels when a British girl is wearing a swimsuit," Makhosi said.

"That was a good answer. Mr. Fields asks funny questions sometimes. He asked me what kind of guys Swazi girls like," I added.

"What did you say, Bulelo?" Makhosi asked.

"I said we like boys who are dark in complexion and athletic, dark like mahogany," I said.

"What did he say after you said that?" Makhosi asked.

"He said nothing. I was holding this picture of the Zimbabwean guy we met during the holidays," I related the incident about the picture of Jama.

"Don't kid us; there is a spark. We know that there is a spark, Twigza, in him for you. You did well by showing him the picture," Sisile said.

We continued with our studying after that. I took out my math book, and I said to Makhosi, "Come and let us work out these problems." She was combing her hair and getting ready to go and brush her teeth. Makhosi had the finest teeth because after eating anything, she would go and brush her teeth.

"I am not mathematically inclined," she said as she walked out with her toothbrush. Whenever she did not want to do anything, you would see the spring in her walk getting stronger. She would smile and look at us as if we did not exist. It was funny that now that we were older, I was noticing different traits in our behavior. Some of us were more adult in outlook and self-presentation. I was still more reticent and still loved a good laugh.

Sisile got a letter from a boy who was at Salesian High School. I think she liked this boy, and because she did not ask our opinion, we did not volunteer any comments. We had come to a stage where we did not say much about boyfriends. The habit of writing the letters together seemed to have died down. While we chatted about the boys, we no longer had the discussion where every word had to be contributed and selected by the voting majority. We did not seem to share things as much. Even in studying, we were no longer that close. We seemed to have learned along the way that we had to take responsibility for the work individually. Sometimes I would ask Makhosi to help me with a problem, and she would say that I wanted to "suck her brains." This sounded funny coming from her. I would feel as if I was a python that was going to entangle itself around a person and suck the brains out through the nose. I would laugh when she said this.

We would do some problems together. Physics was one subject that gave all of us difficulty. We would try out problems individually and compare answers. It was clear that Form IV work was challenging. The fact that we did not have good teachers for mathematics and physics bothered us. We found the work very difficult and knew that we did not have a chance in the examination if we did not put much effort. We would go to school on Saturdays when the teachers from Salesian came to teach us. It was fun to be at school and out of the hostel on this day. After the class, we would go back to the hostel. I would go back to school to work in the library with Mr. Fields after the lunch hour. The weekends would break the routine of the everyday humdrum that boarding school life was.

Chapter Seven

It was one of those boring, cold Sunday afternoons in June when Makhosi and Praisy took off toward Thathuthuthuke Store. They did not want me to go with them. Sisile had gone to Botswana to the international athletics competition, and I was alone at the hostel feeling bored after finishing my James Hadley Chase. I went out to the ring and sat on the cement. I watched as they disappeared behind the gum trees and felt a little bit of discomfort since it was the first time for me to see girls skip and go outside boundaries like that. We all knew that we were not supposed to go beyond the chapel. Crossing the road between the chapel and the grantee's office was just way too much. Even if we crossed, we knew very well that going as far as the road to Mbabane would be punishable with something worse than the big axe and the bucketful of firewood. That is why I knew that Makhosi and Praisy were doing something that was totally unacceptable. I decided to go back to the dormitory and listen to the radio that we had managed to sneak into the dormitory. I put a pillow over my head and covered myself with the bedspread and turned the radio on to LM Radio. They were singing the usual songs like "Is This the Way to Amarillo" and "Vietnam." I hummed under my breath and opened my Bible with my left hand so that whoever came in would think I was reading the Word.

As I listened, I started to reflect on the issue of peer pressure. I noticed that I felt bad when my friends did not want to include me in things even if they were wrong. I had wanted to go with them even though I knew that it was wrong. Why was it that I had not told them outright that they were wrong? Why had I wanted to go with them? My thoughts drifted off into other imaginations, and I switched off the radio. I could hear the band at the boys' hostel, and I knew that the boys were practicing for the next big event we would have toward the end of the year, the Speech and Prize-Giving Day. We could hear the tubas and trumpets from afar. It was good to listen through the window and look at the red cement on the windowsill. We had picked a few Namaqualand daisies and displayed them on the window. Their petals were droopy, and the water needed to be changed. Since Sisile was the one who was cleaning the dormitory, I wanted to make sure that when I saw her, I pointed this out to her. There was no reason why she should not have changed the flowers in our dormitory because she had been gone for two days. The flowers would not have been wilting with a proper change of water. I felt that she had done a shoddy job of looking after our dormitory because it was the only thing she did. We had gone to clean the drains at the Sharpe Memorial Church that Saturday, and I could feel it in the muscles on my back that the backbreaking work of fetching water with the bucket and cleaning the drains with branches of trees had been a bit too much. I missed my friends when the band was playing because we would imitate the boys who were in the band. Killer was in the band, and we would form our own band and imitate him. The girls would sing about me and even matchmake me with one of the band players. We would march when the band was playing as if we were the boys in the band. As I stood there alone, I looked at the school from the window of the dormitory. Its white and red cement walls and light green doors were well set from where I saw it. I looked at the garden in front of me. I could see some thorny hedge with red small flowers. It needed tending, but because of the thorns, nobody got near it. We were lucky that it did not grow to any length. I could see a barren, dry-looking solitary lemon tree that was encircled with stones as if somebody had wanted to mark something. There was also an orange tree and avocado tree further on toward the matron's house. It was nice to look out the window and enjoy the landscape outside the hostel. Some of the tall trees had pink flowers on them. I wondered what they were called.

I moved around the room and then decided to take the radio and go out to the wall near the gum tree that was on the way to the chapel. Sometimes there were girls from other dormitories there who were ready to chat on whatever subject. When I peeped through the door that led to the chapel, I saw a group of girls out there. I knew that I had to check for some one funny whistle-blower who would tell if they knew about the radio. I saw her sitting quietly far from the other girls and knew that I should go and hide the radio where it was kept and just go out and enjoy myself. I went there and sat down. When they saw me, the girls decided that my hair needed a haircut, and they went and got scissors, and they began cutting my hair. We saw the junior matron passing on the way to the chapel, and we did not pay any attention to her. Once in a while we would see a student teacher or one of the "saved" girls going to the chapel to pray. We continued with the hair as I listened at the girls commenting how thin my hair was. I could feel the scissors going through my hair, and the hair falling all over my face. Some of it fell into my eyes and onto my clothes. I wished we had wrapped a towel over my shoulders, but it was too late to do anything since we were almost halfway through.

"Don't cut too much. I don't want a bald head," I said, touching the girl's thigh.

"Cut everything, she must feel how ugly it is to have short hair. Just remove everything." It was Sisile. She was back from the competitions.

"Did you win, baby? Come and sit here, and tell me what it was like," I said, ignoring her teasing.

"Well, I got number one—"

"Up the Reds!" We were all shouting when she said that.

"We took the hundred meters and the long jump, and even though Botswana beat us, we did very well as a team. Lesotho was third," Sisile said, breaking off a dry branch that was hanging off the gum tree. "This branch could hurt someone. Let me go and wash and go and sleep. I am tired. When you are done with cutting your hair, come and join me in the dorm, Twigza."

"Of course, Twigza. I am going to come and tell you the latest."

"About what?" she asked anxiously.

"Just go, I will come soon. I am almost done. Don't be impatient." We watched as Sisile went toward the open door of the dormitories.

It was fun to be in the big dormitory we called "Enqabeni." There was noise all the time. Even now we could hear the noise. We finished cutting the hair, and I picked it up and rolled it into a ball. I went to the big pit to throw it away. To get down to where the girls were sitting, I had to go down the donga and hold on to the gum tree that was near the wall. I jumped down quickly and ran back to the dorm. Sisile was not asleep. I could see that she had just been to the bathroom from the wetness in her hair.

"Twigza, you don't know the latest. Makhosi and Praisy skipped. They went to the store."

"What? Are they crazy? They will be expelled if the matron finds out. Why did you not tell them that?"

"Tell them what, Twigza? You speak as if you can tell Makhosi Rebel 3 when she decides to do something. She never changes her mind. She was just stubborn. I must say I wanted to go with them. They did not want me to go. They said I will be laughing, and they will be found out."

"They were right by not going with you. You cannot take the pressure of such a thing."

"Would you have gone?" I was curious to know what she would say.

"I would have . . . I might have gone. I cannot be sure. Who does not want the adventure of doing such a thing just once? There is fun in being almost caught. You feel like you are a real lawbreaker, a seasoned doer of wrongs."

"I am going back to the girls so that you can sleep. The radio is over there. It is still using the same batteries."

"Bring it here so that I can listen a little," Sisile said, reaching out for the radio.

"Look in there. I am going now." I banged the door as I left the dormitory. I put my foot on the step of the door that led to the chapel and just stood and leaned on the panel that faced the junior matron's door. Right then I saw them.

Makhosi and Praisy coming out of the gum trees. I did not move. They were taking short stealthy steps and walking toward the gum tree where we had sat to cut hair. I watched them, and when they had come out of the gum trees and close to the jacaranda trees, the junior matron came out of the resident missionary's house and walked toward them.

"Where are you from?" She was asking as she moved toward them. I was shaken and wished I could hide. I felt so sad for my friends because they were so wrong they could not even make an argument. I watched as the matron made them put down the things they had gone to buy. They had bought Baker's Lemon Creams in the red box that has the biscuits outside it. They had also bought a tin of pilchards and Simba chips. The matron took the items they had bought and told them to follow her.

I left the door when they disappeared behind the corner to the senior matron's house. I knew that Makhosi was in trouble. She was a prefect in school, and now she had been caught breaking the rules. How was she going to explain that?

It did not take long before Makhosi and Praisy joined us. They told us that they were going to chop wood and dig a new pit near the old one for the whole week.

"Nobody must talk about us at school. The boys must not know that we were punished. If they ask, say you don't know." I listened as Makhosi looked at me. I wondered why she had thought that we would tell the boys about their going to the store. Why would it have been important for us to tell them? I did not understand her thinking. I just listened and knew that this was an agreement. I was surprised by Praisy's nonchalance. She did not seem to care that this had happened and was her usual self. I would have been mortified.

It was strange to go to school without Makhosi that week. Her chair at the end of the class was empty, and since she was the prefect, her absence was conspicuous. The missionaries who were Praisy's guardians came to the hostel to tell Praisy that they were sorry to hear that she had been punished and to say that they still loved her even though this had happened. I was shocked by their behavior. A Swazi parent would have fumed. Makhosi did not have a mother, so nobody came to talk to her.

I got to school that Monday and felt lonely with Praisy not there near me to tease the boys and laugh at them. The "woman of history" was out digging a pit for going out of bounds. I am not sure what UBaba's class in history was like without Praisy and Makhosi. In Zulu, he came in and asked us if we knew what Verwoed asked the Boers. What baffled us was just asking the question out of the blue. In a Zulu class, why were we talking about Verwoed?

"'Waar staan ek?' This is what Verwoed said, idiot? What is the answer? Do you know what the Boers said, idiot? Yes, idiot," he said, pointing at Sisile.

"They said, 'You stand in front of us,'" Sisile answered, sure that the answer she had given was good.

WEEDING THE FLOWERBEDS

"No no no no no. Waar staan ek, idiot?" UBaba said, lowering his gaze and looking at me from the top of his glasses.

"They said, 'You stand in front of the podium,'" I answered, looking at him for his approval because I knew there could be no better answer.

"No no no no no. Waar staan ek? Yes, idiot?" he said, looking at the boy who called himself a lordying and us fruitesters after the words in the "Pardoner's Tale."

"They said, 'You stand inside your own skin?'" he answered quickly, laughing as he did because whenever UBaba said "idiot" in that manner, there would be bursts of laughter.

"No no no no no." He kept prowling and asking us the question for over twenty minutes.

There was a boy who was called the Little 'Un in our class. He shot up and answered and said, "'They said he stands inside his shoes and socks.'" That did not satisfy UBaba.

"No, idiots," he said, addressing us. "He said, 'Ek staan op die Kaffir's sekop,' which means, 'I stand on the Kaffir's head.' The word *Kaffir* was used for black people to disrespect them during the apartheid days." There was a roar of laughter. UBaba started preaching to us about being lazy and being ashamed of ourselves and said that sometimes the way black people behaved, they deserved to be ill-treated. He said that if we were going to behave badly, we would sweep the streets and weed the fields of mealies that were in the eastern Transvaal because if we did not pass, we would have no jobs and go and sweep the streets. After his lessons, we vowed that we would behave well no matter what. After that we would continue with the lesson of the day. On that Monday, we read the story in the Zulu book. The way he said the title of the story made everybody laugh. He would read the words with a Xhosa accent that was unusual. He would say, "Let us read wathi 'Hhhawu hhawu emhlabeni,'" when we expected him to say, "Wathi 'Hawu Emhlabeni.'" There was only one "Hawu" in the story, and the *h* sound was not the vocal one he used. We would imitate UBaba after he has left the classroom and laugh our lungs out. If you were standing and not paying attention, the students would come and hit you on the head and imitate him and call you idiot in the same way that he says, "Yes, idiot."

We were in the science class after school when Killer called me to come and see something. I went to him, and he held me by the shoulders. "Come and see, look."

I looked and saw nothing.

"What must I look at?" I asked impatiently. Just the thought of him holding me in that manner irritated me. It was just that my curiosity had the better part of me, and I succumbed to talking ear to ear with Killer.

"Look, look again. You see. She is wearing a petticoat. She is wearing a petticoat. She is wearing a petticoat," he said as each girl passed and got into

117

class. The sun was in the west, and since the science laboratory door faced the sunset when the girls stepped into class, you could see the parting in between the legs when they were not wearing a petticoat. The silhouette of their legs created a funny partition toward the upper part of their legs.

"You are sick. You are sitting here watching girls in between the legs. You are mad. You know what?" I asked angrily.

"What? Answer my question. Why don't you wear a petticoat? If I can come to class without my underpants, you girls can whine like puppies." I laughed like I have never laughed before. I forgot my anger and just imagined Killer making girls whine. Just the thought was so ludicrous that I could not hold myself.

"Lordying, this fruitester is not serious. She is saying that it is right for this thing to go on." I was glad when the other lordying did not pay attention to what Killer was saying.

When the science teacher arrived, he had us burn some iron rods and observe how they expanded and record the length. I did not like this experiment and felt a bit bored doing it. Since this teacher did not like chewing gum in class, I took my gum out and chewed. He chased me out of the class, and I went and sat outside. After some time, I went to join Mr. Fields in the library. When I came out, the students were walking away toward the hostel. We worked on the books and did not talk much. Mr. Fields told me that we had received a donation of books from America. He said I should draw lines on the cards so that the students can enter their names on them. I was supposed to draw columns for the name of the student and the date on both sides of the card. I drew the lines, and when I turned the card, I did not pay attention. Some of the cards were facing upside down. Mr. Fields did not like that, and he had me do the task over again. After we were done, I dusted the library shelves and took the dusting cloth to the hostel to wash it.

Mr. Fields bought a new bookshelf for the new books in the library. It was white and about five feet long and two feet wide. It stood at the center of the room, and on it we displayed the new books. Many of the *African Writers Series* were displayed on this bookshelf. It needed frequent dusting because the white water paint showed the dust while the rest of the shelves on the walls did not show. The display of the books also made it easier for dust to settle on the space in between them such that one could see where the book had been because in that space there would be no dust while there would be a lot of dust in the spaces in between. I enjoyed working in the library because I got a chance to read all the books I wanted. I took out *Little Women* by Louisa M. Alcott and read it even though its thickness was intimidating at first. I enjoyed the story of the girls. It was good to read about people whose world was more or less like my own. Most of the books we read were by Enid Blyton, and I did not like them as much as this book. They were also older and seemed to have come from a period of their own.

"I also bought you this book. It is a daily read on the life of a Christian. It will help you to understand things and grow. It has passages for each day and a scripture from Psalms and Proverbs," he said, fishing out a black paperback book from his British Airways bag.

"Thank you," I said as I took the book. It had my name handwritten with Mr. Fields's neat handwriting and a short message that said it was from him and the date on which he had given it to me. I looked at the design of the globe on it and then put it aside and continued with the work. We worked on and talked about how the devil tempted Christians. Mr. Fields talked to me about sexual sin, and I listened. He told me that girls in his university used to come to his room, and he had to work hard to avoid getting into relationships with them. After five o'clock, we closed the library, and I went back to the hostel.

When I got there, I took some time and read the book that he had bought for me. It was interesting to read a scripture that shaped each day. The scriptures from Psalms were well chosen. Some of them were the ones that Mr. Fields often quoted. I put the book down when the bell rang for suppertime.

We came back to the dormitory with Makhosi and Sisile, and I took time to tell them some of the things that had gone on in school while they were serving the punishment for skipping and going to the store. "You missed something the week you were punished. You missed UBaba's display of karate in class. He was sweating and kicking all over. He took off his shirt and demonstrated for us how this karate is. We laughed like we have never laughed before."

"What was he doing?" Makhosi asked, her eyes showing that she was curious to hear what we were saying.

"You should have seen the stomach," Sisile said. "He was turning this way and that. If you ever saw a lunatic, that is how he looked."

"What did the other teachers do?"

"We all laughed. We were beside ourselves with laughter," I said and stood up to demonstrate for the girls how he was moving about and kicking in the air. I think I made it more awkward since I did not know what he was doing

"Like the day he demonstrated the malombo beat in class,"

"It was something similar but even better. This is energetic. That day he was just making gestures in the air. It was the way he did the last bit that was funny. He imitated the drummer, and you could tell that it was mostly his excitement with things African because there was no drummer who could do that," I said, imitating how UBaba had shown us how the drums work.

At that time, Makhosi looked at Sisile and laughed. "Ah! The girl is right," Makhosi said, imitating UBaba responding to an answer that had given in response to a question on grammar in class. He had jumped out of his skin with excitement when the girl said the correct answer. He had been making us analyze sentences on the board in grammar exercises. We had struggled with these, and nobody seemed to know the answer. I did not know it even though most of the time I was one of the few students who used to come up with the unusual answers. It was one of those answers that had us all laughing because we were used to UBaba not approving of anything that happened in the school. He called us idiots and criticized the missionaries and their disposition toward black people and religion in blatant ways that left us dumbfounded, wondering what kind of people we would be if we followed his advice. There was something intriguing about the fact that he was an upright man, interesting, a little bit vulgar, but very truthful in his understanding of southern African issues and apartheid. In very subtle ways, he answered correctly after the whole class had failed.

We laughed when he responded so happily and did not call a student an idiot. I think we were laughing because we were surprised that for the first time, UBaba was happy with what we were saying. He had always given us the impression that he was hard to please. We were now accustomed to the difficult questions about Bismark. I was used to the fact that if we were bored, we just needed to answer and say something about black people. My favorite was "Black people are lazy." He would go off on a tangent and start talking about South Africa, and we would hear all the stories. He would talk about the large plantations of maize that were owned by Boers and make it clear to us that we should strive to get to where those Afrikaners were if we were to convince him that we were different from our lot. We listened, and something inside me started to realize that we had different challenges from our fathers.

He would talk about his tough upbringing in the mines, and we would connect with the life of a black South African who grew up where our fathers often went to work. He made us realize what a tough world the mines were and how his upbringing had challenged him to be a different black person in that there was no way he would work in the mines like his father.

"In the mines, they insult you with your mother's private parts. The miners are rude. I am the son of an *induna* [a foreman]. I grew up in the mines. My father worked where it was rough. There was no joke. He taught me how to spread my legs when I wash down there. *UGxamalaze* [spread your legs in Xhosa]." He would go on and on, talking about things that happened in real life that had no bearing on our lesson. We would lose track of the lesson of the day and be happy that we were listening to one of the funniest teachers in the school. Every day was marked by laughter from our class. This laughter could be heard in any class where he was teaching. If we were in Form IV and he was in Form V class, we would wish we were listening to the stories in that class.

One day he told us about the church of Adam and Eve and said this was a church in Durban where people went to church naked. What was funny was when he demonstrated how an old woman stands and watches the men so that if "she sees something go up," she goes and beats it with the small stick. It was not the story that was funny, but the gestures he made with his eyes and his mouth when demonstrating how a "thing" that goes up is beaten when it disobeys the law of the church, which was to have such self-control that you are not tempted by naked women even when they are in the same room. I laughed so hard that day and almost cried.

The lesson ended, and Mr. Fields came into class. At this time, he was helping us with notes on the "Pardoner's Tale." He was wearing a navy blue suit that was not like his trendy everyday look of the man with the moustache, jacket, and bell-bottoms. He seemed to have come out of some era in the past. When he turned to write on the board, we noticed that there was a white thread that had been sewn in a cross at the end of the single-slash jacket he was wearing. He started to write on the board, and the suit would make a hump at the back because the thread would not allow the slash to open and free him inside the jacket so that he can write. Each time he wrote, a concertina-like hump would form on his back, and all the students would laugh. We had never seen Mr. Fields do something funny. He was one of the trendy teachers that we liked. For us, this was his biggest faux pas. He wrote the notes and entertained us with the hump on his back throughout the lesson.

"When his mother packed his clothes, she said, 'My son, you are going to Africa, and these naked Africans have no clothes. Here is a suit from the thrift store. You will need this in the barbaric places that you are going to,'" Sisile said when we were at the hostel.

"No, his mother said, "Let me make sure that your slit will stay open and the suit will not get crushed. I will sew this with white thread,'" Makhosi added to the creativity of the story of the day. I felt sorry for Mr. Fields because he did not know how students like us being black used the power of the underdog toward white people. We often felt that white people could live in their world where we were inferior, stupid, and inarticulate and even hate us; but we had our own fun avenging ourselves for the humiliation we suffered in racist circles. We spoke about "them," and only once did it occur to us that it was unfair to include Mr. Fields among them.

"You sometimes forget that Mr. Fields is white," Makhosi said as we discussed how the missionaries behaved toward us. Most of them had nicknames. There was Magandiyane, Mabhatata, and other weird names that we did not even know how they had come about. What was funny was that the names fitted the personalities of the people in an African sense. Magandiyane was short and bald and very suspicious of the black girls who stayed at his house. In his world, African girls were always thinking about men. For any little offense, his interpretation would go to men, and there would be cases that were brought to the main office and then dismissed when everybody realized that he was a sick old man.

On Saturdays, we went back to school for science classes. We would go behind the school and take pictures near the sisal plants that grew in the flower gardens of the school. I took a photo near the poplar tree, and it came out beautifully. We would wear our clothes on those days because the uniforms were on the line drying and washed so that on the Monday we would look tidy when we went to school.

The dresses we wore on these days left much to be desired. We decided that this was the day when we would break all the rules. There was a transparent blouse that was made of thin nylon and a cotton bra that one of the girls would let me wear. I don't even remember whom these two items belonged to. We knew very well when I wore these that I was provoking the matron to say something about the way the blouse was revealing my upcoming blossoming youthful bosom. Since I would go and work in the library with Mr. Fields after lunch and since the matron had questioned my working with Mr. Fields and pointed out that "this is a man, Mapitsana," as she called me, I knew that I was playing with fire. We took pictures near the sisal plants behind the school; and Diya, (Dear in township Zulu-English as used in a Zulu book *Lemuka Izwe Elihle*), the only boy who bought into the nickname of the Sisters Three, would have us pose in all kinds of poses. This was the time when I honestly thought that I would make the Paris runway, and I would pose in all the poses and make the peace sign. It was just unfortunate that the pictures revealed the stupidity of youth and would never have made it even into *Drum* magazine, the only magazine that had pictures of black women who were looking for love.

When the science teacher arrived, we went to the classroom. There was a boy we had nicknamed the Cannibal because we thought his looks were close to those legendary man-eaters. Since we were afraid of calling him the Cannibal in his presence, we called him the Anial and removed the *c* and the *b*. When he walked into class, we would shout at the top of our voices, "Aniali-in!" This was a way of disguising "cannibalism." Since he was the prefect, I am sure he thought that he was very smart or even handsome because when the girls shouted and smiled when you entered the class, this was a sign of popularity of some sort.

I also had a nickname that I did not like at all. All my friends would call me "Mdi" because they thought it sounded like my surname. While I hated being called by this nickname and felt belittled by it, I felt that showing that I cared was going to make things worse. I just outgrew the name when I left high school.

Wednesday morning prayers were interesting because teachers talked to us about their lives. Mr. Fields talked to us about his girlfriends, and we listened to his stories and felt that we could relate to what he was talking about.

Morning prayers were fun when the teachers sang to us. They would sing Christian songs and play the guitar. Mr. Fields and his friends would sing to us songs such as

> Listen, listen everybody listen
> Come to Christ today

Even though so many pleas were made for us to come to Christ, we did not seem to get the idea. We seemed to be bound not to come close to Christ for any reason. We would go through school with all the hope that if Christ was just there for us as we traversed this part of life and saw us through school and we passed, he would surely have been as good as our teachers made out. I think the prayers we prayed were short after all the sermons, teachings, and chastisements we got.

We would go back to the hostel exhausted after a full day of learning. We would sit around our study tables and read magazines like *Drum* and *Bona*. The favorite page in *Drum* was the column Dear Dolly. Whoever had the latest *Drum* would read the letter that had been sent. The letters were short, and they were requesting Aunt Dolly to give an answer to some of life's dilemmas. Since these were the dilemmas that were facing us, we wanted to know how she would solve them.

"Read, Rebel. Read," Makhosi would insist. She was the one who always borrowed copies of *Drum* from all the students and brought them to our dormitory. We knew very well that we were not supposed to have such literature in the hostel. Not to say that it was ungodly. It was just undesirable because it was thought that it would unfocus us from the cause, which was to make Christians out of us.

"I am reading. Listen and stop saying I must read."

Dear Dolly,

> I am seventeen years old and in Form IV. I am doing very well in my studies. I hope you can help me solve this problem. I am in love with a man. He wants to have sex with me, and since I am still a virgin, I am scared. He is married, and he says he loves me more than his wife. I am not sure how to stop him because I love him very much.

I would read the particulars of the sender that were at the bottom of the letter and glance at the picture of Aunt Dolly in her wig and wonder what wisdom she was about to unleash. She looked wise on the page, and everybody trusted her advice.

"Muntuza, House 5432, Brakpan. She is from Brakpan. What do you think of the letter, girls?" I would ask my classmates and look up from the page and turn to face them. Most of the time, they were sitting on their beds, and I was the center of focus because I was sitting on the table. "There is the letter. Comments?"

"I think this girl is stupid," Makhosi said.

"I think so too," I would add.

"How can she ask such a stupid question? She does not know men. Which man would say he does not love you when you are a stupid virgin?" Makhosi would add. She always got emotional when women made fools of themselves to men. Sometimes I felt that she did not like men. I was not sure about her when it came to issues of self-discipline. I would look at her and wonder if she would ever get married and learn to live with a man.

"Let us read what Aunt Dolly is saying. Listen." My eyes would move to the next part of the story.

"We are listening—"

> You are stupid if you think the man loves you and you are still in high school. You are stupid when you think an older man can love you better than his wife. If you have sex with him, you will become pregnant, and that will be the end of you. Stop thinking about men and concentrate on your studies and grow up to be a charming lady who loves herself. There is nobody who can love you when you do not love yourself enough to realize that you need an education before you can have children. You are about to fall into the usual trap of young girls who have sex, fall pregnant, and then drop out of school. If I were you, I would leave this man and focus on school. It is a good thing that you are still a virgin. That is very good.

"Read the next story, this was a foolish story anyway," Makhosi would say.

I would go on to the next. I would read the first line of each story and skip the story if it was boring and then go on to the next. There were two pages full of such stories so there was a lot to choose from. When I saw an interesting one, I would continue reading. "Listen to this one."

Dear Dolly,

> I am in love with this man. He is the friend of my ex-boyfriend. He started proposing me when I was going out with this guy, and I left my boyfriend for him. In fact, let me say this. I did not really like my first boyfriend. I was just going out with him because my friends told me that it was good to have a boyfriend. Since he was my first, I did not expect much to come out of the relationship; so when the opportunity, came I left him. This guy I am going out with drives a BMW, and he works at the Carlton Hotel. He is the human resource manager. All the people call him boss, and he really makes me feel like a queen. He begs me and talks nicely to me. My old boyfriend did not do such things. He did not even know how to kiss. I was very bored when I was with

him. The problem is that my parents already knew about him, and they liked him. They do not like this new man in my life. They say he is exploiting me. My father said that he will stop paying school fees for me and chase me away from home because he thinks I am selling my body to this man because he is rich. What should I do? I do not want to go back to the old one. I feel confused. Moreover right now I want to just hang in there till I write my school leaving examination and go out to the world. I think this older man will help me to get a job in Joburg when I am done. I have already had sex with him, if I may add. Was this a good decision? I mean to have sex with him? I know that you will say I was selling my body, but I love him. He is giving me new experiences that I need as a woman. I used contraceptives, and I am not pregnant. Please advise me, Aunt Dolly.

Celeste Motsepe—Watville, Benoni.

"This is an interesting one. I think this girl should not have left the old boyfriend," Makhosi would start advising the girl even before we went to find out what Aunt Dolly had to say.

"Makhosi, the guy had no 'kissability.' What do you say about that? Would you like a guy like that? You would also have a problem with him. I do not condone what she did, but I can see that she had a problem. He was young, boring, inexperienced in the things that matter and I guess a bit ugly, even though I am reading into the situation," I would say.

"I think the problem is putting men before education. I think right now this girl thinks she is doing the right thing because she sees a career ahead of her," Makhosi would say. "She should focus on school. You cannot mix school and men. The two do not go together," Makhosi would continue. I looked at her and really thought she sounded like an adult sometimes. I also felt that at times she did not see the dilemma we faced as young people and wondered where she got the wisdom to view things as she did. I would then keep quiet because I could see I was representing the young and childish, even though this was reality.

"Sisile, what do you think?" I turned to look at Sisile. She had her legs astride the bench that we sat on when we were studying.

"I think this applies to all of us. We should not bring shame on our parents by having men, babies, and all that," she would say that and go and take her books and study. She would look at the pages briefly as if she did not want to do the work. Sisile never really studied seriously. She would have her thumb in her mouth or be biting her nails while she looks at the work and continue as if her mind was not really there.

"This one got syphilis from a lover. Wuh! It is reviling." I would read the letters briefly so that the girls can stop me if they are interested in hearing more. The girls would shake their heads as we went on. We would read about men who had polygamy in their households, who were quarreling with their parents, and discuss the issues as if they applied to us. After that we would circulate the magazine to all so that they could read the other articles for themselves. The only ones that we read together were Dear Dolly. If the matron came to the dormitory, we would hide the magazine under the pillow and pretend as if we were not reading anything.

The third term of Form IV was slow. In literature, we moved on to *Lord of the Flies*. We enjoyed the book even though it was about boys who were stranded. We identified with them because we also felt like we were abandoned by our parents in an island where all that was available was religion. We had to drink of it until our stomachs would not hold anymore. The only person who had to put up with being teased in this class was the boy we called the Little 'Un. He had come from Ikhwezi secondary, and he was very young, and having a small stature also added to his predicament.

Besides reading the assigned books, we read our own books and did book reviews in class. Each student would stand up and tell the class about a book that they had read and then sit down. I told the class about *Little Women* by Louisa M. Alcott. The third term was the term my friends Sisile and Makhosi decided to do something that was really out of character. They went out with two policemen. Makhosi anticipated my reaction to this issue and rejected the guy even before I got to meet him. Sisile stayed in the relationship because I remember meeting the guy. The reason why I wanted to meet him was because he had bought her a very interesting novel entitled *The Great Affair* by Victor Canning. We found it amusing because it was about a priest who was defrocked and then ended up misusing the quotations from the Bible. The quote "The Great Affair is to move, but in the right direction" became a household quote in dormitory 55. We were in the last two years of high school, and we could see the future and the freedom it would bring us. That is why after reading the book, I could still ask the two girls what had got into them to cause them to go out with policemen because this was one way of jeopardizing the future that was so close to us that we were to guard it with our lives. Not getting where we wanted to go would have been the silliest thing to do.

"A cop, Diya, tell me, how could you go out with a cop?" I asked looking at Makhosi, hoping that now that she had jilted the man, she could answer the question truthfully.

"I thought it would grow, Diya," Makhosi answered with a sly smile on her face.

I did not let her smile get into me. "You thought what would grow? I don't understand this one," I said to her.

"The love, Twigza, I thought it would grow. Look, at least this other cop you thought was a bad idea bought us a good novel. We would not have known about this book if it were not for him," she said, defending something that I knew could not even begin to be defended.

"You girls were just looking for trouble," I said with a stern look on my face. "Policemen do not think. They beat up people for nothing. I cannot imagine you doing such a thing. Next time, don't do what I wouldn't do," I said, shaking my head.

We ended our conversation and went back to the story of the priest and started teasing another fallen preacher who was hanging around the school those days.

"He does not know the *nduku* [stick] that knows no law." We would laugh and recount how they had found out that he was going out with some of the Christian girls and then suspended him. We felt that they did not understand that he was young and so full of love that forcing him to work among the innocent Nazarene girls was asking for trouble. When we analyzed issues, you would think we knew everything about life.

In English language, we were asked to write a composition about the drought. Makhosi wrote about the death of cattle and told the story of a boy called Dile, which was short for *crocodile*. There had been so much meat that the boys would roast the meat and start fighting over it by throwing it up and competing against each other over who would get the piece of meat. They would throw the meat at crocodiles, and one crocodile had bitten the leg of this boy. It was a good piece to read. Sisile wrote about a man who was so hungry that he went around the trees where chickens slept and waited for them to bomb on top of him, and then he would catch them. We had fun with these compositions. I remember that I wrote a lot, but I don't think my work was as interesting as the work of my friends. It was just error free. When our exercise books came back from Mr. Fields, we all wanted the red ticks. They were few. It was Makhosi who suggested that it was better to get voodoo and bewitch Mr. Fields so that he can mark everything we write as correct. She would demonstrate how he would mark our papers when he was under the spell of voodoo. "Ibaso, ibaso," she would say, imitating how he would respond when he was marking under the spell. We would break out laughing and wonder what the teachers would say if they knew how funny we thought they were. It was nice to get back to our books and then start to plan for another composition.

I would pay attention to the beginning of stories. I wanted to write a catching first paragraph, one that would make the reader not want to put down my story. I would write the openings of paragraphs that I liked at the end of my exercise book together with expressions that I thought I would need when writing. This made me to have a good choice of openings when time for writing compositions came. It also made my mind keep thinking about writing because

I had this archive of interesting openings to try out. I could not wait for the next composition so that I can impress the teacher with my new expressions. I did not realize that I was acquiring an ability to tell like most of the writers whose work I read.

In *Macbeth*, we would recite the speeches of Banquo, Macduff, and the witches. Our favorite line was the one that reminded us of UBaba because it had the word *idiot* in it: "It is a tale told by an idiot, full of sound and fury, and signifying nothing." Everybody knew this line. We would repeat it and laugh each time we heard it. Even though Mr. Fields had taken over UBaba, we still associated *Macbeth* with UBaba when it came to the quotations and teasing other students in class.

Our behavior improved for the better in the last two years of school. The honor was on us to represent the color red so that when people heard us say "Up the Reds," they would know we were good students and also very polite. We read a lot, and it showed in our writing. We had more expressions that showed that we knew what we were doing. The teasing of students also came to a close. Apart from the Ghost of Banquo, there were no new nicknames. The nickname chapter was closed.

I was still Lady Chaucer in the whispers of the students who were always reacting to the fact that Mr. Fields liked us. They did not see that it was because we did well in class. They thought it was because he favored us in all that we did just because we were girls.

Life went on with the usual regularity. The illicit practices also went on unchecked. Letters still came in through PO Box 315. They were still read with the secrecy that the later teenage years created in the lives of Manzini Nazarene girls' hostel students. We still watched the old woman who came to pick up the leftovers at the hostel. We still prayed many a times and called the student teachers "Emastu." It was in this usual Nazarene routine that events took place. Some would be pleasant, and some would be shocking. Life and love still mingled and produced the accepted and unaccepted. Marriages in the church were still taking place, and our lives at the hostel were still punctuated by a few pregnancies among the girls at the girls' hostel. Even though all seemed to be quiet on the boys' hostel front, we knew that there was a lot that went on. The year the bottle store was built just outside the gates of Sharpe Memorial Church at the shopping complex called Lewis Store was a new challenge to the boys who were at the boys' hostel. We knew that the closeness of this liquor store would wreak havoc in the personalities of the boys. It was not unusual to hear that one of the boys at our school had been so drunk when the boys were going to church that the others had to lay him on the roadside, cover him with gum tree leaves, run out of church, and carry him back to the hostel before the boarding master got to hear about the scandal.

We also had our own story of "the waters." A girl who was going out with Sisile's brother who worked at the Manzini Arms Bottle Store had given us a small bottle of Muscatel wine. We had carried this wine to the hostel and after sharing a lid decided that we should get rid of the wine before we got into trouble. We gave the wine to the boys, and they were grateful. It was good to be young and break every rule as long as you were not caught.

All we looked for in life was to break the monotonous routine. We would go out of bounds, and after reading the war books, we would lie down in the grass when we saw the head teacher's car passing and tell the story with such a feeling of triumph that anyone who heard us would have thought that we had done something spectacular. It was good to live from day to day and punctuate each boring day with acts of naughtiness that were typical of children who were bored and wanted to do something.

Chapter Eight

Form IV was a special year because all of us—Makhosi, Sisile, and I—were made prefects. We were called to the front of the school and given pins that had the word *prefect* in silver on a plain rectangular blue background. The pins were about two inches long. Even though they were small, the power they wielded was significant. These pins were fastened to our bosom so that everybody would see and respect us. Makhosi was the head girl, and I was the library prefect. Sisile became the science lab prefect. This meant that we would have to put up with a little bit of bullying by Makhosi, as if what she had been doing already was not enough.

My position was that of library prefect. It meant that I had the privilege of working with Mr. Fields in the library, classifying books and putting cards in them so that the students would find them ready when they came to pick up books to read for pleasure during the library hour. I enjoyed processing the books with Mr. Fields. He bought some books with his own money and also requested books to be sent from America and England. Boxes of books would arrive, and we would unpack them and process them and then put them on the shelves. By the time I left high school, the library must have about three thousand books. For a school of about four hundred students, that was a good library. Since we were also using the library in town, we had enough books to choose from.

Like any other May Monday morning, that Monday of our second term in Form IV began with the raising of the flag. Killer and another boy marched through the glass doors of the school like soldiers on duty. Their hands were on the salute as they pounded in a uniform march as they walked toward the flagpole. They took the corners of the building at angles, acting up with a vigor of such reality that they looked like patriotic idiots who were berserk. When they got to the edge of the front steps, they turned the corner with a soldierly turn that I had only seen in the movies about the Second World War. The exaggeration made their behinds look funny. It was as if their bums were bundled up and acting up for all of us to see what responsible citizens they had all of a sudden become. When you combined the naughtiness of swinging on chairs that they had removed the rubber from the legs of and dashing all over the classroom when Ms. McClou was not around and the marching the two were doing at this moment just made you laugh because it was clear that this was one other stunt that was meant to get the attention of the students. They feigned a seriousness that made one wonder what they would do next. It just brought laughter to all of us. The boots that they wore were also so shiny in front that they must have bought the exact boots that the police wore. When they got to the flagpole, the boy who held the flag saluted and then went to tie it to the string. After he had raised it, they saluted and walked away. It was fun to watch them enjoying doing such an adult task with the real perfection of patriots in the making.

After the raising of the flag, the bell rang, and the two boys joined the rest of us when we went to the assembly hall. There were days when the teachers asked us to choose a hymn of our own choice. On those says, we would choose a hymn and sing and even enjoy ourselves. I liked "Showers of Blessing." When it was sung, I felt the showers falling and the blessings were real to me because in a way we were lucky to be in boarding school when other students were not even able to afford money to be day students even in the cheapest countryside schools. Boarding school was very expensive. Even at that time, we paid a lot since the amount we paid for the whole year was just a little bit below a hundred rands. At that time, that was a lot of money.

We would hear the announcements and then prepare to go out to our classes. We would walk out of the assembly hall through the back door when we were in Form IV and walk past the tap and get down the steps that are near the deputy head teacher's office and head for class.

The day would begin as usual, and all that we did would be routine. It was the afternoons that were different. On Wednesdays we had sports, and some students would take the volleyball and go to the volleyball pitch. They would play under the supervision of some of the teachers.

Netball was one of the fun sports. I remember very well when we played in William Pitcher College in the early seventies. We were so strong that we had defeated all the schools in the area. Even Franson Christian High School was no match for us. The game between us and Franson High School is one I will never forget. I remember the running, passing, scoring, and shouting at the netball field. I remember Sisile at the center or on the wing. I remember how Makhosi would pass the ball to the scorers. She would swing her whole rear end and push the opponent out of position, and once she got the ball, we were sure that it would land right in the hands of the scorer. Watching the netball team was enjoyable, exhilarating loads of fun. From the moment we descended down the steps past the teachers' parking lot to the point where you positioned yourself to watch the girls at it, you knew you were at the right place if you wanted to see real strategy being unleashed on some not-so-good team by our energetic group of players.

The girls would come in wearing red short skirts and white shirts and take over the netball field. They would position themselves accordingly and wait for the referee to throw the ball up so that the two centers can determine which side should choose the pole for scoring. As usual, Sisile would determine if our team would win by making sure that the first decision favored us. She never missed on that one. After that it would be "Up the Reds" all the way.

The netball alias for each player would be shouted as the ball landed in the hands of the player. The names were power names, real names that made us picture success. "Bahoos! Bahoos!" we would say as we encouraged our strongest defender as she reached for the ball while it circled in the ring. If she was successful, we would say the whole name, "Bahoos never dies!" The girls would know that we were fully behind them when we shout their names. We would move from one side of the pole to the other through the guava trees and follow the game to the other pole. At halftime, we would go and listen as the netball teacher coached the team. Our netball team teacher was the home economics instructor. She would impart her own wisdom about the game and advise the girls to close in on the enemy and attack so that we win. We did not want to be put on the defensive by the opponents. When time was up, we would hear the whistle blow and know that it is time to go and take the ball and display our not-so-good talent by scoring. The girls were sweating at that time. They were tired, but happy that we were victorious.

We were still chatting about the match between our team and Franson and demonstrating how the girls were throwing the ball. We wanted to tell the players our version of the game. Since they were tired, we carried the ball back for them. We walked up the steps to the road and started throwing the ball. I was throwing it to Sisile who would catch it and throw it back.

"Yotha Mopho," I said, imitating one of the opponents who had a hand that was burnt. I related to Sisile and Makhosi how we had called her Mopho each time she got the ball. We would say, "Yotha Mopho," referring to the time when King Shaka said to one of his generals he must warm himself in the fire. He had punished him little by little, making him put his hand right in the fire until it got charred. Since Sisile and Makhosi did not see this because they were playing, I would relate the story of Yotha Mopho. It did not occur to us that this was a cruel thing to do. At that time, we would do things that hurt another person in order to see if they would express how they felt about what was being done to them.

We saw Ms. McClou coming down the steps and going to her red Volkswagen and ignored her. I threw the ball at Makhosi, and when she threw it back, I missed it and it went and landed on Ms. McClou's car. She was furious. I went and picked up the ball and did not even pay attention to her.

"You girls should be at the hostel right now. It is half past five." She was already walking to the steps. I thought that she wanted to satisfy herself that there were no girls who would remain behind and not go back to the hostel.

"Yes, Ms. McClou, we are on our way," I said as I took the ball and threw it to the other girl.

"You are going to be punished for this. You must come to my house as soon as you get to the hostel," she said, looking at us with a threatening look.

"For what, Ms. McClou? There is nothing wrong with that." I started protesting against going to her house. I knew that she would tell the senior matron, and then we would be punished because she would think that we had been rude to her.

"I am telling you and not asking you, Bulelo. You know you should not be here at this time."

"Even when there is a game?" I asked. "That is not true," I protested. Ms. McClou did not answer me. She just took out her notebook and noted my name, and I knew that she was going to make an issue out of our being at school past the hour and then cause a lot of trouble for us.

We were used to Ms. McClou making a fuss about rules. She was strict about everything. The way she treated us showed us that she did not trust us. We did not even try to do better in front of her because we knew that as far as she was concerned, we were bad students. When I walked into the front door of the school, it was deserted. I went and opened the storeroom and threw the ball inside and then ran to catch up with the other girls who were already on their way to the hostel. You could tell which girls had been in the netball team because they were walking slowly as if even walking was something that demanded too much effort for one who was as tired as they were.

I was restless at suppertime that day because I knew that we were going to have a showdown with Ms. McClou.

"What are you going to say, Rebel 2? You are in trouble," Makhosi said.

"You too. You were there. What will you say?" I retorted.

"I am not going to that crazy woman. I was playing netball for the school," she said, an angry frown on her face.

"I was also cheering for the school. I am just going to go and hear what she has to say, but I don't think I care about her because she is being a wet blanket. She is spoiling our fun as usual. Remember how she said I was the one who wrote in the library book?" I said, trying to show everybody how crazy this woman was.

"I do," Sisile said, looking at me.

"That too was unfair," I protested.

I did not wait for Ms. McClou to call me. After supper, I went straight to her house. I just wanted this whole thing to be over. I knocked on her door and peeped through the glass door to see if there was any movement from the other side. Right then I saw her coming toward me. She had the little notebook in her hand.

"Where are your friends? You were not alone," she asked, opening the notebook.

"My friends were in the team, and I do not think you should penalize them for being out there," I said, looking at her.

"Go and tell them I want to see them," she said that and walked away. I opened the door and walked out. On my way out, the junior matron saw me. She was walking toward her room.

"What have you done now, miss?" she asked, looking straight at me as if to say, "I know you are in trouble."

"I don't know. I was called by Ms. McClou," I responded.

"You must have done something. She cannot just call you," she said that and then started walking toward the door of her room.

"We were at the netball field, and she came and accused us of being late. The girls took too long to finish," I was relating to the junior matron my version of the story. "She looked at me and then said that I should go and call the others," I said that and then went to my dormitory. The bell for supper rang, and we went to the dining hall.

When I came back from the dining hall, I was with Makhosi and Sisile. We came back and found Ms. McClou and Ms. Cele, the junior matron, talking outside our dormitory. They led us to Ms. McClou's house and sat down on the sofa. They did not even give us a hearing. The junior matron just nodded her head to everything Ms. McClou was saying, and we were found guilty even before the trial.

"Let us go," Ms. Cele said as she lifted herself from the sofa she had been sitting on. We followed her to her room. "You see, if you are going to keep breaking the rules, they will expel you. You should not have been down there at that time." She kept going on, and I resolved that I was going to tell her the truth because Ms. McClou liked to get us into trouble for nothing.

"I would agree if the match had not dragged. You know we were watching the netball match," I insisted.

"I don't know. I was told that you were playing with the ball, so you will clean the bathroom on Saturday morning," Ms. Cele said.

"I don't think it is fair to punish us," I protested. My friends also nodded their heads.

"We were playing netball for the school. We were not just entertaining ourselves by being out of bounds," Sisile added.

"Let us cut this thing short. Just go and do what you have been told." We left the matron's room very dissatisfied with the verdict.

"This is not fair," Makhosi protested. "Maybe you guys should not have been playing with the ball. That is what made us look like we were having fun. Anyway, I am too tired to protest. Let us go back to our dormitory," she added.

"You are right. We will not get anywhere with protesting this one. Anyway, we enjoyed ourselves even though we were not playing. Someone just has to be jealous of our having fun and being ourselves. That is all this is about. Cele is a fool." I was furious as we walked away.

Apart from watching netball, I enjoyed playing tennis. Even though our team was not good, I was selected to play against Saint Michael's High School. Saint Michael's was a girls' school that was run by the Anglican Church. We won against this team too. Their girls were not very good in tennis. For us, it was an easy game. The boy who was coaching us was very happy. He had started coaching us when we were in Form III. By now we were seasoned players. My backhand was much better than it had been at first. One of the Saint Michael's girls had a good forehand. She did hit a few balls that I missed. Since I had learned to volley my serve, I scored mainly on the serve, and that is how we won the six sets.

We were lucky that when we returned to the hostel, we still had some nice things to share. This was because one of the girls was supported through school by some of the missionaries. They would bring her cookies and nice deodorants. One of the deodorants was called Avon Cloud of Roses. We had to spray it from afar, and it would leave a strong scent when it settles on your skin. It was one of the wonders of the missionary world that we enjoyed.

Apart from this, she would also give us scones and biscuits. One time she gave us biscuits and put them on our beds. Sisile bit half of mine and also ate hers. Since I was not in the dormitory when she did it, I did not know she had done it and wondered why she had not given me a whole biscuit like the others. Just as I was about to ask the question, Sisile came in, and I looked at her face. I could see a funny smile, and then I knew what had happened to my biscuit. "Hey you, Rebel, why did you do this?" I said, pointing at the half of a biscuit on my bed.

"I did not think you would notice," she said. I laughed because I had figured out a typical Rebel Sisile act without being told. Her mischief was even more predictable than mine. She had thought that I would suffer through and think that the other girl disliked me and not find why I was given half. She would tell lies so that I could laugh. One day she said one of the lady teachers had seduced a male teacher. Since she was talking about the missionaries, I asked her how she knew that, and that is when she burst out laughing, and I knew that she was just saying that to make me laugh. Everybody knew that I enjoyed a good laugh. I became a victim of all kinds of schemes because of liking to laugh.

One other thing that I liked to do was exercising. We used to exercise for thirty minutes before supper. We would spend fifteen minutes jogging on the spot and then spend the next doing stretches. I would run twenty times in the space that was near the chapel. The girls would cheer me as I made each round. They would laugh and think that I would not finish the twenty rounds only to find that I kept at it and even finished at a faster pace. After running like this, we would go and have a shower and then be ready for the dining hall. It was refreshing to exercise. It gave us something to do.

The last year of school was the most interesting year of our lives. We arrived at school and found that we had a new science teacher who was going to teach us physics and chemistry. We were very happy after the years of torture where we used to play outside instead of having a class and then wait for the teachers who came in the evening. Our teacher was also from York University like Mr. Fields. We believed that Mr. Fields had been the one who had helped in recruiting her. She was pretty, tall, very slim, and had a fine crop of brown, beige hair.

She was faced with the challenge of collapsing the two-year syllabus into a one-year course, and she tried her best. We did all kinds of experiments, and laboratories became places where we would have fun. She had to first get it into us that this was a class because we were used to doing anything that we felt like with this time. One of the games came out of Chaucer's "Pardoner's Tale." It was the time for "counting the florins."

"A bag full of florins, lordyings, what do you say?" the Little 'Un would say, putting all the beakers and tripods in front of his table to make his store.

"You are not supposed to touch anything in the lab when a teacher is not around, you?" Sisile would say.

"Listen to this, fruitester. You say we are not supposed to what?" Killer would say. "What are you? I mean, in the dictionary of fools, what are you called?" he would say with his bullying voice.

"I am the prefect here, and you will behave yourself or I will go and call the teacher." She would stand her ground.

"Go now," the boys would say. "Are you a new girl or just a whistle-blower? Go and tell about us? We will excommunicate you, and nobody will ever marry you. I mean, in the heaven down here. You still need us in your lives, you girls. We are the kings of the earth, do you hear, fruitester?"

Ms. June would come in wearing her floral frock and dragging her Scholls and then look at the commotion and shout, "E—dwa—ard! Edwa—rd! You put those back right now!" There would be commotion in the class as the boys adjusted to the time for learning. It was as if every day for each and every lesson they had to run around and hide their little tricks like mice when they see a cat. They were always being caught in some silly act. I started to be critical of their behavior now that I was a prefect.

I looked at Ms. June as she took out the equipment for the experiments and prepared for the class amidst the commotion and felt sorry for her. What did she think she would find in the depths of Africa? A few saints waiting to enter heaven? I would think and take my tall lab stool and position myself on it and look at her as she wrote the instructions for the experiment. We were going to learn how to make sulphuric acid. She would take a big glass trough and fill it with water and then take a glass cylinder and turn it down. After that we had to complete the experiment using only the chemicals she had put out and then complete the formulae she had written on the board.

"This is one of the experiments that will be in your final examination. Make sure you know it very well," she would say as she wrote the notes on the board. "I want you to calculate the formulae and make sure that you balance the equation for sulphuric acid correctly. You will have no excuse for not getting this correct. I am deducting double marks for any mistake in this one," she would say in her small voice. She spoke as if something was wrong with her. We would watch as her dainty fingers wrote on the board. She wrote as if she did not want the chalk to make her fingers dirty.

She would go on and work on other experiments. She just wanted us to have the basics, and then after that she would drill us in all the important things. We would work on the assignments and then know that we could go and ask her problems after school because she was living with the resident missionary in the hostel in the house just next to the chapel. We enjoyed going to her house to ask her answers to the science problems. We would pick her hair while she taught us, and when we got back to the dormitory, we would have a contest on how many strands of hair each one of us had picked.

Everybody thought that Mr. Fields would have a "spark" for Ms. June. We were waiting to see if there was fire in the works, but Mr. Fields did not give us any sign. Even though Ms. June would come and join us in the library, I did not see much of a spark. Of course the students were asking me if there was any.

We still had science classes on Saturdays because we were far behind in the syllabus. On these days, we would wear our own clothes. There were favorite clothes that we liked such as the *mpimpiliza* and the *nonor*. These two pieces of clothing had to be worn in turns.

"Are you going to wear the *nonor*, Twigza?" I would ask Makhosi because she was the owner.

"No, Twigza, you can wear it today." I would be happy and take the brown corduroy waistcoat and wear it with pride. It would fit on me, and I would feel the dignity of wearing the best piece of clothing of the day.

"I will wear the *mpimpiliza*," Sisile would say as she picked out the three-cast Dutch piece of navy blue-and-white paneled skirt. This skirt was about one foot long. Since we were not allowed to wear dresses that were too short, we knew that we were challenging the matron in wearing this one, but who cared? We would walk in our brown sandals and go off to school. It was good to appear in these two pieces of clothing. They were the ones that marked our heroism. We ended up duplicating the *mpimpiliza* by tearing one of my skirts that had box pleats and sewing a six-paneled skirt like the *mpimpiliza*. At that time, we would both wear the two *mpimpiliza*. The original *mpimpiliza* was beautiful, and the other one hung like an umbrella because we had not evened out the angles when we cut the panels. With the rudimentary sewing skills we had then, there was not much we could do. I wore it with pride all the same even though it hung like an umbrella on me.

"Let us go to the back of the school and take pictures," Makhosi would say. We would call Diya, the photographer, and he would come with his camera on his shoulder. We would go to the back and take photos in the flower gardens of the school. I liked to stand near the sisal-like plants in the latest pose of the day. We took pictures in front of the school in all kinds of clothes.

We would even borrow a camera and take pictures in pants at the hostel. Since Ms. June wore pants, we did not see anything wrong with wearing them. We would hide the camera and go and take turns taking pictures at the back of the chapel. It was good to be at the school and enjoying ourselves. All we had to do was to hide the clothes like pants and the camera from the matron. They were part of the secret corner of our lives that she had nothing to do with. When we took trips to the farm, we would run ahead so that we could take pictures. When the matron asked us what is in the bag, we would take out the biggest guavas and give them to her and tell her that the whole bag was full of guavas. Seeing the big guavas, she would believe us, and we would run triumphantly after pulling a fast one on her and go and laugh when we knew that she was out of earshot.

We read war books when we were in Form V. We enjoyed the stories about when the soldiers have to lie down in the grass when the planes were passing. This was a stunt that we decided we had to learn because it would be useful in our escapades. We liked to go for walks toward the farm. There was only one bad thing about walking that way. The head teacher lived on this route, and he was one person who would see us and know that we are out of bounds. We would take off on the road that was used by trucks when they brought hostel supplies. It was a back road that went behind the dormitories of the student teachers. There was a thicket and undergrowth from the thick forest of gum trees that surrounded the hostel. On this side, they grew on both sides of the road; and when the road ended, it formed a T-junction with the main road that was between the girls' hostel and the school. We would take this road and walk past the houses of the missionaries. They were fenced with nice hedges that had purple blooms of the most beautiful bougainvillea and hibiscus plants. Beyond the missionary boundary, we would look on to the landscape that leads to Elwandle, a place that was on Swazi Nation Land that had nothing to do with the mission and boarding school. We would walk on slowly, and when by any chance we saw the head teacher's car, the wild cry "Go down!" would be the only one to announce that if you remain standing, we would all be in trouble because we were way out of bounds.

We would lie down flat on our stomachs, and the sound of the car would come closer and pass in a flash, leaving a cloud of dust behind it, and then after peeping to see if things were safe, we would rise up and go our way.

"That was close, Twigza," Sisile would say. "That was really close." We would take off slowly and go our way talking about our escapades as if we had just done something really triumphant. Ahead of us, we would see the old farmhouse. It was a yellow house that was in the middle of the forest. It was big and looked disheveled as if nobody lived there. The old woman who used to take girls home when they were pregnant would appear on the door, and her husband would follow her. We would hide so that they wouldn't see us because we knew that she was the friend of the matron. We knew that she would tell her if she saw us so far away, and we would be in trouble.

"We have to go back. This is it for today," Makhosi would say with a serious, determined look on her face. She had the look of authority on her face whenever she said it was time to go. Since she was the head girl that year, we tended to listen to her though not all the time. I would constantly try to get her to flex the rules a little bit because we were now in charge of the school. There needed to be some form of real democracy so that the students could feel that life is not about rules and also that it is the privilege of those who govern to make and break the rules. The rulers had to know that we the people made the rules, and therefore we had to question everything so that the yoke that sits on our bodies does not get too heavy. We did not want the juniors to see us exercising power like them and breaking rules. Something about being a senior meant that we alone had the permission to break the rules. That is why the juniors were not allowed into our dormitory. Makhosi would terrorize them, and I would feel sorry for the "people." I would know that my heart goes out to them. What was wrong with them rubbing shoulders with the bosses? Why did they have to be in awe all the time? This was a question that I did not know I would spend the whole of my life trying to ask in different ways, settings, and genres.

"They must not come here. We do not want children here," she would say with a seriousness that made me wonder why power sat so fittingly on her. Makhosi was the daughter of a prince; and her father was a chief of the Khoza, Lavumisa, and Ntondozi chiefdoms that I knew. I just did not think that so early in life she should live the life of a ruler over the ruled. The traces of Rebel 3 had matured over the years into a woman with a springy walk and a small frame that carried power, a flashy smile that turned into a fierce look with the spur of the moment. The power of renunciation seemed to be a gift that she had groomed effectively while I was preoccupied with the gift of love. Since I believed in my virtues, I was silently critical of her scaring tactics when she scared the young Form Is from our dorm. I felt that it was unfair because the Form Vs we had found had liked us. We had been their pets, and they would do naughty things in front of us, like putting the panties in between their bums and walking about as if this was normal. Something in me would always side with the powerless of the earth. Between pity, inferiority, shame, and powerlessness, I could not place my feelings.

To me, they were all the children of one Africa, one God, and therefore should have been in the world to have a long and endless laughing spree.

Makhosi was different from me. She was a fearless girl and very adamant when she set her mind to it. Her terror-filled gaze had got her into trouble when she first arrived because the principal had accused her of giving her the look and made her clean the toilet for the whole day. Being the new student and being punished did not soften her. I remember the day we had to answer to the matron why we had refused the beige bedspreads. It was quite a situation. It all started when we arrived for the year. The hostel had three colors of simple quiltlike bedspreads that were made out of a cotton design of chainlike patterns that ran all over. These were reversible. There were green, blue, and beige. We disliked the dullness of the beige ones. We had never had those throughout our lives at the hostel, only to find that in our final year, we were stuck with the dullest color of all the bedspreads. We knew that one of the student teachers had been distributing them, and when we asked them for another color, they refused. Everybody who saw the bedspreads on our beds laughed because they made our room look very dull. We all used to say they were the "donkey color." I was cleaning the dormitory that week. I watched as the girls took other bedspreads and not these. They piled them on top of the bookshelf. I wrapped them nicely in a newspaper and threw them on top of the suitcases. We did not know that the matron had come around and seen that our room was in all colors because the girls who did not have an alternative bedspread had just left their beds uncovered. When the matron saw this, she was mad.

On Monday during study time, we went to the dining hall; and while we were sitting there, she came and called us and told us to go back to our dormitory. We went back and sat on our backs. She went and called the resident missionary, and together they came to the dormitory.

"My children, I want to know why you are not using the bedspreads," the senior matron asked.

"We do not like them," Makhosi answered. I hid behind the door and started laughing mischievously. I was lucky that the matron could not see my face.

"Who said you should use bedspreads when you like them?" she continued to ask. Her voice was soft but angry.

"We did not know that we have to use them even if we do not like them," Makhosi answered.

"This is very serious behavior. You can lead a strike when you behave like this. Do you want to start a strike?" she continued.

"Not necessarily," she answered again.

"Did you do this deliberately out of stubbornness?" she persisted.

"Not necessarily," Makhosi answered again

"Where are the bedspreads?" the senior matron asked.

"They are up there," I answered from behind the door. I stood up and pulled the bedspreads from on top of the suitcases.

"You have that bedspread on, Bulelo. Where did you get it?" the matron asked, pointing at my bed.

"I borrowed it from another student," I answered and went and sat on my bed behind the door. The resident missionary said, in funny SiSwati, that she agreed with the matron.

"Take these bedspreads and put them on your beds now, and when you are done, you can then go to the study," she said those words and closed the door, and then together with the resident missionary, they walked toward the end of the corridor.

I peeped through the door until I saw the door close, and when I was sure they were out of sight, I started talking. "She does not know how lousy these bedspreads are. We are the ones who must put up with this lousy donkeylike color. Just look how lousy and dull our room looks now," I said as each student put the bedspread on the bed.

"I agree with you, these are lousy. We were just better off doing without," Sisile added as she took the bedspread and spread it on her bed. She folded back the part under her pillow and tucked the three sides under the mattress. I had to agree with the matron that the room did not look dull. There was some order that was brought about by the uniformity. It sort of made the room look like a ward in a hospital, but it did not matter.

"Let us go to study time before the matron comes back. If she finds us here, she will not be happy with us," I said as I opened the door and ushered everybody out.

We walked through the long corridors of the dormitories and wondered what the other students would think of us as we came into the dining hall late when all was quiet. The junior matron was standing near the tables that we used to iron on. These were against another table. She looked at us as we entered. We crept in and sat down. Study time was quiet, so quiet that you could hear the humming sounds of the fluorescent lightbulbs on the ceiling. Every student had her eyes on her books. Sisile was busy biting her nails as she studied and seemed to be half concentrating on her work. She never did her work seriously. It was a miracle that she passed.

I got in and pulled the bench and sat down. I did not entertain the stares from the other students. If they were curious, they would have to eat their heart out because I was not going to offer a single word. I went through the things I had to do because I knew that we had lost half an hour in our ordeal with the senior matron. That night we replayed the incident and thanked Makhosi for being bold and taking the heat. "You did well, Rebel 3. You answered her," I said, looking at her as she put on her nightdress.

"She just thinks we will lead a strike. That is very extreme. Just reacting to something we do not like does not necessarily mean we can lead a strike," she added. We switched off the lights and carried on our debate in the dark.

"She was just angry for something so simple. It's as if anger is the only response she knows. It's unfair. It is unfair." Right then we heard the door open, and the lights were turned on.

"You are going to the mountain on Saturday. You are making so much noise that I have been unable to sleep," the junior matron said from the door. She was wearing a blue coat. We kept quiet and feigned sleep, and then she switched off the lights and went back to her room. Her room was round the corner from us. It was a corner room on the other side of the wall. Even as we retired, we knew that we had been done for. There was a sadness in knowing that the week had come down on us with two bad incidents. I did not like the thought of chopping wood on the Saturday. With that feeling, I drifted to sleep.

We woke up early that morning, and each and every one of us covered their bed with the bedspreads. We did not want to get into trouble. School started early, and it was UBaba who was conducting morning assembly. He asked us to sing a song of our choice. We chose the second song in the Alexander's hymns, "Be Not Dismayed." We sang it, and its words of comfort got to me because I needed comfort after such a week.

He read from Psalms and did not do much preaching except pointing out that we needed to improve our behavior and work at it since it is a lifetime thing. After hearing a few announcements about music, we were soon on our way to class. We got to class and waited for the events of the day to begin. This was a good time to chat. Praisy and I would sit and wait for the other students to enter the class. We would watch as the Form IV students pass to go to their class. We were still chatting when UBaba came in. He had in his hand the Zulu book. He spoke to us in English as he settled into the chair behind the table.

"You know what, I often hear preachers saying that they want to go to heaven, they want to go to heaven. Do you know what happened in Johannesburg? One preacher kept saying he wanted to go to heaven and *tsotsis* heard him. They decided to go to his house at night. When they got to his bedroom, he was wearing pajamas.

"'You said you would like to go to heaven?' they asked. 'We have come to send you to heaven.' They took out a revolver and pointed it at him. Do you know what he did?"

"He shivered and cried," one student answered.

"No," UBaba said, shaking his head. "Yes, idiot!"

"He prayed to God," I answered.

"No," UBaba shook his head. "Yes, you, idiot, what do you think he did?" He was pointing at Makhosi.

"He begged for mercy," Makhosi said.

"Now I will tell you because you have failed to guess. You know what he did? He urinated." There was a roar of laughter at this unexpected answer. We had all expected an answer that would show that the man of God was ready to meet the Creator whom he loved. To learn that he was so afraid that he urinated on himself made us roar with laughter. UBaba knew that he had scored a point with us because in his sermon he had been brief. The opposition and open protest to Christianity of the type we were being put through was his way of balancing our education. We knew that he did not care about salvation. He was just a teacher who was doing a job that he loved badly. Sometimes I wondered why he came to class so regularly. Telling naughty stories and making us laugh seemed to be more important to him than teaching.

After his class, Mr. Fields came to our class. He talked to us about charlatans and explained that the Pardoner in Chaucer's "Pardoner's Tale" was a charlatan and warned us that there were such people in life. He told us about geldings and said that these were people who were eunuchs. We listened to his teaching and learned about the seven sins. Avarice was the most important one. Since it was the moral of the tale, we repeated it in the Latin, *Radix malorum est cupiditas*. We were quiet that day and just enjoyed listening to the lesson and reading together the sections of the "Pardoner's Tale" that were assigned to us. It was good to be in Form V and enjoying what was the best teaching since we had started high school. I think what made Mr. Fields's teaching interesting was that he identified with us and wanted us to enjoy our lessons. He also treated us more as his friends than as students4. He did not put himself way above us so that we felt alienated. We connected to his mind and the lessons he taught us quite easily. His poise and softness were a combination that did well for his execution of the teaching task.

After he had left, we relaxed. I looked back and saw Sisile looking at me. Right then the boy who had written a letter telling her that she must "strike while the iron is hot" passed near the door. He might have been going to the boys' toilet. I shouted "Strike!" He did not hear me, but Sisile heard me and stood up to come to my desk. She knew that the boy would pass again, and we would shout again. We waited till he passed and then shouted. This time Makhosi finished the idiom with "while the iron is hot!" The students laughed because they understood the joke. We had told them while sitting in the auditorium waiting for the science teacher.

The next teacher was the head teacher. He had come to teach us geography. We were doing the geography of North America. He had our test papers from the previous Friday. He gave them out, and I could tell that he was not pleased with our grades.

"You did not do well in this test. The diagrams were small," he said. I had drawn my map and made it small, and I had shaded it with crosses. I liked it, but

I could tell from the points that he did not like the fact that it was so small that he could not tell which was Lake Huron, Erie, and Superior. Lake Michigan was easy to see because of the shape of the peninsula. I looked back when he talked and tried not to feel the hurt because instead of scoring twenty-five marks, I had got only thirteen.

That day he began his lesson on the tundra. It was interesting to learn about faraway lands. We identified with the Eskimos because their igloos were round like the beehive huts that we built in Swaziland. We turned to our atlases in order to look at the map of North America and locate the places. It was interesting to learn that there were long summers in the tundra and that the cold season also lasted a long time because it confirmed that what we learned in physical geography about the revolution of the sun and its rotation were facts that are observable and can be studied in the lives of the real people who live on the poles. We felt that we were lucky to be living in the Southern Hemisphere because we did not have landmasses that stretched to the poles that had populations on them. We felt lucky to be living in the tropics because our temperatures were mild.

We would do calculations of time in the geography class and learn about the Greenwich meridian and the international date line. All these were interesting things to learn about. It was interesting to learn that people in Tokyo were fast asleep when we were awake. It was interesting that one could calculate what time it was over there. We were expected to know these facts because in the final examination we were going to have to answer questions on them. When the teacher had finished teaching, he went out, and it was time for break. The electric bell would ring, and you would hear it throughout the entire school. Soon after that you would hear the screeching of desks as students pull out their chairs. The sound of laughter and commotion could be heard from outside. We would walk out of our class and watch as the students in the junior forms got down from upstairs. They would go into the steps as if they were falling into a shute. They would be laughing and yelling, and the boys would pass near us and go to the boys' side. Their side was to the left of our classes.

We would stand outside near the window of the of the head teacher if we did not go to the front of the school. It was nice to bask in the sun in the winter. Once in a while we would watch as a teacher went up to the teachers' toilet. Students would laugh and say that they did not think that teachers went to the toilet. Break would be short, and we would soon find ourselves back in class. When there was no teacher, we were happy because it was time for us to read our novels. We would bow our heads and put the book on the lap.

Lunchtime would seem to be far off as we waited and read to pass time. It was as if we lived for the breaks. We would be happy when the siren from the mission rang to announce the beginning of the lunch hour. That meant that we had to go to the hostel to eat. It was good to have something to look forward to even though going for lunch meant the usual meal of beef stew and mealie rice. We walked toward the hostel in groups. Each person would walk with a friend. Sometimes we would see the woman who lived at the farm as she walks home from the teacher training college. She was old now. Each time I looked at her I wondered how many girls she had escorted home because of pregnancy. I wondered what she said when she got to the homes of the girls. I dreaded talking to her because to me she symbolized the end of a student's life. I was glad that I had come this far without ever getting into the kind of mischief that led to being sent home with this woman. I did not even want to think what I would do if I was ever in such a situation. I walked to the hostel and wished for the future that I could see in front of me. When I passed the dining hall, the cooks had already set the tables. They were putting our meal on the tables.

The matron saw me as I passed and called me. She told me that I had a letter. I went to pick it up. It was in an airmail envelope, and I could see the foreign stamp on it. I looked at the handwriting and knew that it was from my uncle who was studying at the Malawi Polytechnic. He was telling me that he would come home that summer and also that he was counting on me to do well in the examinations. I read the letter several times. I went to the dormitory and told the girls what it was about. It was not one of the letters that the girls would clamor to read. We were still talking about the letter when the bell rang. We made moves to go to the dining room for lunch. When we got there, one of the girls started the song "We Ask You Our God to Bless Our Food." We would sing with our eyes closed. The last note on the "Amen" was followed by the sound of benches being pulled against the floor. After that it would be the sound of cutlery on the enamel plates. Apart from the matron moving up and down to supervise our eating, there was quiet. After five minutes, the bell that announced that we were free to walk away would ring, and the light eaters would file out of the dining hall.

Chapter Nine

I got the letter over the holidays. It was addressed to me in an unusual handwriting. I could tell from the way my father held it that he had read it. He did not say anything, even though I could see that he was not particularly amused. I pretended not to be interested in the letter and went to buy milk at the store. I was anxious to know who the letter was from, so I did ran all the way and came back. I made sure that I took the letter where I could read it alone.

When I opened it, I was surprised. I did not know that this boy knew my name, let alone my address. We had read the *African Writers Series* with my friends, and the word *Bakweri* was one word we used for most boys who talked to us. I put it down and thought about how I would reply to it. I reread it to see the words *I love you*, and I started to feel my heart beating inside my chest. He was a very handsome young man, athletic and tall, with a mahogany complexion; and every girl in the school liked him. I felt flattered to be chosen by him. His was the second letter that I had received that term. The other letter was from Mr. Fields. He was talking about the apostle Paul and how we should deal with the Christian life. He had drawn a diagram of the two carts, one for feelings and one for facts. I understood the letter and found that right then I could apply the knowledge he was giving me. My feelings were all over me about this boy. The facts seemed to follow in the other cart.

This relationship was a battle of the spirit because I had changed a lot after Mr. Fields's talk about Christianity. I was a bit unsure how to deal with the issue of this boy now that I had given my life to the Lord Jesus. I grappled with the idea of saying no and knew that it was not what I wanted to say. Like in the Millie Jackson song, if loving him was wrong, then I did not want to be right.

I took a pen and went to my room and wrote the reply. It was a short reply, consenting to the issue of love even though I was not very sure what I was saying. It felt good to be loved and to love somebody back. I did not see it as a weakness or a betrayal of the Lord Jesus. The only thing that worried me was that I knew that most of the boys in my class were not Christians. They were just nonchalant souls when it came to these issues. I knew where they were because I had stood on the borders for a long time, watching the indoctrination of the Nazarenes as if it was an age-old drama. Some of them were actually more lost than others because they were outright harassing us. There was one boy who liked to rush to the door when girls were entering so that he can press them to the door or even touch them in a silly manner. I always felt humiliated by his behavior and the shamelessness and crudeness with which he was doing this. This one other boy was nice. He had tried to open the door for me, and I said no and held it for myself, and I remember him commenting about how he was trying to be nice, but knowing the boys in my class, I had been adamant to be myself and not some "softie" that anybody could treat in any manner. I thought about those days and felt funny that here I was ready to write a letter of love. I thought about my friends and wondered how they would react to my writing the letter. It was a trying moment. When I finally put a full stop on the letter, I knew that I had taken one step in a direction I had never envisaged myself taking.

I felt the truth of these words when I was writing the letter. I wrote that I was surprised to get a letter from him but felt strongly that I should agree to his request because it is the right thing to do. I wished him well and told him that I would see him when schools open. It came just like in the movies and read like a Tracy Rosewarne poem.

> At the age of Romeo, standing in a hot, high school room
> Lines of Shakespeare and love
> Stammering out of your mouth,
> You imagined what it would be like for you
> to be Romeo
> and to have found your Juliet.
>
> (Tracy Rosewarne)

I was reflecting on these lines when I walked on the car road to post the letter. I walked to the Ngwenya post office myself. It was quite a long three-mile walk, but I did not mind. I was committed to seeing the letter into the post office box myself. I got there and bought a five-cent stamp and put it on the letter and gave it to the man behind the counter. I did not want my father to see this letter because in it there was a picture of me I had taken standing near the poplar tree that was in the garden below the Form V class. It was my favorite pose. My thoughts always went to this boy after the letter had been sent. So this was the thing called love. It made you feel warm at times and unfocused at others. It felt good anyway to have someone I could call my own. I wished and hoped that the young man would love me back the way I loved him.

When I went back to school, I was dying to tell my friends about the letter. I met Sisile near the post office as usual on that school come of our last term in school. "Twigza, the Bakweri wrote me a letter," I told my friend when we met.

"Which one, Twigza, which one?" She was laughing and looking at me in the eyes. The gap in her teeth and the dimples made her curiosity seem even more girlish and funnier.

"I mean the one and only Bakweriman."

"You mean 'the body?'"

"Yes, I mean 'the body,' Twigza. Folks, yes, Folks," I added.

"You mean the Father of the Tigers?" Sisile added.

"Yes, I mean Folks. He is a handsome guy. I like him."

The young man had a football alias that was very unusual, but since he was a great soccer player, the name had taken.

"That's great. He is a fitting Bakweri, Twigza. He scored the only goal against Malawi." I was relieved that my friend agreed with me in that this was a great guy.

"Let us go this way. There is a young man from Saint Christopher's that I want you to meet. His name is Mdu. He lives at Standini over there. I met him this holiday." We walked past the banks and turned to go down to Ngwane Street. We got into Enterprise Stores and picked up some toiletries. I bought some petroleum jelly and Country Club, the only perfume we used at the hostel. It was cheap but had a sweet scent that left us smelling good. We walked out of Enterprise and walked toward Young's Butchery. We were just crossing the road to go to the library when the boys appeared from nowhere.

"Sisile, how are you? Meet my friend Mavusana."

"Twigza, this is Mduduzi, and Mdu, this is Bulelo, my friend." We finished the greetings and then told the boys that we were going to the library.

"Can we go and buy some ice cream at the Punch Bowl? I will buy you some." I walked with Mavusana while Sisile walked with Mduduzi. We were near the library when we saw the Bakweriman down the road. He was wearing a red jacket as was typical of all Manzini Wanderers Football Club soccer players. When we saw him, Sisile said, "Excuse us, my friend needs to talk to this guy," and we walked away from the two boys toward the Bakweri.

"How are you?" Sisile said when we met with the Bakweri.

"I am fine, how are you? Bulelo, it's good to see you. I am going this way. Where are you going?" he asked.

"We are waiting here for these two guys. After that we will go to the library. We need to check out some books."

"I will catch up with you. I want to go and get some keys from a friend of mine there at the bank so that we can go and play music at his house." He said that and looked at me. It was a stolen look full of feeling. I felt a stab in my heart. "See you later," he said that and walked away.

We went back to Mduduzi and Mavusana. They were sitting under the umbrellas. We watched the Bakweri as he disappeared up Nkoseluhlaza Street and joined the two boys under the shade. It was nice to eat ice cream. After that we all stood up and went to the library. We checked out some books and then went to sit on the tables to read. The Bakweri found us reading, and he greeted the other boys. He said, "Bulelo, let us go. I am not breaking up something here, guys. I just have to go with her." We walked out of the library and took the road that goes past Dups Bazaar and walked down to the Umzimnene River.

"How was your holiday?" I asked him.

"It was good. I missed you guys and thank you for accepting to be my girlfriend. I feel honored to go out with you," he said.

"I think you are a special person too," I added. I was happy that I found it easy to relate to him. I had thought that it would be difficult. Although I was a bit unsure of myself, that feeling soon wore off as we talked about our families. He told me that his sister was in America studying nursing. Most of the things he was telling me were not new to me because his family was well known to us at Manzini Nazarene High School. His father worked at the pharmacy, and one of his sisters went to Saint Theresa's High, and the other one went to Saint Mark's High School. I was a bit unsure about his sisters, but I was assured that what we had between us did not touch any other person.

We walked past Trelawney Park, and when I looked back, I saw Sisile and Mduduzi. They were behind me. They were walking slowly and looking down. I wondered what they were talking about. When we got to the park, we sat down and chatted about life. It felt good to be in love with someone. It was a young love that brightened my world and made the sky even brighter.

After some time, we walked to the house of the Bakweriman's friend. When we got there, the Bakweri opened the fridge and poured two glasses of Fanta orange.

"Leave the door open. I want my friend to see us when she passes. We won't stay long because we have to go to Mr. Fields's house." I walked to the door and opened it.

"What is it with you girls and Mr. Fields? He likes you, and we have started to think he does not like us. Anyway, you guys are smart. Who wouldn't like you?" he said, looking at me and smiling.

"Don't laugh. It's not about that. He teaches us a lot. He talks about God, and I think he is the only teacher who has made sense to me on this subject," I added.

He walked over to the wall near the sofa. There was a Sanyo stereo next to the wall, some records, and a sofa. I went and sat on the sofa.

We played some music. The song that he played was Barrabas's "Only for Men." It was a nice song. It went on and on about women and money being for men. I enjoyed the beat of the music. I walked out to see if Sisile and Mdu were coming up the road. When Sisile saw me, I indicated to her that we were in the house. We played music and drank some Fanta orange. It was good to be young and listening to music. We played on until Sisile came in through the door.

"Well, how are you, guys? Mduduzi has gone. He had to go to the bus. It leaves at three thirty," she said and sat down. I went to the fridge and poured her a glass of Fanta orange.

"What is Manzini like? We went to the countryside for the holiday," she was asking the Bakweri.

"The usual. We had a beauty contest in Manzini Wanderers, and guess who won the contest?"

"Do we know her?" Sisile asked.

"Yes, from our class," he added. I started thinking of all the girls that I associated with Manzini Wanderers. I could not come up with a name.

"It is a hard question. Just tell us," Sisile added.

"Praisy. She scooped the prize. I could not believe it," he said and handed us some sandwiches. We ate them and then danced some more to the music. We played reggae music by Bob Marley and the Wailers. We also played a song "Do You Remember the Days of Slavery?"

"We better get going if we are going to go to Mr. Fields's house, Bulelo," Sisile said.

"We have to go, and thank you for everything." I gave the boy a hug, and we walked out of there.

"He is a nice guy, Twigza. I like him. He is also easy to get along with," Sisile added as we walked up the hill toward Raleigh Fitkin Memorial.

"What about Mduduzi? I think he is a handsome young man. I like him," I said to my friend.

"Look at this," Sisile said, showing me a picture of Mduduzi. He was standing against a tree, next to the main building on the Saint Christopher's grounds.

"I think he is a handsome guy. You haven't told me what you really think," I pestered Sisile.

"I like him, but I have to think. This was our first real meeting. He talked about a lot of things. I had to ask him about his past. I think I heard that he was going out with a girl from Saint Michael's. I do not want to get into a situation."

"It is good to be careful, but don't be too untrusting. It is bad for a relationship," I warned.

We got to the hospital and decided to take the road that went past the nurses' college to get to Mr. Fields's house. When we got to the gate that let do the mortuary, the guard asked us our names. We told him that we were going to say a few words to Mr. Fields and we would soon be back.

WEEDING THE FLOWERBEDS

"Go, I think he is at home. I did not see him leave," the guard said. We walked in the direction of the small yellow house that had a small verandah in the front. We got to the door and knocked. The door was open. We looked in, and at the back we saw Mr. Fields. He was wearing his swimming trunks. We were surprised. When he saw us, he stood up and came to greet us. He told us that he was having a suntan because he was going to the seaside with his friends.

"Come in and sit down. Let me change, and I will come and serve you some lemonade," he said that and went into his bedroom.

"The man Chaucer, Twigza. He basks in the sun for hours," we said, whispering to ourselves.

"Now, what did you do at home?" he asked. When he appeared, he was wearing a pair of white shorts and a yellow vest.

"I just read books and visited with friends," I answered.

"I was at home, and we visited my grandmother in Endzingeni," Sisile said.

"So now you are back and school begins tomorrow. I have been working on your revision for this term. I think we are doing well. You passed very well, which is good," he said, indicating some work he had in the red file that he used in class. We chatted, and then he asked us when we are supposed to get back to the hostel.

"At half past five," I answered.

"You better get going, and thank you for coming. Bye," he said as we stood up to go. We walked out and went out, and he walked with us. We decided to go through the hospital this time. We walked on the long covered corridors. When we got to the tuckshop of the hospital, he said good-bye and told us that he would go and check if he had any letters. We turned left to go to the gate that was near the emergency ward. He walked toward the outpatient department.

"I love you, Bulelo," a voice said from the door of the emergency ward. It was a young man who was in white. He had always said he loved me. Each time we went to the hospital, we would find him busy going up and down. He came out with a wheelchair and pushed it out of the gate to a green car that was parked to the side of the gate. He was wearing white as usual.

We passed him and laughed. "Even if you can laugh one day, you will marry me," he continued. I laughed and looked to the right. There was another of the hospital usuals, a fattish man who always wore a smile. He was a relative of Sisile.

"Sisile, here is your uncle," I said laughing.

"How are you?" the man asked. Even when he spoke, you could tell that he had a speaking impediment. He was raking some leaves near the gate. You could see that he had just finished the inside. The evergreen plants that grew in the gardens were shiny, showing that they were well taken care of.

"I am fine, how are you?" Sisile said to him. We stood to chat with him and then quickly told him that we were in a hurry and walked away. "It is good to see him. He is a very nice person," Sisile said as we walked off.

We got to the hostel at twenty past five and went straight to the senior matron's house. We walked into her dining room quietly. "How are you, matron?" We greeted her standing at the door.

"How are you, my children?" she said in her hoarse voice.

"We are fine," we replied.

"Go to the dorms and get ready for supper. I will see you at suppertime." She sat down. We walked out and met other students at the door. They were also almost late like us.

We walked out and went to the jacaranda tree and took our suitcases. We always left them there on the first day of school. We took them up the stairs and headed for the dormitories. In the dormitory, we found Makhosi and other girls.

"Guess what girls. Bulelo has a new Bakweri," Sisile said even before she could put her suitcase down.

"Just put the suitcase down and tell the story. It is juicier than that. She also has a new find, you girls, so I will wait for her to go on," I said as I put my suitcase down. The lockers of the two girls were already full of nicely folded clothes. I sat down. I had to let Sisile do her locker, and then I would be the last one. I did not have a chance because I knew that she would disapprove of the way I threw the things into mine. I decided to take my time. I took out my sheets and made my bed. The bedspreads were piled on the bookshelf. They were the same old beige that we did not like. Anyway, we were past our protest now. I made my bed and then started to fold my clothes on the bed.

"You had better fold the clothes there on the bed. You are not making the usual mess with those clothes. I won't let you."

"Sometimes you are a hell of a perfectionist. I am not, and it is fine," I said.

"Twigza, it is not fine on the first day of school. It is just not fine." I did not argue, so I went to the top of the bookshelf and ate some of the food that was laid out there. There were chicken, scones, avocado pears, and peanuts.

After Sisile had finished folding her clothes, I folded mine. I was in the middle of folding the clothes when the bell rang. It was time to go to the dining hall for supper. We walked out and made for the dining hall.

All the girls were present, and the junior matron was standing near the window watching over us. We got into our positions, and one girl started the song "We Thank You God for Our Food," and then we began eating. The only sound that you could hear was that of the cutlery against the enamel plates. After five minutes, the bell for the end of supper rang, and we went out. We were not going to eat sandwiches when there was so much food in the dormitory.

We walked back to the dorm, and the story about the Bakweriman resumed. Makhosi was happy for me, and so was everybody. Makhosi told us that she had got a job at the industrial sites in Matsapha that term. She told us how the

Chinese owner of the factory would say to her, "Amini, Amini, too much *mabele*," and touch her bust. We laughed when she told us that "Amini" was the way the Chinese pronounced the surname "Dlamini."

"It sounds like they are saying Amin like in Idi Amin," Sisile added. From that day, the Chinese were called the Idi Amins of Swaziland.

We sat down and ate together while we looked at the nice clothes that Makhosi had bought. She had bought a brown-and-white dress of the softest crepe. "For the final social dinner," she said. She had also bought a pair of cream white patent shoes. They had a thick belt that had perforations and fastened on one side.

Sisile took out a long floor-length floral skirt with a frill. "Uyaca," she said, meaning a stylish long skirt in Zulu. She put the skirt against her body.

I took out the denim sandals and the black-and-white dress that my parents had bought from Square One. I also had white platform shoes. "These are lovely," the girls said, indicating my shoes. We all took turns trying on the long skirt. We agreed that for the social we would wear long skirts.

Right then Praisy came in to tell us about how she had scooped the prize for Miss Wanderers. We were interrupted by the bell when it rang. We went to the chapel for the first time and listened as the matron preached. I don't even remember once what her sermons were about. The junior matron, I remember how she used to remind us of Jeremiah 33:3, that the Lord says we should call on him, and he will answer us and tell us all the mysterious and hidden things. We knew that in our moments of difficulty, this verse would stand us in good stead.

The following day, we went to school. We were surprised to find UBaba because we had said good-bye to him for the second time before schools closed. He came into class with the Zulu book and a bottle full of a white cream. "Yes, idiot, do you know what this is?" he said, pointing at Makhosi.

"It is . . . It is . . . It is . . . ," Makhosi stammered in an unusual way. I could not tell what was wrong with her.

"Idiot, stop telling the story that has no end. Do you know the story that has no end? It goes like this. Once there was a king. He had a beautiful daughter, and he decided that the young man who would marry her would be the one who would be able to tell the story that has no end. All the young men in the land wanted to marry the king's daughter. They all came to prove themselves. Each young man would tell his story, and unfortunately for all of them, the story would eventually come to an end, and they would go home defeated. One young man came in after a long time when the king was sure that there would be no clever young man who could marry his daughter. He told his story. 'There was a big bun. It fell at the foot of a big hive. A bee came out of the hive. It circled the bun and then flew away. Another bee came and went round the bun and eventually flew away. And yet another bee came. It circled the bun and eventually went out. And yet another bee came . . ." Mr. Khoza was indicating with his hands as he showed the bee going round the bun. What was funny was watching him do this. We laughed our lungs out at Makhosi who was standing now and not saying anything.

"You see, idiot. Answer the question, and stop telling the story that has no end," he said, looking at Makhosi.

"I think it is a pomade for the face," she said at last. "That is the word I was trying to remember," she said and sat down.

"No, idiot, you, idiot, what is this? Do you know?" He was talking to me now.

"I think it is a cream for some lightening the skin," I answered.

"No, let me tell you all. This is very good stuff. It is for the hair. It will make you have a beautiful Afro hairstyle like the African Americans. You see, the hair must not be short and kinky like this. You can lengthen it with this stuff. It is five rands. You apply it and then comb it through. Anybody who has five rands, I will give it to her," he said that and put the bottle down and then went to sit behind his chair. We continued with the lesson for the day.

That day the girls lined up in the staff room with their money. UBaba sold them the white stuff. Everybody who had money bought it and went to the hostel with it. When we got to the hostel, the girls put the stuff in their hair. Some were scalded at the bottom of the scalp. Some got good Afros. Some had sleek hair on one side. I was surprised when I saw the outcome of the contents of that bottle. I wondered what the matron would say because one of the rules of the hostel was that we should keep our hair short. We were not allowed to use chemicals in our hair. We knew this because there had been a strike in the late sixties, and the girls had used chemicals in their hair in protest and gone wild, so using chemicals in the hair was likened to protest.

I saw some of the girls looking beautiful, but those who had damaged their hair immediately went out to the cement near the gum tree to cut their hair. The matron did not mince words when she saw the girls who had used the stuff at the chapel. She made it clear that if they did not cut the hair, she was going to cut one line from the forehead to the back and another from the left ear to the right ear. I laughed when I saw the girls whose hair looked as if something had licked them. The hair would be flat on one side and stand on edge on the other. The girls were quite a sight. A few of them lived with the hairstyles for a number of days, but the whole thing had to come to an end before the matron ended it with a rough show of cruelty.

I took the bottle that had the stuff and looked for the instructions. There were none. There was just an address that said the stuff was made by some company in Isando in South Africa. I wondered how UBaba had come by this one. I felt that if there ever was a charlatan, he was one. He seemed to do the oddest things and get away with them. Like the day he came and demonstrated karate in class.

When he saw the girls after they had applied the stuff, he complimented them. "You see, this is beautiful. You look like real ladies of the world," he said. The girls did not talk about how they had got into trouble with the matron over what they had done to their hair, nor did the principal of the school talk about the issue. It was one issue that was hushed. It made us realize that the head teacher had a soft spot for UBaba. Small wonder we had said good-bye to him, and he was back.

Life was a bit of living in the shadow of a warm cloud when I knew that somebody liked me in class. Everybody could handle it except Killer. In the science lab, he could not help asking me what it felt like openly.

"So you two are in love. What does it feel like to have someone for yourself?" Killer said, whispering into my ear. The other students were busy studying, and we were having our usual talk before the physchem teacher arrived. "I just want to know how it feels. Do you feel like you are grown up now that you have him?"

"Oh my goodness! There you go. What do you think? It just feels fine. Do you understand? You sound jealous. Grow up. Life has to be lived at a different level sometimes. After all he is a handsome and athletic guy, and you are not." That was enough to get Killer to go back to his part of the table. He went to join the other lordyings in playing with the pipette. I was surprised that Sisile did not shout at them because then she was the one who was the laboratory prefect. Instead she moved some beakers to the shelves and carried on with studying the chemistry problems we had been given. I always had problems with balancing chemistry equations. I did not really understand what I was supposed to do, and the Nove did not worry when it came to things that involved mathematics. At that time, she had accepted that we were poor in math. She would just simply say, "It is the math. Don't calculate to the final end. Just write the formulae and leave the problem like that. You will get most of the marks." We got used to writing problems out and leaving them at the end when we were supposed to calculate and got used to the fact that this was all we could do.

When she came in that day, she was wearing a black-and-yellow blouse. Her thin waist made her skirt move about this way and that. The skirt also seemed to be too heavy for her thin, tall frame. She had already laid out the experiment and went on to teach us what to do. We listened carefully and watched closely what she was doing. She seemed to use her fingertips when holding everything. Even though she had a dainty look, she had a very strong fiber in her. After the lab, we went back to our class. We knew that in English, we were to get back our essays because Mr. Fields had been marking the long essays throughout the time we were away. He came in with our exercise books and gave them to me and Sisile to give out.

"Lady Chaucer," the students whispered as I passed out the exercise books. I did not mind because I was used to this type of teasing. We passed out the exercise books and then sat down to look at our work. I had three red ticks for using good expressions and two spelling mistakes. There was a big capitalized *careless* near each one of those and an exclamation mark. That did stab my pride a little bit. I exchanged my exercise book with Sisile afterward and read how she had written about the man who used to steal chickens, and later when I gave Makhosi my exercise book, I read about the boy and the crocodiles. It was good to have our work back.

We started discussions on different types of compositions. We studied descriptive ones and comparison and contrast ones. The Bakweriman had also written an exceptionally good composition about the "killing of the bull" at the Lusekwane, an event that was part of the Incwala that was held to celebrate the first fruits of the year. I am not sure what he got, but I got seventy points. This was the best that Mr. Fields could give you. He never went beyond that when he was awarding marks.

"I enjoyed your essays. They kept me busy during the holidays," he said that day when we were working in the library.

"That is good. We enjoy writing them too. We have fun when we write, and I think today we will discuss them at the hostel," I commented.

"This past weekend, I donated blood to a man who had my blood group. They looked for everybody in the hospital, and I was the only one who could help," he said while drawing lines on the cards. "It was just funny to see my life being drained out of me," Mr. Fields added.

"I thought they always kept blood in a blood bank there. We have gone there to donate sometimes. I could not even fill a pint. They had to stop me from doing it, but I got the bottle of Coke," I said as if the Coca-Cola was the most important thing.

"I filled a pint very quickly. My blood group is rare. I felt good that I could help someone," he continued.

"Did they give you Coke like us?" I asked.

"No, that is done to encourage you to donate," he said. "What are you looking at?" he said, looking at me.

"This photo. It is the photo of a guy we met when we went to Ephesus House with some of the girls. Makhosi gave it to me. She said that this guy sent it to her. He is from Zimbabwe. His name is Jama," I said, holding the photo so that he could look at it.

"Well, you will soon wear the color of this boy," he said, laughing.

"I think he is cute. Not that much, but just the idea of him sending the picture to Makhosi is an interesting idea," I said, putting the picture in the pocket of my blouse. I continued working on the cards. I was still working when the Nove came to the door. She came in and chatted with us. She was not interested in what we were doing. She just looked around and then walked out after some time.

"Sometimes I wish she could put more meat on her thin frame." I heard Mr. Fields say to himself. I was not sure what to say, so I kept quiet. I thought it was his way of saying we should not think that he intends to go out with her. We worked on silently, and after some time he asked me a question, "What do you think of all the books that I have bought? Would Ms. McClou have bought these books?" He was laughing when he said that because he knew that he was using a name I had used in my composition when I described some of Ms. McClou's weird behaviors.

"She would never! She only kept the library going. She did not think of buying new books. We are grateful that you have even used your own money to buy us all these books. We are enjoying them. Many students have started to enjoy reading for pleasure," I said. We worked on, and when it was time to go to the hostel, we closed the windows of the library and locked the door and walked down the stairs. I took the way to the hostel and then decided to go and check if Sisile had closed the lab. She was still in there. I helped her to clean some beakers, and then we locked the lab and walked up together. We felt privileged to work with the teachers instead of going to the boredom at the hostel. By the time we got there, it was already close to suppertime. When we got to the dormitory, the bell rang, and we made our way to the dining hall.

Life was routine at the hostel. Apart from a few happenings, things were a bit dull. We tried to keep ourselves busy by trying on our clothes. These days it was our preparations for the final social that made us work even harder at finding something special to wear. We had decided on long dresses. My uncle came to visit me, and he gave me money. I asked the home economics teacher to buy me material and sew me a long dress. She bought a checkerboard material that was blue and white, and from it, we sewed a halter-neck dress and lined the frills with a red-and-white elastic ribbon. Everybody worked hard to get something special for the event. We paid two rands and gave the money to Mr. Fields who was the one who was going to organize the dinner for the big event.

"What will you wear, Rebel 3?" I asked Makhosi when I realized that she was not working hard at buying a long dress.

"I will wear a dress. It might not be long, but it will be beautiful. Take my word for it," she said with her usual self-assured manner.

"I will wear the dress that is being sewn in the home economics class," I added. "I think it will be beautiful."

The event that caused us excitement that term was the invitation to Mr. Fields's house. One of the girls told us that he had asked her to go and clean the house that Saturday. When he finally told Makhosi, who was head prefect, that he was inviting us to his house, we were pleased. At first we were not sure if the senior matron would allow us to go. When she actually agreed, we were very happy. We were dressed in our casual clothes when we went there.

We walked past the teacher training and some of the houses where the other teachers lived. When we looked back, we could see the girls' hostel behind us. It looked like a distant land on the hill, a place of mysteries amidst poplar trees. There was a steeple on top that made the place look as if it had come out of an era way back in the past when there were guards who watched things in the surroundings from a tower. Looking at it from a distant as we did while walking, it looked like an enchanted place and not the place where we spent hours and hours trying to get shaped into people who would leave and be able to do well for themselves.

"I wonder what the matron thinks of our going. Maybe she did not approve," Makhosi said.

"Like when I first had to go and work in the library on Saturdays, she was against it. Look how much work we have done. We could not have accomplished so much if it had not been for the extra work," I added.

"The senior matron does not think about life. She just thinks we must keep out of mischief," Sisile added. We got to the gate that was at the back of the hospital, and the security guard asked us where were going.

"We are going to Mr. Fields's house. He has invited us," I answered.

"Well, I did not see him leave today. He is still there," he said that and went to sit down near the gate. We proceeded past a building that seemed to have a boiler because there was a lot of coal piled next to it. The laundry of the hospital was also at the back. We walked on the black charcoal that was on the road that led to the little yellow house. It stood alone close to the hospital. We could see that the door was open from where we stood. When we stepped on the half-enclosed veranda, we peeped in and saw Mr. Fields. He was sitting on a chair. He was playing his guitar. He put the guitar down and came to the door. He let us in and showed us where to sit. He took out some snacks of peanuts and sweets and gave them to us. After pouring us glasses of lemonade, he sat down. We chatted about class and told him some of the stories about UBaba's class. We told him about the story of the bee and the bun and also the one about the church where the Christians used to leave their shoes at the door and then the *tsotsis* came and stole them. He also told us stories about his family. He told us that his brother was in high school in England and showed us photos of himself when he was a baby of about six months. He was wearing a dress and looked like a girl in the photo. I laughed and my leg, which was always uncontrollable when I was treated to some laughter, kicked that bowl of peanuts, and they got spilt. I did not make much of the behavior, but I was not proud of myself either. We always wanted Mr. Fields to think well of us. Seeing me at my worst behavior was something that I always avoided. I think just because he was nice to us, we also wanted to be nice to him. We started singing together while he played the guitar. We sang, "In the Stars His Handy Work I See."

> In the stars his handy work I see
> On the wind he speaks with majesty
> Then I saw him face-to-face
> And I felt the wonder of his love
> Then I knew that he was more than just
> A God who didn't care who lives away up there
> Now he walks beside me day by day
> Ever watching o'er me lest I stray
> Helping me to find the narrow way
> He's everything to me.

We also sang Mr. Fields's favorite song, "Give Me Oil in My Lamp." He played the guitar to this one, the way he would do at school.

> Give me oil in my lamp keep me burning
> Give me oil in my lamp I pray
> Give me oil in my lamp keep me burning
> Keep me burning till the break of day

Then we will sing

> Hosanna, sing
> Sing Hosanna,
> Sing Hosanna, to the King of Kings
> Sing Hosanna to the King.

As we chatted, Mr. Fields told us that he had invited some of the teachers, and some missionaries had refused to come to the dinner because black teachers were coming. We could tell that he was annoyed by their behavior because of the tone of his voice. He said that he did not see why people would travel all the way from overseas and then refuse to share a moment with others and argued that Jesus lived among all types of people. It was after two hours when we finally said good-bye. We walked back to the hostel feeling like we had gone out on some outing of some sort.

On the way, we met the boy who was our tennis coach. He was from playing tennis.

"Who were you playing with?" I asked him.

"By myself," he answered.

"Can you please play with us for a short while," I insisted.

"Where are you going? I don't want you to get into trouble," he said, taking out the tennis balls out of the Dunlop container.

"We will not get into trouble. The matron said we could go and play," I continued.

"Come down then. There are four rackets. Some of you will have to count, but since you are all learning, you can take turns after fifteen minutes," he said that and walked toward the court. We followed him. We were excited, and running with Sisile, I got there and went to pick one of the rackets. They were all wooden rackets except one. I picked it up and noticed that it was no longer very straight. The surface for hitting the ball was a bit twisted. It was a very subtle twist that you noticed if you were observant.

"What caused this racket to twist?" I asked the tennis coach.

"I think somebody left it in the sun. That is why it is like that," he answered. "Take it and come and stand close to the net. I will throw the balls over, and you girls must hit them back. Don't allow them to land. Do it with your backhand and your forehand. Be alert so that you can change your footwork accordingly." We knew by then what he meant by footwork. We had been playing for quite some time. It was good to have a coach once in a while. We just wished that we practiced regularly. With the rigidity of the school's timetable, it was hard to get time to come out and practice.

We played for about forty-five minutes, and then Makhosi said that time was up. We picked our things and then headed for the hostel. When we got to the hostel, all the girls wanted to know where we had been. We told them that we had been to Mr. Fields's house. They were envious, and the Form IV girls told us that he did not like them. They told us that he had shouted at them when he went to their class and said that they did not take their work seriously. We told them that in our class, he had never shouted. He seemed to have a lot of respect for us, just as we had respect for him.

When we went to bed that day, we talked about our visit to Mr. Fields's house and recounted all the stories about our teachers. We believed that some of them were very good people. Even though we teased every one of them, we liked them. We teased the head teacher about the way he sang. He also used to like to say to the student who could not sing, "All Africans can sing except you." We would laugh because we thought that he was also one person who could not sing. We felt that he was the last person to say that anybody cannot sing. We also gave him a nickname about his nose. I am not sure why, but we found this name already there. It was students who had come before us who had nicknamed him Emanose. They had composed a long poem about him and said it with a Shangaan accent. Whenever the students saw him walk away or drive away, they would recount this poem.

The big event of the last term was a trip to the Bible school in Siteki to sing at the opening of the school. We got into the bus and drove all the way. Mr. Fields went with us. He laughed when another girl teased the boy who called himself

Sweet Saliva and said, "Mathamnandi is a chap and a half." There was a roar of laughter in the bus. We passed the Highway Drive Inn, and some of the boys tried to be witty by saying we were drive-in material. We fought back hard and humiliated them for saying that. It was nice to be on the bus and drive all the way with the students. I had never been to Siteki. I enjoyed seeing the beautiful landscape. When the bus started climbing up toward the top of the mountains as we neared the town, I looked back at the landscape. I wanted to see the land as it looked down below. It lay green beautifully marked by patches of fields. There were cattle that were grazing here and there. When we got to Siteki, we noticed that the town was very small. The street where the Bible school was, was all there was. We drove into the premises and got out. We waited for our turn to sing Handel's *Messiah* piece "For unto Us a Child Is Born," and when we were called, we went and lined up in front of the audience. We sang the song, and there was applause at the end. After that we went to the bus and drove back to Manzini. It felt good to drive into the town that had become home to us for all our school days. We could see the Nazarene as we drove toward the river valley of the Umzimnene River. It is as you near Moneni that the whole picture fades and your view focuses on the immediate surroundings. After that you drive into town and feel that you are in the real Manzini with people going up and down.

Chapter Ten

My last report had shown me that I was doing well. Preparing for the last examination had to take off from there. I tried to maintain focus and work hard. Math was still a strain, and science was a challenge, but with the help we were getting from the teachers, it was clear that we were going to "lick" the exam. "Licking it" was an expression we had come up with as we progressed in the preparation of our lives in the different examinations we had gone through. Those who did not pass well were told that they must not accompany other students to the examination room but focus so that they can do their best in their work.

The last examination began with the practicals. We did the physics examination first. As usual we tabled everything correctly and left off where we had to do the calculations as the Nove had told us. The examinations that followed came a few weeks after that examination. Studying became something that we did every day. Apart from that, we worked on improving our looks for the social. We braided our hair before we slept or pushed it back because we wanted to have beautiful Afros when we went out for this event.

"The great affair is to move, but in the right direction," Sisile said when we had finished studying that day. "What are we going to do when we finish?" she asked, looking at the book by Victor Canning.

"I am definitely going to the university. I am sure about that," Makhosi said, looking up from her notes for geography. "We have to practice labeling this map of the Great Lakes. There was a question on this in last year's examination. It might come up again," she said, holding up her exercise book and showing it to us.

"I think we should label the map of Japan. All the islands, Honshu, Shikoku, Kyushu, Okinawa, and what Rebel 3? What is the fifth island?" I asked, looking at the old examination paper in my hand.

"I don't know, and I don't think I will get this one. All I know is the question about the deepest part of the world," Makhosi said.

"Well, if you think that is all that you will be asked, you are not serious. We are going to write essays in the examination, not one-word-answer questions like that. I think I will study the map of Russia and South America. We had better make sure we know all these things. There is no way we can pass if we don't know much," I added.

"We should also practice calculating the time. It is important to be able to mark in the international date line of the globe and be able to count longitudes from the Greenwich meridian. What if we get such a question? Look at this past examination paper. Here, do you know this?" Makhosi asked. She had all the examination papers that her cousin who had written O levels before her had collected. The papers made it easy for us because we were able to practice how to answer questions.

We were still studying when the door opened. It was the junior matron. "You know you are not supposed to study on a Sunday. Apart from that, you are making noise. I will come back and check what you are doing," she said and walked out of the dormitory.

"Draw the spookie so that we can study. We cannot afford to be following rules of the Sabbath when we are faced with such a big examination," I said as I took the other examination paper and looked at the questions.

After finishing working on geography, we took the Zulu book and started to go through the proverbs. I read each proverb and asked the girls to give explanations to what it meant. "Look, Rebel 1, you have to be able to use the proverb in a sentence. You cannot just recite what is in the book. Everybody knows that. When I read a proverb, I want you to explain and then give me a sentence in which you are using it," I said, insisting.

"You are driving us too hard with this thing. We will pass this. Who would fail Zulu? I think we should move on to Bible knowledge. I want to write down the facts about the story of Zacchaeus. Do you know that story?" Sisile asked.

"Let me see your notes. I wrote summaries of the stories in mine. You should do the same. It will be difficult to remember these notes if you have written them like this," I said, showing her how I had marked my margins and put an asterisk against each story.

"What is this?" She asked. "You mean for each story I should do this?" Sisile said.

"Yes, you had better. How else will you remember? You will not learn this by osmosis. Do it and it will be easy," I insisted.

"That's a tall order, my dear. I cannot, will not, and would not," she protested.

"Why wouldn't you do it if you know it will help you to get good grades?" I asked.

"I am just not the good grades type. I learn easily when all the things are right there in some way, not any particular way as such," she explained.

"What you are justifying is haphazard jumbling up of things. The way you fix your locker and the way you study are so different. I wish you did your schoolwork the way you do cleaning up, Sisile," I said, annoyed.

"It doesn't matter. As long as I don't fail. I will get there eventually. Let us do more Zulu. I can handle you on the proverbs. Come to think of it, why is it always you who asks us about the proverbs? Bring the book here. I need to ask you to answer," Sisile said.

I took the book and gave it to her, and she started to ask me questions. I had looked at the idioms and proverbs so many times that I knew everything. I could use them in sentences just as well as I could explain what they meant.

"I am scared of the final examination. I think it will be difficult. What do you think, Rebel 2?" she asked, looking at me as if she needed reassurance.

"You will do well, don't worry. You have worked for almost five years now. There is no way you can fail this examination," I assured her. "You just need to have a strategy for passing and figuring out what each examination question needs," I continued.

"I have been praying in the chapel each and every day. I am praying because I hear prayer works when everything fails. I want to go to the university. This is the second year since they opened. We all have to go there," she said, looking at the books as if they were the ones that could block us from going through the examination.

"I am going to the nurses' college," Sisile said.

"What after five years here you mean you are going to the nurses' college? You think you can handle wounds, dead people, and all that? I am too squeamish to think about that profession. Look at this scar. The day I got hurt here on my leg, I decided that nursing was something I would never ever go near," I said, showing her the scar on my leg.

"What happened?" Makhosi asked.

"I was riding with my uncle, and when I was getting off his motorbike, I scratched my leg on the number plate. At first I did not even see that I was hurt—"

"Why such a huge scar?" Makhosi said even before I finished explaining.

"There is white flesh here. It was white at first, and then it filled with blood, and I started to bleed. I mean real bleeding. I was taken to the hospital, and I got seven stitches," I added.

"You see why nurses are needed. You need people who can help when you are hurt. They are useful people," Sisile said.

"You, you are joking. You can never be a nurse. Do you remember how you behaved when the javelin hurt the teacher at school?" I said.

"I ran away. That was a deep wound," Sisile said. "I could not handle what happened there. Now I am a grown-up," she added.

"They will also train you in how to handle patients," Makhosi added. I was surprised that everybody seemed to agree that it was a good idea to go into nursing. I had thought everybody would want to leave the Nazarene mission after all the years. We argued about careers until it was time to go to the chapel.

WEEDING THE FLOWERBEDS

We half listened to the sermons in those last days. We knew our days were numbered at the school. Whatever they were doing to prepare us for the outside world had to be in the polishing-up stages at that point. Anything that the gospel had not done up to now had to be left to life. There, truth about what we would become lay between the books that Mr. Fields had given us on Christianity and the experiences that we had had with our friends, the matron's daily sermons, and UBaba's near-blasphemous teachings. Somewhere in between was where our lives were balanced and ready to venture into the outside world. If we had been disciplined, life was going to prove to us how good everything was for us. If we had been resisting the religion, we had been spoon-fed that would also prove itself in the outside world. The world loomed before us like a big Gehenna—something of a Sodom and Gomorrah, if not a Babylon—and there we would go, the last children of Israel ready to be swallowed and enter the Sinai Desert without our Moses who had led us through the last five years.

The day of the last Speech and Prize-Giving Day came. I walked out to go to that Speech Day fully assured that I would scoop a few prizes. I had become accustomed to getting a few. I was wearing my red tunic and black shoes with the red sole when I walked out of the hostel. My friend Sisile was with me. We were following the other girls and running behind them because we had delayed while combing our hair. When we walked down the road and passed the toilets at the high school, we could see the girls disappearing near the teacher training college.

We walked on half running and half walking because we were way behind the other girls. We were near the hedge that grew along the path that runs along the road near the tennis courts when we saw the car of Dr. Samuel Hynd, the head of the mission station. It was a green station wagon that had tinted windows. Its Chevrolet make was out of the latest American models. We had seen this car passing near the school and dreamt what it was like to sit inside it. When he stopped for us, we hopped in. We sat behind him and Mary Wise, his wife. Everybody loved Mary Wise. She would preach with the women, wearing a black skirt and yellow blouse like everybody. We loved her as if she was our mother. They greeted us, and we responded and started admiring our surroundings. The car was as luxurious inside as it seemed on the outside. It had a white leatherlike finish that was incomparable to anything we had ever seen. We looked out as the building receded and wondered if the students could see us in there. It was in the cradle of luxury that slithered toward the Sharpe Memorial Church for what would be the last Speech and Prize-Giving Day of our lives. The ride was the first and the last we would ever take in such a car, but since it was our special day, we thanked God that we had been honored in this manner. When the head of the mission station parked his car under the conifers outside the Sharpe Memorial Church, we stepped out and walked round the building to go to the side of the girls from the girls' hostel. We joined the others and sat where we usually sat for the service. There was a lot of room because the student teachers were not in the church. A prayer was said at the beginning of the actual ceremony.

The first speech was the report of the head teacher as usual. He stood before the school and gave a summary of the triumphs of the year. We knew these already and listened thinking that it was our parents who should pay attention to what the year that was had laid at the feet of their children. He ran through all the victories. It had been a victorious year where both the trophies for the main music pieces for the mixed choir had come to our school. The trophies were raised as the events were announced. The victories in athletics were also mentioned, and the trophies earned from those were announced. We had won the National Spelling Bee Competition for the Year, and the team that had represented our school was called, and the whole of Sharpe Memorial roared with applause as they went to receive the national prizes that came from the Ministry of Education. The National Writing Competition Prize had also come to our school. The Student Writer of the Year was one foxy Rebel. She stood up to go and receive the prize of the year from the Ministry of Education. The Biggest National Prize went to the Bakweriman. It was a sports bag by Adidas. After all the national victories were announced, we sat down to listen to the last speech that was focusing on us the high school graduates of year of our Lord nineteen hundred and seventy four.

We sat down and listened to the main speaker for that day. It was none other than the head of Franson Christian High School, a Mr. Xaba from Southern African General Mission. He talked about how Nazarene schools had improved to the nation's highest levels in education. He congratulated the head of the school on his work in making sure that we excelled both academically and in social activities like music and athletics. His speech turned to us graduates of the final year of the school. He thanked our parents for paying the fees and seeing us through what was a quality education. He thanked them for raising us to be the children we were and said they had made an important contribution to the nation in investing in us. He turned to us and told us that the outside world loomed before us like a nice place. He said that is where we would be proved if we had learned to keep time because after the last few bell rings that we would hear in the school, that would be the last ever that a bell rings to let us know it was time to do a particular task. After this, if we had not learned how to use time, it would be the world against the principles we had learned and the real failures that mark lives of indiscipline that we would have to face. He said we should remember lessons such as the prodigal son and the Good Samaritan and take what was good in what we had been taught and apply it if we were to live fruitful lives. He said if our lives were going to leave the Holy Spirit behind, we would have left behind an important friend who would guide us all the way. All these words were landing on deaf ears because our eyes were on the annual prizes for the school. The last Speech Day did a lot to impress upon us that the time had come for us to go out and be "the salt of the world." "And if the salt has lost its taste ...," continued the speaker. He talked on and on, and when he folded his notes, we waited for the next item.

When the prizes were called, it was Mrs. Xaba, a white American lady, who came up to shake our hands and pass them on to us. I got three prizes that day, one for religious knowledge, one for English language, and one for being second in the class. Makhosi got a prize for excellence all round and English literature and geography. Sisile got the sports prize. It was a small prize that was accompanied by a gift from the Ministry of Education for the International Prize of the Year for the girls. With those prizes, we sat down and listened to the conclusion of the events of the day. Afterward the graduates were called, and each of us received a Gideon's International New Testament in red. It was a small Bible that one could fit into a purse. We took our presents and went and sat down. After all the events, it was time to listen to the music pieces we had been polishing up for this day. The mixed choir of the school, which consisted of girls and boys, stood up to render the main piece of the year. It was a song about our own country that was composed by the nation's composer, Mr. Hugh Magagula. It was a beautiful melody that pointed out the importance of knowledge to Swazis and the place of our country in the whole continent.

> Swaziland, live lenjabulo
> (Swaziland, land of joy)
> Sitichenya ngawe
> (We are proud of you)
> Noma umncane
> (Even though you are small)
> Utel' emachawe
> (You have given birth to heroes)
> Wakhulisa sive
> (You have raised the nation)
> Waba neligama, Swaziland
> (You have a name Swaziland)
> Namhla iAfrica iyakhula
> (Today Africa is growing)
> Nelwati nalo luyachubeka
> (Even knowledge is growing)
> Uze ube sibonelo kuko konkhe Ngwane
> (Be an example in everything Ngwane)

Inhlanha nenala akwehlele kuwe
(Good things and plenty must come to you)
Sinikel' impilo yetfu
(We offer our lives)
Isebentele wena
(To work for you)
Majaha akitsi
(Our young men)
Nani tintfombi
(And you young women)
Khutsalani
(Be hardworking)
Nihole Sive sakitsi
(And lead our nation)
Sibe nebucotfo
(To have integrity)
(You have a name, Swaziland)
Namhla iAfrica iyakhula
(Today Africa is growing)
Nelwati nalo luyachubeka
(Even knowledge is growing)
Uze ube sibonelo kuko konkhe Ngwane
(Be an example in everything Ngwane)
Inhlanha nenala akwehlele kuwe
(Good things and plenty must come to you)
Phambili, phambili
(Forward, forward)
Sive sabokhokho
(Land of our fathers)
Inhlanhla nenala
(Good things and plenty)
Akwehlele kuwe
(Must come to you)
Uyinqaba Swaziland
(You are a fortress Swaziland)

After singing this song and knowing we were expressing sentiments that we needed to carry with us into the future, we sat down as if we had just uttered one of the most important prayers that had been written for the nation by its own Handel. It was a song through which we reiterated what we were to our country. We went to sit down after telling everybody through Hugh's music that we were prepared to serve our country with integrity after getting as good an education as we had got.

The other forms also rendered their pieces. Afterward we stood up to sing a piece from Handel's *Messiah* that was being sung by all the school that year, "For unto Us a Child Is Born." We also sang a love song that we felt the head teacher had made us sing so that he could express love to a special someone far away. It was a beautiful melody entitled "I Could Not Breathe the Parting Word Farewell." It was a fitting song because we had finally breathed the parting word *farewell*, and we were saying the real farewell to what had been our home for the past five years. We knew that there would never be any years like these. They had been the most adventurous years with knowledge that we would ever have. They were years that had left their mark on us. They were years we would remember with nostalgia all our lives. They were years we would look back at with pride because they had made of us people whom the world would be proud of. We filed out of Sharpe Memorial Church that day knowing that we would live to tell what all the years of learning had done to our lives. I knew that these years would be years that I would look back at and wish that any child could have for the richness of experience and the absolute truthfulness about the basic truths about the world they had given to me. I vowed to tell in times to come what they were like.

"Sisile, let us go and line up for the drinks at the high school," I said.

"No, let us first go and see if my father's car is out there. We will just peep, and then we will know that they are there," she said as we ran to the other side of the church. We saw the blue-and-white Datsun and knew that Sisile's parents would be there. I knew that even if my mother was there, she would have to go to the bus, so I just looked at the crowds and saw other parents. We saw Makhosi's grandmother Gogo Ndlaleni Vilakati. She was standing near a solitary palm that had yellow fruits high up on its stem near the leaves. Some of the fruits were on the ground, and she was stepping on them. She came toward us holding her hands on her back as usual. She had her blue *doek* on her head and walked barefooted. We went to her.

"Gogo, Makhosi is that side. We are going to the high school for cake and drinks. Let us go," we said and walked with Makhosi's grandmother. She had fine wrinkles on her face. Her eyes were a glowing pair that peered at us with effort as the grey on them was starting to impair her vision. She looked up at me as if I was too tall for her.

"You are becoming tall, Bulelo. You children have become very tall. Just yesterday, you were this short," Grandmother said as we walked up the road to the high school. She was a short woman and walked with a gaiety that was unusual for someone her age. As rumor had it, we guessed her age to be in the eighties or nineties. She would touch her forehead against ours each time and tell us that she wanted her long life to rub off on to us. We enjoyed walking with her and asking her questions about what they used to do as girls when they were young. One time she told us that when they were girls, they used the bark of a certain tree for sanitary pads. She said they would pull off this bark and twist it to soften it and then use it. We would listen with amazement at her stories. As we walked up to the high school auditorium that day, we knew that it was the last time that we would walk on the grounds of the school with grandmother Vilakati telling us her words of wisdom. When we got to the school, we showed her a place to sit on the benches in the auditorium and went to get cold drinks for her. When we came back, she took out some roasted peanuts and gave them to Makhosi. We said thank you and went to join the other students.

Sisile's mother was there with a tin full of scones. We took the scones and went up to the hostel to drop the prizes. We threw things on the bed and headed back to the auditorium to enjoy the events of the day. We were at school until it was close to time for us to go back to the hostel. That day our talk was about the Speech and Prize-Giving Day.

"Twigza, we drove to the Speech Day in 'the car,' all the way from near the teacher training college right to the church," I said to Makhosi who was sitting on the bed, eating scones from the big cake tin that Sisile's mother had brought.

"Twigza, it is pure luxury inside," Sisile said. "Nothing like anything you have ever seen. It is scented inside. The windows go down on their own," she added.

"The windows, Twigza. They are nothing like anything you have ever seen. They are electric; they go up and down, not this winding up and down we do. Twigza, the air conditioner! It is so cool inside the air makes its own breeze. You are in nothing but heaven, Twigza." Makhosi looked at us as we described the car.

"I envy you girls for that. I should have been there. We walked out first because we wanted to elude you and go and check to see if the *Nuntius* was ready so that we would sell it as soon as the speeches were over. We were asked by the deputy head teacher to sell it to you, guys. Look at our picture in here. By the way, what does the word *Nuntius* mean?

"It's a Latin word. It means messenger or announcer. Look, the man Chaucer, he is standing in the middle," Makhosi said, showing me our class teacher's picture in the *Nuntius*.

"Look at Bulelo, look at her legs. They are the longest in the class," Makhosi said, laughing at me.

"Talk about long legs, girl, look at you over there," I said, pointing at Makhosi. She was standing near Mr. Fields. We went to the prefect's page and pointed out a few students who were on that page. "It was a wonderful year, girls. The music was good. What was Ms. McClou doing in the hall? She just wanted to spoil our fun. Did you see her eying us with 'the look?'" I said to Sisile.

"She wanted us to come back because it was time. I think now that she does not teach us, she misses harassing us. That is why she makes sure she is a demon in our lives," Makhosi said, and I wondered where she had got such an insight about Ms. McClou. I always thought she had just signed a contract with the devil to frustrate us wherever she saw us.

"Look at her here. She is with the Form IIs. Wow, look at the figure and the hairstyle, Twigza. The same over the years never to change again! The stilettos are still the same white ones that she wore when she taught us in Form II. Have you ever heard her sing? I stood next to her once when she was singing 'He Owns the Sheep on a Thousand Hills.' It was a rattle of a voice. If you have ever heard the hissing of a snake and then combine it with the bleating of a hoarse goat, it is sick," I said as I imitated Ms. McClou's hoarse voice. The girls laughed as they listened to my rattling voice. I rattled on and on, repeating the words of the song.

"Bulelo, you are exaggerating. There is nobody who can sing like that." It was Makhosi, defending her.

"Fine. One day you will be blessed and sit near her and hear her yourself," I said and took one of the scones and ate it.

We were interrupted by the bell that was announcing suppertime, and then we filed out of the dorm and went to the dining hall.

The final examinations were the main thing that we focused on after Speech and Prize-Giving Day. I studied geography all night on the time on which we were to write English language and went to class drowsy. I learned a lesson of a lifetime. I vowed that I would never cross night as I did that day because if it had been another subject, I would not have known what to do. When I got to the examination room, I found that I had to write a composition about a sewerage tank that had broken. I did not know what the word *sewerage* meant even though I could work out what to write. I got out of the examination room unsure of what the result would be. Like any examination, I was just glad that it was over.

Mathematics was a hurdle to jump over. I had tried to study, and what made things worse was that our teacher was not around on the week that we wrote the examination. We decided to go and ask the Nove all the math problems. She did not explain much because she could see that she would confuse us. We were happy after the science examinations because we found that most of what she had taught us was stuff that was in the examination. When we came out of the examination, she asked us which questions we had attempted to answer; and when we told her the questions, she said we had chosen well. She knew that with our background, there wasn't much she could expect; but for all the work she had put into teaching us, we wanted to make sure that we made all her effort worthwhile.

The day we had been waiting for came, and we dressed up for the social. I wore my halter-neck blue dress of blue-and-white checkerboard-designed material and my white shoes. It felt good to wear *uyaca,* as Sisile called the long dresses.

"Rebel 2, Bule girl, you look stunning, Twigza," she said and turned to look at her back. She patted her behind in the usual way and said, "Well, my back is not going to make much out of me, but this skirt feels good," she said and started putting on her brown shoes.

"Twigza, you look good. I can see your dimples and the gap in your teeth, baby. You look like the heavens!" I said in the usual hostel talk. We were fond of trying on our clothes and creating our dreams about our future. It was one pastime we enjoyed. Like typical southern Africans, we always had to come to terms with our behind. A little heap here and there did not do harm; but as the African heritage did it to us, the bigger was sometimes good, but the biggest bad. I had to assure my friend that her behind did not matter at a time like this. God had bestowed her with a figure like a tree, and standing inside that long skirt did all there was a piece of clothing could do for a girl at seventeen.

"Makhosi, I think you look great in that," I said, complimenting Makhosi. She was wearing a beautiful soft crepe navy blue dress that had red flowers and a hugging bodice. It was not long, but it was beautiful. "I had thought you would wear the brown-and-white dress and the cream white shoes," I said, trying to suggest that I thought that those colors would be better for the evening.

"I will wear that tomorrow. You know I have to look beautiful even tomorrow. This is your day, girls. Have fun. I am the head prefect after all. I am supposed to hold the fort and let you flap your wings sometimes." She was laughing when she said that.

"Let us go. We are supposed to go to the resident missionary's house and wait there. Mr. Fields said that he will walk with us to the George Hotel," Makhosi said, giving the instructions in her usual way.

We walked out and went to the resident missionary's house and waited. There were two sofas and a shaded lamp in her house. We sat on the sofas and chatted. When Mr. Fields appeared at the door, he was wearing an Afro shirt that was made out of java print material. It was cream white in color. He wore it over cream white jeans.

"Well, are you girls ready to go?" he said and went to the resident missionary's room to tell her that we were going. She came out to see us off and told us that she would follow us by car. She asked if any of us wanted to ride with her, and Makhosi said she would ride with her. The rest of us walked with Mr. Fields.

It was a long walk to town, but since we were happy to be celebrating five years, we did not mind it. We walked through the mission and made it into town. We crossed the Umzimnene River and headed up Ngwane Street to the George. Manzini is very quiet at night. Apart from few grocery supermarkets, it is dead. A few bars are open, and since we did not have much to do with those, we passed and went on our way silently. We passed some men, and they made funny comments about this white man and these "birds." We did not pay attention to them.

When we got to the George Hotel, we found that a room had been booked for us. We walked into the room and found that the tables had been laid. White tablecloths and silverware marked the places where we would sit. The boys from the Form V class were already there. They had taken their seats in some of the chairs. We took our chairs and sat down. The Nove was the last to arrive with the resident missionary. She was wearing a beautiful long pink dress that had puffed sleeves that were tied down with thin pink ribbons on the upper part of the arm. Our teacher looked stunning in that dress. Her beautiful curly brown hair fell over her face and created an angelic impression out of her thin, long face. She wore flat cream white shoes. The resident missionary was wearing a simple long cotton skirt and a white shirt. She looked beautiful. I enjoyed watching her cheeks and the gap in between her teeth. She reminded me of my mother because she also had the gap in between the teeth.

We sat down and talked about the menu. The waiters came in to serve us hors d'oeuvres as we talked. They served us some creamy stuff that was on biscuit like wafflelike pastries. These were passed around, and we used the small saucers that were on the tables to eat them. The menu was passed around, and we ordered the soup of the day and then waited for the waiters to serve us. It was a time for listening to advice from the teachers. They were not formal with us on this day. They just talked in a casual manner. Even the head teacher was relaxed. He showed us that he had enjoyed having us at the school. After some time, our soup of the day came, and we started eating. We were impressed that we had an a la carte menu. We had thought that we would be served one dish since we had paid only two rands.

The second course was the actual meal. Mr. Fields had ordered filet mignon, and I ordered prawns on curried rice. Makhosi ordered a salmon on a pastry blend. Everybody got what they had ordered. We ate our food while the teachers talked to us about the world. They were very happy that we had reached this stage in our education. The waiters came in to take the soup bowls, and we continued to eat. The sound of cutlery on china was all you could hear as people ate the food. I ate slowly and took in the scene quietly. It was a dinner like no other. We knew that it would be years before we were treated to such food and such honorable company again.

After the main meal, we had sweets. There was a choice of a blended pears and cream or a peaches-and-ice cream combo. I chose the blended pears and cream. Makhosi and Sisile had the peaches on ice cream. I looked at the Nove as she ate her food. She was sitting on the other side of Mr. Fields. The energy was good in the room. A part of the evening reminded me of the pictures of the last supper with Christ. The only difference was that the tables were arranged such that we were sitting on all the four sides of the room. The space in the middle was empty. Diya, the photographer, took some photos of the occasion. We posed standing up and sitting down.

After the meal, we spent time talking, and then we discussed how we would go home. Praisy wanted to go and sleep at her sister's place. We decided that the first thing we would do would be to walk her to her place near Standini, and then we would go back to the mission station. We left the George Hotel in groups and walked through Manzini around ten o'clock. I did not find it difficult to walk in my new white platform shoes. We walked into Nkoseluhlaza Street and took the full-length street from the top and walked in the direction of Dup's Bazaar. The mannequins inside Truworths and Edgars were staring at us in their trendy clothes. They seemed to be spiteful of the night and us as well. We passed the post office on our left and walked toward the Standard Bank. The CNA had beautiful displays of stationery that were tantalizing to the eye. We could see the latest Crazy Horse displays inside the windows of the Jet Set Store. We crossed the street that separates the two banks. The lighting inside Barclays reminded me of the days when I would go to the bank with my parents.

We crossed the street that separates Barclays, and it was quiet in the main streets of town. Except for the blinking of the traffic lights as they changed from red to green, the only lights were from the business buildings that were waiting for morning to come so that they could open the doors to the customers who started milling around town as early as seven o'clock. We walked on quietly knowing that we had the whole town to ourselves. We passed the Spar and walked toward Tops and Half Price. At the corner of the Punch Bowl, we turned as if we were going to the main Manzini market.

We turned and walked as if we were going to the bus rank and then walked on toward Umzimnene River. I had thought that we would cross the Umzimnene, and yet we did not. Diga, Praisy's sister stayed at a place that was adjacent to the bus rank. We got to the door of the house and knocked. They opened, and she went into the house. After that we turned and retraced our steps and went back to town. We walked as if we were going toward Dee Bee Supermarket and then turned left and crossed the Umzimnene River and started going up the hill on the way to the Nazarene mission. The boys were waiting for us on the other side. I was not sure if they had been following us or what. When we crossed the Umzimnene River, we could hear them from behind us. Now it was Sisile and me and Mr. Fields because Makhosi had chosen to drive back in the deputy head teacher's car together with the Nove. We walked on in the night and talked about all kinds of things. We thanked Mr. Fields for the dinner, and when we got to the hostel, he opened the door for us and then went into the house, and we sat down and chatted for a little while. After some time, he said good-bye, and we went to our dormitory. It was about twelve o'clock when we got back to the dormitory. The other girls were asleep. We got into our beds tired but excited about what had been the very last event of the year.

We woke up and went to the boxroom to take the trunk boxes. We packed the books and blankets in them and then took them to the jacaranda tree and then packed the clothes we had worn the previous night in the suitcases. When we took the morning bath, we knew that it was our last bath. The other girls were envious of us as we got ready to leave. We washed and went to wear our home go special dresses. I wore my black dress with the high bodice with the floral pattern of red and green. I was a small Christmas spectacle as I got into my white platforms. Sisile wore a beautiful Delswa skirt of the latest soft crepe. It had an elasticized waist, and it made her stomach look flat. She wore the skirt with a beautiful knitted woolen sweater. Makhosi had on the famous white-and-brown dress and the cream white shoes. I had worn that dress a couple of times. It was time for the trendy clothes that we had and not the *mpimpiliza* and the *nonor*. After we got dressed, we took our suitcases to the jacaranda tree. We came back and said good-bye to the girls and stepped out into the world in the latest fashions. It was sad to look at the flower beds from inside the courtyard that was near the sinks and know that we would probably never see them again. I took in the hostel and looked up the pit past the small brick house and remembered the big axe and *entsabeni* up the mountain where we would chop wood when we had been punished. I thought about the people who came for leftovers. They were still up there sorting their food after our breakfast of bread and thin, sour porridge. I knew that theirs was a mixture of sour porridge, bread, and tea all mixed up. I waved at them and then walked back to the room.

"Twigza, your father is out there. There is the car," Makhosi said, showing Sisile the white canopy that was on the blue Datsun through the window. It was already parked under the big jacaranda tree.

"Twigza, we will take your trunk box and leave it in the bus with my father," Sisile said as she took her big throw-over rug and the red coat that had a white fleecy collar. "Kisses for the babes, Twigza, and hugs for the Sisters Three. Be good and don't do what I wouldn't do," she said that and headed out of the dormitory to go to the car. I ran after her when I realized that she had left the cake tin that was on the shelf. I caught up with her and accompanied her to the senior matron's house.

"You are leaving, girls. Have a good journey, and thank you for being good here at the hostel. God bless you," the matron spoke very nicely to us, and we walked out.

"How are you, my children?" Sisile's father said as he loaded the trunk boxes on to the Datsun. "Sisile, you know which bus we will put this trunk box in. We would take the suitcase if we had room, my child." He said as he put my trunk box in the car. Sisile jumped into the back, and I went to the side window and said good-bye to her. When she left, I went back to the dormitory to see how Makhosi was doing. She was ready to go.

"Let us go and put my trunk box under the tree. We will go to town and hire a taxi to come and take it home. First I will hop over the fence and go home. Let us go. Twigza, I will see you in town." When we walked through the door, we saw Makhosi's grandmother. She had come through the path that went through the gum trees near the pit. "I am going up the hill. Twigza, we will meet near the library in about two hours. If I don't see you there, I will write," she said that and walked up toward the pit; and I went toward the dining room, entered the hall, and came out on the other side. I had a black handbag in my hand.

The jacarandas were in bloom that November of the last day of our end-of-the-year term. It was as if they were saying good-bye to us. Passing the jacaranda tree that was near the hostel reminded me of the many times we had swept the dead jacaranda flowers in the years when we had been at school. We had swept the dead brown jacaranda flowers off the walkways and paths around the hostel. We knew every yard of the school with our hands. Weeding the flower beds had been one of the things we had spent most of our time doing. Here we were taking our suitcases from under the jacaranda tree for the last time. We were going home never to return to the place that had been our home for the past years. We had mixed feelings about leaving. There were warm feelings of loss and the sadness of parting. There was the sadness of parting with friends as the students watched us disappear on our way away from the hostel. They were peeping at us through the windows, the way we had done.

I looked at the high school for the last time. I really felt that those red, white, and green walls had given more to me than I had given to them. I hoped that I would keep all that they had given. When I was near the teacher training college, I looked back at the girls' hostel. I could still see the top of the hostel and the mysterious little roof that I had never even gone into. It was right on top, and it still held mysteries I did not know about. Standing there, the girls' hostel was just the red bricks and cream white paint that I saw through the line of poplar trees. I thought about the first day I had arrived. I had not known then that this was the girls' hostel. I had taken in the whole place at a glance and felt lost. Right now, the place did not hold mysteries anymore. It had unraveled all that there was about it. I felt as if the mystification of me and my spirit as it had unfolded, that there was something I could touch at that moment. There seemed to be a new me that had developed that was different from the little girl who came to this place five years ago. I wanted to hang on to the old self and keep some of the new. I was very unsure what to discard and what to take as I walked away. I looked at my suitcase and wondered where I was going. I seemed to be walking away from home. I just prayed that the spirit of humanity and the truths about life that I had heard there, or whatever it was, would stop haunting me and leave me to go to the world as any person would. I was still thinking about this when I saw Mr. Fields. He seemed to be coming from his house. He stopped and said good-bye. He said that we should check on him whenever we came to Manzini and walked away from us. As he walked away, I realized that here was a teacher who had had a big influence on my life. He had become more of a friend than a teacher without losing any of his dignity. He had taught us about Christ in a loving sort of way. What he had imparted would remain with us for the rest of our lives.

I walked past the Sharpe Memorial Church and knew that the NYPS I had attended that week would probably be one of the last services that I would be a part of inside that church. That service had probably been the last time when I would be among the voices that sang in the well-lit church on Wednesday evenings. There would no more be preaching and praying in my life. I was going back to my Methodist background, where salvation was not a daily thing that was preached about three times a day. My grandfather, who was a lay preacher in the Methodist church, had died during the time we were writing examinations; so even at home, the year when my high school education ended was the end of an era in my life and the church.

As I walked away, I thought about the events of the previous night. I remembered how we had walked on this same route after dropping Praisy at her sister's place. I was still thinking about our meal when the Bakweriman appeared from direction of the road that goes to William Pitcher College. I guessed that he was from his home.

"Can I help you? How are you anyway? What happened to you guys last night?" he asked.

"Nothing really. We went to Praisy's sister's place to drop her and then went to the hostel. What happened to you?" I asked.

"We followed you, and realizing that you were being escorted, we went to the hostel. I just came from home to drop my things," he said as he heaved the suitcase up. We walked to the bus stop, and when we got there, the bus had already come from Big Bend. We told the conductor to put my suitcase on the bus and then checked my trunk box and took a walk. We walked all over town and met some of our friends from school. It was the real beginning of a new freedom. It was a freedom we had waited for, for quite a number of years. Now that it was here, we wondered what we would do about it. After hours of enjoying the walk in town, it was time for me to go back to the bus. I got to the bus and found that it was ready to pull off. I got in and sat down near a man. I was still sitting there when the vendor we called "Ngcam Ngcam" came in to sell his wares.

"*Ingcam ngcam*, mothers and fathers, the children will ask for sweets at home. A packet of sweets is fifty cents. A comb for two rands. We are eating also, and children need to eat when you get home. Bananas are one rand. Apples too for two rand," he said, and when he saw that there was nobody who was paying any attention to him, he walked out. I saw him get into the Swaziland National Cooperatives, a red bus that went to Goedgegun. Later he went into the Injabulo Bus Service, which went to Golela. I admired his patience and wished that I had as much patience to do the same thing in the buses for the whole day. I thought about when I had first seen this man. It was as if each time I had been to the bus rank he was there. I wondered how much money he had made from this suitcase of wares and felt that it was by studying him that one can learn what perseverance is. I was not surprised when I later heard that he had built a store from the money he had made from selling things in his little suitcase.

The bus pulled out on time on that day and went toward the countryside. Even though it was full, I did not really care. I just cared about the fact that I was leaving behind a life that was like no other. I looked at the mountains through the window and thought that I was blessed to be alive and able to see such beauty. Our country was beautiful. I could see the blue sky and the white clouds as the bus traveled on the dirt road. I knew that I had begun the long road toward what the real life and its challenges would bring. I said a little prayer in my heart and hoped that after all life was a blessing that was lived with hope, and I was ready to do nothing but hope for the best.

> We're are all a part of everything
> The future, present and the past
> Fly on proud bird
> You're free at last.
> (Charlie Daniels)

The End

Printed in Great Britain
by Amazon